GIOVANNI VERGA

GIOVANNI VERGA
A GREAT WRITER AND HIS WORLD

By the same author

Giovanni Verga's La Lupa, Philosophical Publishing House, London, 1968

The Stornello and its Flowers, *Biologia Culturale*, Rome, 1969

Luigi Capuana's Comparatico: a story which made literary history, Ciranna, Rome, 1970

Il comparatico di Luigi Capuana e gl'inizi del verismo (con traduzione inglese), Collana di Narrativa, Ciranna, Rome, 1970

Operanatomy: an eclectic introduction, Orion, Messina, 1971 (*distributed by Grant & Cutler Ltd*)

GIOVANNI VERGA

A GREAT WRITER AND HIS WORLD

by

Alfred Alexander

GRANT & CUTLER LTD
LONDON

First Published 1972 by

Grant & Cutler Ltd, 11 Buckingham Street, London, W.C.2

SBN 900411 35 X

Printed in Great Britain by Redington & Co., London & Surrey
Set in Times Series by C. E. Dawkins (Typesetters) Ltd., London.

Contents

LIST OF ILLUSTRATIONS

Frontispiece--photograph of Verga taken by Grita in Catania
circa 1912

*   *   *

Illus. 6, 7, 8, 37, 39, 40, 48, 49, 50 and 55 were taken by Verga and catalogued
and copied by Ins. Giovanni Garra Agosta, who also supplied illus. 24

The colour photographs for illus. 29 and 30 were taken by Valerie Macready

Dr. Lucio Sciacca very kindly granted permission to use his photographs illus.
5, 10, 41 and 42

Salvatore Reina supplied illus. 4, 16, 36, 46, 47 and 51 as well as the last
photograph of the Postscript

Jennie Dallas supplied the drawing for illus. 21

Illus. 9, 11, 32, 43 and 44 are photographs taken by the author

A LETTER TO THE AUTHOR
(*translated*)

I have enjoyed our many talks over the last few years, and feel, as you do, that the existing biographies of my uncle fail in several respects to do him justice. I am very pleased, therefore, that the first English book on Giovanni Verga should be yours, and can see several reasons to warrant its success.

First, your sincere affection for and understanding of his writings; further, your thorough knowledge of the conditions in Sicily, and of Italy's literary situation in his time; and lastly, your keen desire to expose and redress the wrongs from which he has suffered and which affect some aspects of his work to this day.

Fifty years after the death of Giovanni Verga a formal authorization for a biography is hardly necessary. However, I confirm with great pleasure that I have given you every right to publish the letters and photographs we have selected together, as well as the information arising from our talks.

I would like to add a personal comment. Years ago, when *I Malavoglia* was ignored in Italy, Giovanni Verga wrote that it would "disclose a fine state of affairs if the first proper account of this book had to come from beyond the Fréjus."

It seems equally odd (though it does not surprise me) that the first book which shows a full appreciation of Giovanni Verga should come from beyond the English Channel!

With best wishes for your task,

yours,

Giovanni Verga fu Pietro

*The writer of this letter is Cav. Giovanni Verga, Verga's nephew (his brother Pietro's son), and his only heir and representative.

PREFACE

Giovanni Verga has been dead for more than 50 years. Recognition within and without Italy was slow, but he is now accepted as one of the great novelists and short story writers of the 19th century.

Adequate translations of his main works have failed to make the impact they deserve, probably because they lose too much of their flavour and character in the process; further translations are unlikely to remedy this.

The result is that few people in this country know of Giovanni Verga. A number of Italian biographies are available, but practically nothing has been written on Verga in English and it is high time that such a book was published.

My aim has been to reveal the man himself, to state his position as a writer, and to describe his background and the setting in which he lived. Also, to portray those of his contemporaries—many of them household names—who were his friends or enemies, and to draw attention to the injustice that is still done him in the matter of *Cavalleria rusticana*. Finally, to explain why the period of his great creative writing was restricted to relatively few years out of a life that lasted over 80.

I am fortunate in being able to reveal much that has not been told before. For this I have chiefly to thank Verga's nephew, Cavaliere Giovanni Verga, who over a number of years has not only given me access to the information I required, but freely and generously of his time as well.

I must also thank Professor Gino Raya, Italy's eminent Verga scholar, for his encouragement, his help and his friendship; Giulio Cattaneo, the author of a well-known Verga biography, for permitting me to use some of his material; Dr. Andrea Cavadi, the director of the library of Catania University, as well as members of his staff, for their cheerful readiness to assist with—and to solve—a variety of problems; and, last but not least, Professor Emilio Interlandi for his amicable advice.

CHAPTER I

A SICILIAN BACKGROUND

A SICILIAN BACKGROUND

OUR great storytellers were not always cherished by their contemporaries, and this disregard has goaded posterity at times to excessive zeal. By ancient tradition the seven Greek towns of Smyrna, Rhodes, Kolophon, Salamis, Chios, Argos and Athens wish to be known as Homer's birthplace; it seems hardly surprising that two Sicilian towns, Catania as well as Vizzini, should both claim Giovanni Verga as their son.

Verga's parents were married in Catania in 1838. It was not a peaceful period in the life of this trouble-torn town. One year previously, a violently staged insurrection had been viciously suppressed, and a few months after their wedding there occurred one of the worst outbreaks of cholera ever recorded in the district.

Little is known about Verga's father, a gentleman who applied himself assiduously to the management of the family estates. He was cultured, fond of reading, and possessed a liking for the occult. He took a keen interest in the education of his first-born, particularly in his studies of Latin and history. Although a "liberal" (a term loosely applied to those opposed to the Bourbon monarchy), he played no active part in political life, nor was he prepared to support revolutionary movements—even if he did approve of their aims.

More is known about Verga's mother. Caterina di Mauro was a distinguished and charming woman, born of a gifted family. According to a contemporary, she was regarded as an intellectual, "at a time when this word did not yet convey that element of sarcasm it does now, and when ladies of her standing either could not read at all, or restricted their reading to the stories of St. Genevieve and St. Agatha." Domenico Castorina, a well known writer, was her cousin. His work was so highly thought of in his time, that he was considered the equal of Catania's most famous son, the composer Vincenzo Bellini, and was referred to as the "Bellini of Poetry".

Caterina di Mauro, probably more liberal in outlook than her husband, and certainly more inclined to take an active interest in ideas she believed in, is reported to have read and approved a book which had been the cause of a grave scandal. The book, *La Vie de Jésus* by Ernest Renan (1823-92), an audacious and erudite historian, divested Christ of his supernatural element and presented the historical Christ as a spellbinding Galilean preacher. The impact of such writing on Catania may well be imagined: the Bishop offered a *triduum*—a three-day prayer—"so that the Lord may forgive the French writer his sacrilege", and many citizens thought that the Antichrist was at the gates of the town.*

It is essential to grasp the background of political events in Sicily during the first half of the 19th century in order to understand the social conditions which prevailed in the island during Verga's childhood. An unexpected connection with Great Britain is here revealed, a connection which influences the cultural background of educated Sicilians to this day.

Once a British administration was established in Malta, which is as close to Sicily as Newhaven is to Dieppe, two irreconcilable political systems became divided by a channel only 70 miles wide. The Bourbon monarchy's autocratic rule and Britain's liberal democracy represented fundamentally opposed principles of government, freedom and thought. The British influence which extended across this channel to Sicily was the more immediate and effective because there was no language barrier. The British system worked in Malta until 1921 in Italian: every pronouncement or government directive, with its element of British democracy, was therefore immediately understood and readily disseminated in neighbouring Sicily. This had a profound influence on political events. Some relevant data on the history of Malta and of Sicily are given in Table I opposite.

Since the first part of the eighteenth century the ancient kingdom of Sicily had been joined with the kingdom of Naples, the largest state in Italy, under the rule of a branch of the Spanish Bourbons. It was a backward state, and in Ferdinand, King of Naples and Sicily, whose reign began in 1759, it boasted one of the most reactionary kings in Europe. Yet he survived both the explosive impact of the French revolution on Italy, and the Napoleonic invasions and settlement of the peninsula. He was temporarily deposed by Napoleon, who made Naples in 1806 a client kingdom.

Sicily was an island in a sea dominated by a British fleet. Imminent danger of its invasion was averted in 1806 when an English force, which was strengthening a Bourbon army and was com-

*Federico De Roberto, *Casa Verga* (ed. C. Musumarra), Le Monnier, Florence, 1964.

TABLE I

From A.D. 1090 to 1530

MALTA	SICILY
	i.e. for 440 years, the two islands belonged to the same realm: this followed the conquests by the brothers Robert and Roger de Hauteville, sons of Tancred de Hauteville, from Normandy. Robert was later called "Guiscard", i.e. the Clever; his line became extinct. Roger took Malta from the Arabs; his son, crowned in 1130 Roger II, King of Palermo, succeeded to the whole realm. He was followed by his second son, William (the Bad), 1154-1166, who was followed by his son, William (the Good), 1166-1189. Difficulties of succession then arose, leading to the massacre of the "Sicilian Vespers" in 1282 and to the decline of Sicily.
	In 1410, Sicily and Malta were appended to the Kingdom of Naples and Spain.
In 1516 occurred the unsuccessful Great Siege of Malta by Sultan Soliman. In 1530 Emperor Charles V (of Habsburg) gave Malta to the Knights of St. John after their expulsion from Rhodes by the Turks.	In 1693 Catania was totally destroyed by a violent earthquake. Ferdinand, King of Naples and Sicily, reigned from 1759-1806, when he was deposed by Napoleon; British forces subsequently garrisoned Sicily and
In 1798 Napoleon gained control of Malta. English occupation followed in 1800, and this meant, at least in theory, reunification of Sicily with Malta	within the Kingdom of Sicily, as Nelson upheld the contention that the King of Sicily, as rightful successor to Charles V (see above) was the legitimate sovereign of Malta. This view was rewarded by Ferdinand IV who gave Nelson in 1799 the Dukedom of Bronte in Sicily (a title now held by Lord Bridport; see illus. 3).
In the Treaty of Amiens (1802) it was intended to restore Malta to the Order of St. John: the Maltese protested against this, as it would have signified a return to French influence.	A British type of Parliament was introduced in 1812.
The Treaty of Paris (1814) confirmed Malta as part of the British Empire.	The English flag was flown side by side with the Neapolitan flag until 1814 when the departure of Lord William Bentinck with an Anglo-Sicilian force was followed by the abrogation of the British Constitution of Sicily.

manded by Sir John Stuart, defeated the French forces under
Regnier in the battle of the vale of Maida in Calabria. This was
an event considered important enough to be commemorated in the
name of one of London's new, wide thoroughfares: Maida Vale. In
consequence, the main centres in Sicily were, after 1806, garrisoned
by British troops, and Lord William Bentinck was despatched to
Sicily in order to protect the island against Napoleonic aggression.
It was a sound choice, for Lord William understood Napoleon's
tactics, having been present at the "miracle" of Marengo in 1800,
where he observed Napoleon's power to assess and exploit a rapidly
changing situation.

Lord William was a British officer and statesman of democratic
training and convictions. The absolute powers of the Bourbon King
Ferdinand IV—suspended though they were by the presence of a
British garrison—were anathema to him, and he proposed to force
the autocratic ruler to adopt constitutional methods. The old tripartite
Norman constitution with its baronial, ecclesiastical and imperial
representation did not appear worth revivifying, and he promptly gave
the Sicilians the blessing of a British political system, with its two
chambers, the Lords and the Commons. This Sicilian Parliament, a
true daughter of the Mother of Parliaments, had an importance
which far outlasted its rather short life. It was a first taste of "English
freedom" for the Sicilians and the taste remained. To this day,
Sicilians speak with affection of English freedom, likening it to a
cake with a taste and texture which is gradually improved and per-
fected by painful effort and slow legislation, a cake which is the
property of all, but is never to be eaten. This is contrasted with
"French freedom" which to the Sicilians appears as if it were personal
property, with everyone violently claiming his individual morsel of
the cake. Illus. 1 shows the title page of the "Hansard" of this British
parliamentary offspring: the word Bill, which does not exist in
Italian, is a memento of its ancestry.

In an interesting book* first published 15 years later—it was
forbidden reading in Sicily during Verga's childhood—the public
reaction to the Bentinck measures is referred to as follows:

"Inexpressible joy filled the hearts of the Sicilians. They felt that
the year 1812 marked the beginning of a new era, an era which would

---

*The title of the book is reproduced in illus. 2. It was printed (outside Italy)
in 1827, without the author's name (probably Count Giovanni Aceti). Its
first Italian edition (Oliveri, Palermo)—still anonymous—dates from 1848.

RACCOLTA

DE' BILLS, E DECRETI

DE' PARLAMENTI DI SICILIA

1813. 1814. E 1815.

PER SERVIRE DI CONTINUAZIONE

ALLA COSTITUZIONE POLITICA

'DI QUESTO REGNO

FORMATA L'ANNO 1812.

PALERMO)(1815.

1   The front page of Sicily's "Hansard"
Bills is *not* an Italian word

DELLA

SICILIA

E DEI SUOI RAPPORTI

COLL'INGHILTERRA

ALL'EPOCA DELLA COSTITUZIONE DEL 1812.

2   *Sicily's link with Great Britain*: the book was forbidden reading

DUCEA DI BRONTE
CACCIA VIETATA

3   Lord Nelson's (now Lord Bridport's) Duchy of Bronte is well enclosed and poaching
(rabbits and quails) is discouraged

finally settle the destiny of Sicily and bring back the beautiful days of its ancient glory."

The family of Giovanni Verga had a double connection with the "British" Parliament of Sicily. His grandfather's eldest brother, Barone Fontanabianca, was a member of the "House of Lords". The grandfather himself, another Giovanni Verga, sat in the lower chamber as member for Vizzini, a constituency 25 miles south-west of Catania, where the Verga family had their estates. Giovanni Verga belonged, therefore, to the landed gentry of Sicily, and his descent from a cadet line of the Fontanabianca family entitled him, and his brothers, to use the prefix *Cavaliere* by birthright—a prefix comparable with Honourable in the British aristocracy.

In 1815, Ferdinand IV returned in a new guise: he was now Ferdinand I, "King of the two Sicilies", but he was again invested with his previous absolute powers, and had every intention of exerting them in spite of an unwilling populace. As soon as the British protectorate of Sicily had come to an end, and Lord William Bentinck had left with an Anglo-Sicilian expeditionary force for Leghorn, Ferdinand abrogated the British constitution. Parliamentary efforts to save it proved quite futile and the optimism it had engendered collapsed. The two chambers were swept away by the violent political developments which followed. This caused a distinct cooling off in the friendship between imperial Britain and the Bourbon monarchy, a relationship which had been based on Napoleon as the common enemy. The period of direct British influence in Sicily had ended.

However, a phase of strong indirect influence was to begin. Sicilian memories of "English liberty" were kept green by the example of Malta, whose economic and political development began to diverge sharply from that of Sicily, once her sister island. Selected data for a comparison are given in Table II on page 7.

British sympathy had been alienated by the Bourbon attitude, and refugees from Bourbon oppression found help as well as traditional British asylum in Malta, where a Sicilian "Committee of Liberation" was established.

For geographical reasons, British influence in Sicily became strongest, and most direct, in Syracuse and Catania, the two seaports nearest to Malta's Valletta. Of these two, Catania, with 70,000 inhabitants, was a far more important city than Syracuse, and it was here in August 1837, the year in which Verga's parents were betrothed, that revolt broke out. The embittered people of Catania knocked down the statue of Ferdinand I which stood in front of the ancient university, broke up the insignia of the Bourbons, tore their flags, slashed the portraits of the sovereigns and hoisted yellow flags.* A town council proclaimed independence. This audacious venture, a breakaway atttempt rather in the tradition of classical Greek city-states, ended after violent but hopeless resistance against a quickly despatched and well equipped Bourbon army. It was followed by severe counter-measures, and by the public hanging of the leader of the revolutionary movement, Barbagallo Pittà. His death, for the "freedom of Italy", together with that of eight others, is now commemorated on a stone in the Square of the Martyrs at Catania.

A school-teacher from Vizzini, Giuseppe Paternò, wrote a remarkable pamphlet published shortly before his death in 1968, which described the repressive measures following this ill-fated rebellion. Writing "in the shade of a huge oak tree" at Campoliberto, high up on the hillside near Vizzini, on land which he had inherited from his grandparents, Don Giuseppe (b. 1818) and Donna Vanna (b. 1825), Paternò felt it his duty to record for posterity what his grandparents told him during the long winter evenings of his childhood:

"Thousands of police informers (*sbirri*) swarmed like bees round the Catania of 1838-40. The people were muzzled and shackled. Officials, officers, aristocrats and ecclesiastics, who during the short spell of revolution had sworn allegiance to independence, now had to swear allegiance to the Bourbon King, during enforced feasts and compulsory jubilations, and Te Deums accompanied by bombs and cannon. Terror reigned, and executions by shooting occurred regularly. Four thousand cavalry, armed with rifles and cannon, and led by Marshal Saverio del Carretto, subdued Catania with blood and terror, driving the town to despair. Any pretext was sufficient to arrest, prosecute and condemn citizens."

During this period, political attachments were often proclaimed by different types of beards.

"It was sufficient for a young man to wear a pointed beard of the Mazzini type, or for an old man a round beard (Cavour type) or a forked beard (Garibaldi type), and the police informers would cut these beards off with their scissors. Even the ribbons of green, white and red and other colours which were attached to the bridles or manes of horses,

*The yellow flag was the banner of independent Sicily.

TABLE II

MALTA		SICILY
Malta becomes part of the British Empire	1814	The Anglo-Sicilian Army under Lord William Bentinck leaves Sicily for Leghorn
The British Exchequer contributes £600,000 to aid Malta's economy	1814	The "British" Constitution abrogated. Reinstitution of the Bourbons to absolute power. From 1815 onwards they reign as "Kings of the two Sicilies", Ferdinand IV (see Table I) becoming Ferdinand I in this new appellation (1815-1825)
Stability of government Maitland Reforms Trial by jury introduced 1829 Council of Government—as precursor to representative legislation—introduced 1835	1815	Anti-Bourbon Revolt followed by reprisals in Palermo 1825-30 Francis I 1830-59 Ferdinand II, the "Bomb King" (re Bomba) 1837 Revolt in Catania. Independence of 1838-39 Severe reprisals. Execution of Barbagallo Pittà
	1840	Birth of Giovanni Verga Severe cholera epidemic
1847 More O'Ferrall Civil Governor	1848	Revolution of 12th January. Independence under Ruggiero Settimo September bombardment of Messina
	1849	April: Catania sacked by Filangieri May: Fall of Palermo
Taxation approximated to British pattern Abolition of sinecures New constitution of Council Schools opened in all country districts Legal procedure simplified and approximated to British system. Police established on English footing	1851	The Aberdeen letter of Gladstone: "the Bourbon regime is the negation of God erected into a system of government"
Unprecedented prosperity in connection with the Crimean war Extension scheme of great harbour begun	1854	
New military defences, municipal improvements, embellishments and amenities constructed.	1860	1859-60 Francis II—end of the Bourbon Dynasty Unification revolts as result of the unification of Northern Italy under the House of Savoy; Garibaldi's 1,000 land at Marsala. Battle of Calatafimi. Conquest of Palermo (27th May) Plebiscite (21st October) Protests against Land Reform and Flour Tax Massacres of the gentry

mules and donkeys were cut off, because humble peasants, and their
animals, too, could be accused of liberalism. Cigarettes which came
from Malta in boxes of the three colours were confiscated: every trace
of revolution and of the revolutionaries was to be eradicated. This was
particularly so in Catania, where hidden newspapers, books, pamphlets
and other printed matter could easily arrive from Malta. Bourbon police
inspectors, their long rifles slung across the shoulder and with pistols
in their belts, were accompanied by their informers. They would sit down
and drink with the people, in order to make notes about any anti-
monarchical or revolutionary views they heard expressed. Thorough
searches were made, even in the niches and crypts where the friars kept
the bodies of the recently deceased Father-Guardians and other brethren
for drying out, as well as earlier corpses which were already wrinkled
like parchment. Not even the dead found peace and eternal rest in their
cold and humid abodes, because the Bourbon authorities feared that
weapons or gunpowder could be hidden below the tunics, and in the
grooves below the feet of the mummified cadavers. Such was the
Bourbon repression in these holy places."

If the conditions prevailing just before the marriage of Verga's
parents were deplorable, they were soon to get worse still.

They were married in Catania on 15th August, 1838. Giovanni
Verga's mother owned a house at No. 8 in the town's Via
S. Anna (illus. 4). It was to be the house of his birth, the
home he retreated to after his journeys, and the place where he
eventually died. The father's home was at Vizzini, a small town of
about 10,000 inhabitants, in whose district the family held substantial
agricultural properties, particularly at Tiepidi. The Verga family
house, the so-called *Palazzo Verga* (illus. 5), was in the centre
of Vizzini facing the square, with the Piazzetta S. Teresa at its rear,
the little square which through Verga was to become famous (see
p. 98 and illus. 25).

A short time after their wedding, the young couple moved
from Catania to Vizzini and, a little later, to a villa in Tiepidi,
between Vizzini and Licodia Eubea, at the foot of Monte Altore.
Shortly afterwards hell broke loose in Vizzini. Paternò describes it
thus:

"In that horrid summer cholera raged terrifyingly. The town seemed
deserted, and everyone who could possibly do so went to live in isolated
houses, villas or huts in the country. All public offices were closed and
all public services were abandoned. No gendarmes, and not even the
half-dozen or so public scavengers, could be found anywhere. The
corpses had to be buried in the underground vaults of the churches or in

4   Verga's house in Via S. Anna with a commemorative
plaque between the first and second windows

5   Palazzo Verga in Vizzini. The lane on the extreme left leads to
the Piazzetta S. Teresa, of *Cavalleria* fame

6   Vizzini from Via S. Antonio

7   Vizzini from Via del Pericolo

communal graves, for at the time of the Bourbons the town did not possess a graveyard. The stiff corpses of their relatives, enfolded in counterpanes or bed sheets, were carried away by the bereaved families.

"Vizzini was without water, without light, without drains and without cesspits. Its roads were impassable. It was forsaken by the administration and by all officials as well as by the decurions (lieutenants) and the centurions (captains) of the Bourbon gendarmerie. There were no sanitary services, no doctors and no medicines, and in the absence of drugs all the two pharmacies could do was to crush herbs and seeds. Under such conditions lived the people, together with their beasts of burden (horses, mules and donkeys) and hundreds of pigs which roamed the streets. There were no hygienic measures whatsoever. No advice was to be had, nor was disinfection available. All of this contributed to a rapid spread of the disease, particularly in the summer. It was the people's habit to dry their washing on the roofs, where containers of fruit and other produce were drying in the sun. The water in the reservoirs, which were filled with rainwater from the roofs, was frequently contaminated.

"The epidemic completely paralysed and interrupted all communal life, and not only every small hut in the fields, but even caves, caverns and grottoes served as a refuge. In order to avoid cholera, no one bothered to report or register births or deaths. Anyway, utter chaos prevailed not only in the municipal offices but also in the churches. News from the town only became known when a courageous man dared to go to Vizzini and upon his return related his sad list: the news of victims would then spread from house to house, and from hut to hut, in the various districts of the countryside.

"Neither spiritual nor material assistance was available to the afflicted. All parish priests, vicars and priests went to the country to save their own lives, and to avoid becoming infected with the terrible disease. For five months the cholera killed men and women, the old, the young and the infants. Only in the countryside did the people escape."

The epidemiology of the cholera held no problem for the populace. Long before Robert Koch had discovered the comma bacillus of cholera, they knew exactly where the disease had come from: it had been foisted upon them by the rich, and by the nobility with the support of the Bourbon administration.

"And whenever they saw dustmen pouring out buckets of quicklime to disinfect the squares, streets and passages, they yelled 'Morbu Borbonicu'."

The real sources of the epidemic were, of course, the water

supplies—which had been contaminated with the vibrio, the microbe responsible for cholera. This also explains why the people who had gone to the country generally escaped the epidemic. Contaminated roof waters, as Paternò believed, may well have initiated the epidemic. For an epidemic to spread rapidly a major communal water supply had to become infected: this was neither known nor seriously suspected at the time. The general practice of putting damp straw in front of the entrance doors of the houses was a pathetically futile precaution, though in ridiculing such a measure it should be remembered that in England this same practice was recommended, and adopted, during the foot and mouth epidemic of 1967-8—with as much scientific justification as during the cholera epidemics of a hundred years before. Another practice, by intention preventative, which was frequently resorted to, was the shooting on sight of suspicious strangers believed to be carrying the disease. This added the senseless murder of a few innocents to the holocaust.

During the epidemics, it was a family duty to bury the dead. The 8- to 9-foot loft ladders that practically every household possessed lent themselves well for use as stretchers. The corpse's stiffness, the *rigor mortis,* begins in the case of cholera soon after death. In some muscle groups it lasts a short time only, but in others it appears late, and is rather prolonged due to the violent cramps which accompany this frightful disease. For this reason, the bodies remained stiff for a considerable period, and this stiffness facilitated their transport on ladders.

In his booklet, Paternò is claiming that Verga was born at Vizzini at the beginning of this epidemic, on 24th June, 1840. This is conjecture; what is certain is that he was christened at Catania either on the 2nd or the 8th of September. When Benedetto Croce wrote a critical essay on Verga in 1903, he asked Verga for his birthdate. Anxious to be exact, Verga made enquiries at the Catania municipal offices and wrote to Croce that "I now find that I was born on 31st August! So here I am, a week or so older than I thought, but with unchanged appreciation and affection for you".

That the epidemic caused delay in the registration of births is easy to understand. Emilio Interlandi, a poet and teacher from Vizzini, has drawn attention to certain contradictions in the Catania register entries in support of Vizzini's claim that Verga was not born in Catania, but in Vizzini. A powerful argument against this is that Verga always enjoyed an affectionate and intimate relationship with his mother; no doubt she would have told him had he been born in Vizzini, even if this meant admitting a violation of the registration laws.

Five of the six children of Verga's parents survived. Giovanni was the eldest, followed by Mario, Rosa, Pietro and Teresa. They were an upper middle class family, and maintained a reasonable standard of living. There was no shortage of food, nor of domestic help in the house, but available spending money was often limited; it depended upon the prices received for citrus fruit and olive oil, as well as on the rents. All these were likely to be unfavourably affected by Sicily's recurring troubles, her civil disorders, epidemics and earthquakes, and the permanent poverty of the tenants. Verga was conscientiously aware of the family's circumstances and when he had to draw on family finances while living away from home he felt rather guilty. He was not a spendthrift, but was used to living "as a gentleman" and would have found it distasteful to abandon this standard.

In recollection, Verga looked back with pleasure on a happy childhood, its winters generally spent in Catania and its summers in or around Vizzini. Outside the home, things were not so happy. Verga's eighth year, 1848, was a year of revolutionary outbursts throughout the world. The upheavals of 1848 actually began in Sicily, where the bubble of discontent burst in Palermo on 12th January. Disturbances in other towns followed quickly. Catania rose on 25th January. There were insurrections in Messina on the 20th, and in Trapani on the 29th.

A self-styled Sicilian Assembly met in March 1849, and declared that the Bourbon dynasty had ceased to reign; Sicily, under the presidency of Ruggiero Settimo, declared herself part of Italy. It had seemed an opportune moment, as the Bourbon rulers in Naples faced serious trouble on the mainland. Practically the whole of Sicily was soon in the hands of the insurgents—with one fateful exception: in Messina, the revolutionaries had failed to dislodge the Bourbon troops from the town's citadel, where they held out in a state of siege. The Bourbon ruler, Ferdinand II (generally referred to as "The Bomb King", *Re Bomba*), sent a powerful army under General Carlo Filangieri to Sicily, as soon as the conditions on the mainland had developed in his favour and permitted him to do so. Landing near Messina on 3rd September, 1848, they relieved, and were themselves reinforced by, the troops who had held out for seven months in the citadel. After three days of severe fighting, Messina was captured and sacked.

From Messina, Filangieri's army advanced southwards, committing vile atrocities in its progress. Catania was invested and, following the Bourbon King's ultimatum of 7th April, 1848, taken after violent fighting, plundered and sacked. Final victory for the Bourbons came in May 1849, when the Palermo "Assembly-government" surrendered on the promise of a general amnesty. In spite of this amnesty, Ruggiero Settimo and 42 others were executed shortly afterwards.

Re Bomba's military success thwarted the historically interesting attempt of Sicilian liberals to obtain British aid and sympathy through a proposal to replace the Bourbon rulers by a constitutional monarchy of British type. A new King of Sicily was to have been nominated by Britain's government.

Verga's teacher, Antonio Abate, had taken part in Catania's resistance. Wounded in the fighting around Catania's Porta d'Aci—the city's gateway leading to the area associated with the ancient myth of Acis and Galatea—he returned to Catania, after fleeing to Palermo, to "await the fury or the clemency of the tyrant he had offended". The clemency shown to him—he was not prosecuted—did not change his views, and when Verga, who at the time of the battle of Catania was nine years old, came to Abate's school, he was strongly influenced by the anti-Bourbon sentiment and revolutionary fire which still inflamed his teacher.

The two severe cholera epidemics of 1854 and 1855, during which Verga's family moved to his mother's villa on the slopes of Mount Etna, intensified Catania's anti-Bourbon discontent. A few years later, the Bourbon dynasty eventually came to an end. Its last phase reveals another link between Sicily and Britain. The Bourbon gaols were full of political prisoners, many of whom had been transferred to prisons around Naples, where supervision was easier. Among the prisoners, who were kept under horrifying conditions, were men of exceptional qualities. Gladstone spent the winter of 1850 in Italy, and Sir James Lamaitis, a well known Anglo-Italian, drew his attention to these facts. After some investigations Gladstone wrote his famous "Aberdeen letters" to Lord Aberdeen, in which he described the Bourbon regime as the "negation of God, erected into a system of government". These letters startled the whole of Europe. They are still remembered in Sicily, and are one of the reasons for the alleged "anglomania" of Sicilian society.

In April 1860, insurrections flared up all over the island. Encouraged by the rumours of the impending, and later by the news of the successful, landing of Garibaldi's expeditionary force of "the Thousand" at Marsala, and their victory at Calatafimi, these insurrections quickly gathered momentum.

In Catania, where the terrible events of 1848 were still painfully remembered, insurrection could possibly have been prevented if the Bourbons had taken heed of the advice of their local commander, General Clary, who recommended that the tax on flour be abolished immediately, and public construction works initiated.

The tax on flour was hated and detested: it was regarded as the most insulting and vile exploitation of the poor that the Bourbon system could devise. The tax had to be paid—in the old Sicilian currency of grains, tarì and ounces—whenever grain was milled into flour, a process which had to take place at the water-powered mills. It invited evasions, and the corn growers conspired with the millers and the pasta-makers to get the flour on sale without it.

The collection of the odious tax itself was comparatively simple, for the situation of the mills was conspicuous, and supervision therefore relatively easy. Every evasion, once discovered, was severely punished. When the King was eventually prepared to take Clary's advice, and abolished the tax, it was too late: the Bourbon dynasty was swept away in a violent revolutionary rising.

The hated rulers had gone, but unfortunately one of the main grievances against the old regime not only persisted, but became even more difficult to bear than before.

The crux of this matter was the presence of an impoverished, land-hungry peasantry, in the midst of enormous tracts of land owned by the Crown, the Church, the universities and the high aristocracy. There existed, therefore, a desperate need for land reform and dissolution of the large estates. This, in principle at least, had been admitted by the Bourbon rulers, and the splitting up of the crown lands had been accepted as inevitable. Ever since 1848, sporadic outbreaks of unlawful occupation of crown lands had occurred, violently carried out and equally violently suppressed.

The democratic politics of the Garibaldi movement encouraged the aims and ambitions of the social revolution. When the new leaders came to power, the relics of the feudal land system were abolished, and the estates were split up, just as the people had been promised. During this process, however, certain circumstances arose which could well have been foreseen, but, in fact, were not.

Firstly, when the estates were split up and were sold by public auction, the land was bought not by the peasants but by the middle classes (*borghesia*) and the minor aristocracy. For both these groups, acquisition of land proved a heaven-sent opportunity for narrowing the gap between themselves and the grand aristocracy, the minor aristocracy being in many respects nearer to the *borghesia* than to the nobility proper. The peasants were left out; even if some of them could have afforded the purchase price, the selling authorities of the communities, comparable perhaps to Rural District Councils in England, favoured the *borghesia* as purchasers. But this was not all. Further disappointments for the peasantry were in store. Under the feudal system, they had enjoyed commoners' rights over the crown lands, the church properties and the large baronial estates. They possessed grazing rights, timber rights, fruit-picking and hay-cutting rights, and in some cases cultivation- and harvesting-rights as well. In the eyes of the movement for social betterment, such privileges had been regarded as inadequate; now, with the lands sold, and enclosed by their new owners, they had been lost altogether.

The disappointing truth therefore dawned on the peasantry that, instead of gaining the longed-for ownership, they were now, in fact, losing what barely satisfactory rights and privileges they had previously possessed.

The fact that this did not result from deliberate injustice, but merely from the failure of the authorities to foresee the results of their own actions (a proportion of the crown lands should, of course, have been assigned to those who had held commoners' rights over them) hardly mattered now; it was too much for a disappointed and desperate peasantry to bear. It produced the violent and terrible outbursts which are referred to as the "massacres of the gentry". The worst of these outbreaks occurred in the communities of Biancavilla, Bronte and Acireale, in the province of Catania. The savagery and the cruel rage of the infuriated masses, who, wearing white berets* and armed with axes and sickles, stormed the towns with the cry *"Viva la libertà!"* is almost indescribable. The most barbaric assaults and the foulest murders were committed. Verga has described the violence of those days in *Libertà*, a short story of literary as well as of historical interest. At the time of the massacres, Verga was 20 years old, and no doubt had

---

*The wearing of hats was restricted to the upper classes.

accurate reports about the tragic excesses which had occurred so near to his home. The outbreak described in Verga's story is generally accepted as that at Bronte, a township 2,000 feet up in the Etna range.*

The story *Libertà* is a depressing lament for Verga's *sventurata Sicilia,* his beautiful and unfortunate island home; man's cruelty to man had been endemic there for longer than almost anywhere else and ever since the days of the torture of the Athenian prisoners in the stone quarries of Syracuse, outbursts of violence and vengeance had followed one another interminably. The kind of events described in this story are little known in this country, and the story is therefore given in full, in a new translation.**

LIBERTÀ

by

GIOVANNI VERGA

The tri-coloured handkerchief fluttered from the bell tower. They sounded the tocsin, and in the square they began to shout: "Long live freedom".

Like the sea during a storm, the mob foamed and surged in front of the "Club of the Gentlemen". Outside the Town Hall, and on the steps leading to the church, was a sea of white berets. The axes and sickles glittered . . . soon they burst into one of the side streets.

"It's you first, Baron, because you ordered your field guards to flog the people." Right in front was a witch-like woman, her old hair bristling. Her nails were her only weapon.

---

*Bronte was one of the townships founded by Charles V, above the valley where in 1040 A.D. the Greek General Maniaces, aided by the Norwegians and Normans, had defeated a large army of Saracens. In 1174 Margaret, the mother of William II, founded the Benedictine Convent of Maniace there; the monastery itself was later suppressed. In 1779, Ferdinand IV gave the whole district to Lord Nelson, creating him "Duke of Bronte", with the ducal seat at the Castle of Maniace, where Lord Nelson's heirs still live with some residuum of ducal splendour (illus. 3).

**It was first published in the *Domenica letteraria* and reprinted in a collected volume of short stories (*Novelle rusticane*) in 1882.

"And then you, you devilish priest, who have sucked the soul out of us!"

"And you, rich feaster, who got so fat on the blood of the poor that you can't even run away now!"

"And you, coppers' nark, who brought to justice only those who have nothing!"

"And you, gamekeeper, who have sold your own body and the bodies of your neighbours for two tarì a day!"

Their blood was boiling, and it poisoned them. The sickles, their hands, the stones—everything was red with blood.

"The gentlemen! The Hats! Kill them! Kill them! Down with the Hats!"

Don Antonio was making for home by way of the short-cuts— the first blow sent him falling onto the footpath, blood all over his face.

"Why do you want to kill me?"

"To the devil with you!" A crippled youth picked up a greasy hat, and spat into it.

"Down with the Hats! Long live freedom!"

"You, you as well"—they yelled at the cleric, who had preached Hell to those who had stolen bread. He was just returning from saying Mass, the consecrated host in his fat belly.

"Don't kill me—don't! I am in mortal sin."

His mortal sin was Lucia, whose father had sold her to him when she was 14 years old, during that hungry winter, and who supplied the "wheel"* and the streets with ragged urchins.

If that houndsflesh had only been of some use, they could have had their fill of it now. They were like the hungry wolves, who do not think of filling the stomach when they come across a flock, but kill in rage. They tore the flesh in front of the doors, and on the cobblestones, with blows from the axes.

The lady's little son who had gone to see what was happening was the next victim. He was followed by the chemist, who was just closing his shop in a hurry.

Don Paola was returning from his vineyard, astride his donkey, the half-empty pack-saddle behind him. He still wore the little old cap which his wife had embroidered for him as a girl, long ago, before the blight had hit his vineyard; she and the five children

*For an explanatory note on the wheel see p. 73 and illus. 20-22.

8   Via S. Antonio, Vizzini. Photograph taken by Verga in May 1892

9   Bronte . . . "at the bottom of the small street which went steeply downhill,
the fields of the plain and the deep woods on the side of Etna could clearly be
seen" (p. 19))

10 and 11 (inset) Catania's Elephant: made of lava tuffs and carrying an Egyptian granite obelisk, it served as the turning point of an ancient chariot racecourse

were waiting for what little food he had in his pack-saddle. In front of the big gates she saw him fall. "Paolo, Paolo!" The fellow right in front caught him on the shoulder with a blow of the axe and, while he still clutched the doorknocker, blood pouring from his arm, another got at him with a reaphook and disembowelled him.

The worst of all happened when the notary's son, a golden-haired boy of eleven, was knocked down by the mob. His father had tried to pick himself up two or three times, and before he was dragged away to die on the refuse heap, he had called out to him, "Neddu! Neddu!"

Neddu ran away in terror, unable to scream, his eyes and his mouth wide open. They threw him to the ground. He, too, lifted himself onto his knee, just as his father had done: the torrent went over him. One fellow kicked him with his hob-nailed boot in the cheek and smashed it in: the boy still begged for mercy with his hands. He did not want to die, no, not as he had seen his father murdered. It was heart-rending. The wood-cutter struck him down, as an act of mercy, with a powerful blow. He held the axe with both hands, as if he was felling a 50-year-old oak, and he trembled like a leaf.

Someone yelled: "Never mind! He, too, would have only become a notary." What did it matter! Now that their hands were red from so much blood, they might as well spill the rest.

"Let's kill them all! All the Hats!"

What made their rage boil over now, was no longer the hunger, the whippings, or all the iniquities to which they had been subjected; innocent blood did it now. The women, with their bodies covered in tattered rags, were even wilder than the men. They shook their thin arms and shrieked with high-pitched voices.

"You—you came to pray to the Lord in a silk dress!"

"You, you didn't like it when you had to kneel next to the poor!"

"And you, and you . . ."

They rushed into the houses, up the staircases, and into the bedrooms. They tore up the silk, and the fine linen. There were many precious earrings on blood-encrusted faces—and many gold rings on hands that tried to ward off the blows from the axe.

The Baroness had ordered her guards to barricade the front gates with beams. Big carts, loaded with filled barrels were drawn up behind them, and her field guards fired from the windows, intent on selling their lives as dearly as possible in their last and desperate stand.

To start with, the mob could not advance against the shooting —keeping firearms had been punishable by death.

However, they soon broke through the main gates, yelling "Long live freedom!" They streamed into the open courtyard and, jumping over the wounded, they rushed up the flights of stairs. They did not bother with the field guards. They could come afterwards! First of all, they wanted the body of the Baroness, with her fine skin, and flesh made from partridges and good wine. The Baroness ran from one room to the other—and there were many rooms. Her hair was dishevelled, her babe was in her arms. You could hear the mob yelling through the maze of rooms, irresistibly approaching like a river in flood.

The eldest son, 16 years old—still of tender flesh—tried with trembling hands to buttress the doorway, and shouted "Mama! Mama!" With the first push they turned the door on top of him. He tried to hang on to the legs which trampled him down. Almost out of her senses, half crazed, and holding her hand over her baby's mouth so that he should not scream, his mother had fled to the balcony. The other little boy, almost demented, too, attempted to defend her with his own body, and tried to clutch the edges of those axes with his little hands. The mob separated them in a flash. One man took her by the hair, another gripped her body, a third got hold of her dress, and they lifted her over the railings. The coalman tore the baby from her arms. His brother saw only black and red when they trampled him down and broke his bones with kicks from their hobnailed boots. He bit one of the hands which had tightened around his neck, and did not let go any more. Axes could not strike in the scramble and, held up high, they glittered in the air.

In that raging carnival of the month of July, in the midst of the drunken shouts of the hungry mob, the bell of God continued to sound the alarm right until the evening. No midday bell sounded, and no Ave Maria—just as in a country of Turks. Eventually, tired from the carnage, dejected and subdued, the mob began to disperse. Each one tried to avoid his companions. Before dark, all the doors were closed in fear, and the lamps burned all night long. The only noise in the streets was the dogs' dry gnawing of bones while they rummaged in corners, in the light of the moon. The moonlight made everything white, and showed up sharply the wide open gates and windows of the deserted houses.

Came the break of day: a Sunday, without people in the square,

and without the sound of the Mass bell. The Sacristan was in hiding.
The priests could no longer be found. The first few people who
gathered on the square in front of the church looked with suspicion
upon one another. Each one thought of what his neighbour might
have on his conscience. When there were more of them, they started
to grumble: how could they remain without Mass on Sunday, like
dogs? The "Club of the Gentlemen" was closed. No one knew where
to go to, how to get orders from the employers for the next week.
The tricolour handkerchief still dangled limply from the bell-tower
in the yellow heat of July.

The shadows in the church square were slowly getting shorter.
The people huddled together in one corner. In between two little
houses of the square, at the bottom of the small street which went
steeply downhill, the yellow fields of the plain below, and the dark
woods on the side of Etna could clearly be seen. Now they could
divide those woods and those fields among themselves. Each one
calculated on his fingers how much should be his lot, and looked
askance at his neighbour.

" *'Libertà'* means that there must be something for everyone!"

"Do these fellows, Nino Bestia, and Ramurazzo, imagine that
they can continue with the arrogance of the Hats?"

"If there is no surveyor left to measure, and no notary to write
it down, could not everybody take what he wanted for himself?"

"And if you eat your share up at the tavern, has it all got to be
divided afresh?"

"Thieves, that's what we all are, all of us."

"Now, as *'Libertà'* has come, those who want to eat for two will
have their own feast day, just like the gentry had theirs!" The
wood-cutter brandished his hands in the air as if they were still
wielding the axe.

Next day it became known that the General*—the one
whom all the people feared—was coming to dispense justice. You
could see the red shirts of his soldiers, as they slowly ascended the
ravine towards the little town: it seemed as if all they had to do was
to roll stones from above to squash the lot—but no one moved. The
women cried and tore their hair. The men, dirty and with long beards,
sat on the hillside holding their hands between their thighs.** They
watched those tired young men arrive, bent under their rusty rifles,

*General Nino Bixio, who commanded the government's troops, was
despatched to restore order.
**A favourite posture of rest.

and in front of them, all by himself, that tiny General on his big black horse.

The General ordered some straw to be brought into the church, and he sent his boys to bed, just as a father would do. If they did not jump up at the sound of the trumpet, well before daybreak, he would swear like a Turk and ride his horse right into the church— that was the sort of man he was. Five or six men he ordered to be shot right away, Pippo the dwarf, Pisanello—the first few they came across. The wood-cutter cried like a child when they made him kneel against the wall of the churchyard: he thought of what his mother had said and of her screams when they tore him away from her arms. From afar, and from behind closed doors, these rifle shots which followed one after another sounded rather like the fire-crackers on the day of the Festa.

Later, the real judges arrived; gentlemen with glasses who had been clambering up the hill on their mules. Tired from the journey and moaning about their discomfort, they interrogated the accused in the convent's refectory. They were sitting sideways on the high-backed refectory chairs, and every time they moved, they groaned "Oh!"

The long trial just didn't seem to come to an end. Those who were found guilty were marched on foot into the town. They were chained together in pairs, and made to walk between two lines of soldiers with muskets at the ready. Their womenfolk followed, running along those long country roads which wind their way between the ploughed fields, the cactus plants, the vineyards, and the golden-coloured crops. They were panting and limping. At the bends of the road, when the prisoners' faces became visible, they would call them by name.

When they arrived in the town, the men were locked up in a prison as big as a monastery, iron grilles at all its windows. If the women wanted to see their menfolk, they could only do so on Mondays, from behind an iron gate, and in the presence of the warders.

The prisoners never saw the sun, and in that perpetual shadow the poor fellows became yellower and yellower. Every Monday they would speak less, reply less and complain less. If their women did hang about the prison on any other day, the guards threatened them with their rifles. The girls did not know what to do with themselves, did not know where to find work in the town, nor how to get their daily bread. A bed of straw at the stables cost two *soldi* and the white bread, which could be eaten in a single mouthful, did not fill one's stomach. If they squatted for the night in the church porch, the guards would arrest them. One by one they went home, the wives first, the mothers afterwards. A good many of the girls just disappeared into the city, and were not heard of any more.

Those who had stayed at home returned to the tasks they had carried out before. The gentlemen could not work their land with their own hands; the poor could not live without the gentlefolk. They made peace. The chemist's orphaned son stole Neli Pirru's wife, and this seemed to him the right thing to do in order to take revenge on the murderer of his father. She had certain qualms from time to time, and feared that her husband would slash her face when he came out of prison, but he would just say: "Don't you worry—he won't come out any more."

By that time, few people thought about them any longer. Only a few mothers and some old men did, when their eyes wandered towards the plain where the city was, or on Sundays, when they saw the others talking meekly, beret in hand, to the gentlemen in front of the clubhouse. The devil always takes the hindmost, they thought.

The legal proceedings didn't take a day less than three years. Those three years of prison, without ever seeing the sun, made the accused look like the dead and buried when, handcuffed, they were led to the law courts.

All the people who could possibly do so had come along. The witnesses came, the relatives came and many who were just curious came along too as if they were going to a fair. They wanted to see their fellow-villagers again, now, after they had been packed into that hen coop for so long a time. And what sort of capons they had become in there! With his own ugly face, Neli Pirru had to see the face of the chemist who had made himself his "in-law by fraud".

One after the other they were made to stand up.

"What is your name?"

Each one heard himself called by his full name, and heard what he had done. The lawyers, their wide sleeves dangling, were kept busy in between their chatterings. They got worked up and foamed at the mouth, and then wiped it up immediately with a white hand-kerchief, and took their dose of snuff.

The judges dozed behind the lenses of those spectacles which made the hearts of the prisoners freeze. In front of them sat 12 gentlemen in a row, tired, bored, yawning, scratching their beards and chatting. They considered themselves lucky not to have been the gentlemen of that other little place up yonder, when they proclaimed *Libertà* there!

The accused, poor devils, tried to read the expressions on their judges' faces before they left, to talk among themselves. They waited, pale, with their eyes fixed on the closed door. When the jurors came back, their chief, the one who always talked with his hands over his belly, was almost as pale as the accused when he said: "Upon my honour and my conscience . . . "

The coalman stammered when they came to handcuff him. "Where are you taking me to? To prison? Why? I didn't even take a hand's breadth of land . . . They all said there was to be *'Libertà'*!"

★   ★   ★

This story closely mirrors events which had actually taken place. Verga always adhered to strict incidental accuracy, regarding it as a fundamental requisite for "true" writing. Later generations accepted Verga's descriptions to such an extent that disputes about certain features of a locality, or certain customs at social functions, have been known to have been settled by quoting from Verga stories.

What clearly emerges from this story is Verga's infinite compassion for the doomed—on whatever side he finds them. The tragedy of the deeds is as explicit as the tragedy of the retribution. He does not approve of the deeds, but his understanding of their underlying reasons emerges as clearly as his criticism of the method and the manner of the justice dispensed.

The mob's violence had important consequences. The middle classes and the minor aristocracy rightly held the inefficiency of the democratic government responsible for their plight. The government had encouraged the aspirations of the populace and had promised the people land reform. When that reform came and did not turn out as the peasants had hoped, and when violence occurred in many places, the government and their executive proved quite unable to give adequate protection. Never, the gentry vowed, must such circumstances be allowed to arise again. They realized that it was an absolute necessity that they should be able to protect themselves.

During the disturbances of 1848, a National Guard had been formed, originally composed of volunteers from the bigger towns' middle classes. For the country districts, this Guard was quite inadequate, mainly because its movements were far too slow. A different type of protection was now necessary, a force closely in contact with the peasants, capable of preventing a repetition of those outbursts of ferocity and, best of all, capable of intimidating the restive peasantry altogether. Small units, even individual men only, though of the right type, had to be found, and to be placed in strategic positions. Such people were now looked for and recruited. What was needed was a type of private bodyguard, or private police force, controlled by the local gentry. Applicants should be strong, impressive in appearance, and should themselves be well capable of violence and of intimidation. It was not necessary to be particularly scrupulous; on the contrary, one could almost say that an applicant was the more suitable the fewer scruples he possessed. Plenty of applicants came forward. Quite obviously, the biggest bullies promised to be the most successful intimidators. Those were now selected and duly equipped with weapons and some money. The organisation, if any, was rather loose, and varied from place to place.

Soon the new force started to enjoy themselves enormously: poachers had been turned into gamekeepers. They were engaged to intervene on the side of law and order. They did so, but they quickly learned to feather their own nests at the same time. No business was concluded, no sale of mule, horse or land could take place without some profit of their own accruing simultaneously. Those peasants who did not want to conform, soon learnt what it cost to oppose them. Success came readily to them, and it came even easier once they realized that they could make their position stronger and more secure if they made certain "pseudo-laws". These rules outlawed the giving of information or the reporting of misdeeds to the state's executive. "Manliness requires", so they blared, "that in questions involving personal honour no outside interference between offender and offended must be tolerated." This "manliness" principle became the rule of *omertà*, and demanded, in fact, compulsory connivance from all who knew about their crimes. The population learnt, or had to learn, to respect this rule. At times it may have appeared tempting or expedient to comply with police or army requests for information. Protected by uniformed executives, one could feel quite safe in answering their questions. The executives, however, were only casual visitors; the others stayed for good and all those who had talked out of turn had lessons of reprisal taught to them and to their families. The next time the police came, no one had ever seen or heard anything. Thus the Mafia was born, a sorcerer's apprentice scheme, if ever there was one!

The name "Mafia" itself is most probably of Arabic origin. It was the slang name for a district of Palermo, the *Borgo*. The *Mafiosi* conformed to a pattern, the *tipo mafioso*: proud in bearing, strong and fierce, prone to violence, with a flair for the ostentatious in attitude and dress—fellows who wore their caps in a special manner, right over the ear. Curiously enough the name "Mafia" only became generally used as the result of a play: *I Mafiosi della Vicaria** was first performed in 1863, when Verga was 23 years old, two years before he left Sicily for Florence. Verga frequently alludes to the *"tipo mafioso"* in describing bearing and attitudes, but does not use the term "Mafia" in his writings.

How did the Mafia manage to survive? They were neither the first nor the only terror organisation in Italy. Others had come and gone, but these thugs and bullies had learnt a lesson from their brethren on the mainland: one must never keep any records, lists of members, or addresses of sympathizers. It only brings danger, and makes things easier for the executive.

The organisation which had taught them this lesson was the Camorra. At one stage, the Camorra was so powerful in Naples that no merchant dared to trade without their "help". They indulged in a "bureaucracy", and this proved to be their doom. Nothing is left of them now but the name "Camorrista", an expression with which Italian, and sometimes American, politicians belabour one another on suitable occasions.

What is the historical significance of the Mafia system? The units were small. A few people, known only to one another, formed a *coscia* or "leg". Soon they had a "leg" wherever they needed one, a system which Hitler's National Socialist Party in Germany for example adopted with great success, with the difference that the "leg" was called a cell (*zelle*).

*Giuseppe Rizzotto (1828-95) is generally regarded as the author of this play. He was, however, only the actor-manager responsible for its successful performances in many places, among them New York. In a recent publication, Francesco de Felice states that the writer of the script was the schoolmaster Gaspare Mosca. A *capo mafia* jailbird related to him the play's events, which commence in the prison (*vicaria*) of Palermo. In the play's first scene, the prisoners learn to fight with knives under a pseudo-military discipline (*Verga e la tradizione verista in Sicilia*, Giannotta, Catania, 1966).

The cell system was not the only Mafia export; all protection rackets are of mafious origin. Certain legal and quite permissible business activities also, it is said, derive from Mafia practices. The credit-card system for example is claimed to be a Mafia invention, its "mafiosity" consisting in the failure to disclose to the public the fact that the organizers demand a percentage of the price (generally 5-10 per cent) from the supplier of the goods. Certain connivances met with in trade union practices are also possibly of mafious origin.

While the general situation in Sicily during Verga's youth was troubled and complex, his own personal circumstances remained sheltered and pleasant. He lived in a happy family circle, within a civilized but, in comparison with other parts of Italy, rather backward setting of liberal, provincial *bourgeoisie*. Outside his sheltered home reigned constant political unrest, thriving illegality and abysmal poverty. The middle classes' distrust of the peasants, which stemmed from the massacres of the gentry, had led to a rift of extraordinary depth within the population, some aspects of which persist even now.

The acquisition of land by the middle classes had narrowed the gap between them and the grand aristocracy, but had widened the gap between this new social layer and the Sicilian "primitive". Such a gap existed, of course, in other countries, and Disraeli's novel *Sybil, or The Two Nations* pinpoints its English equivalent. However, the rift was much more severe in Sicily than anywhere else, and far more difficult to bridge because of the lack of education and of opportunity.

In general, the educated Sicilian neither cared for nor understood the attitude of the "primitive", and the two strata lived far apart, as if in separate worlds.

Verga's literary importance is based on his psychological understanding of the primitive, an achievement which came to be referred to as "the lyrical insurrection of the Sicilian primitive". He was led towards this understanding by the power of compassion, with which he was born.

It remains to be shown how he came to be interested in the lives of the peasantry; how he gained in his youth that insight which, maturing within him, led him to greatness, and eventually—if too late for himself—secured fame and recognition for his name.

CHAPTER II

EDUCATION IN CATANIA

M ERELY to have access to education was, during Verga's childhood, a privilege in Catania, and it was a privilege reserved for comparatively few. The general standard of education was utterly deplorable.

The scholastic regulations in force required every town of more than 4,000 inhabitants to have a "Lancasterian" school, while "simultaneous instruction" was to be available in smaller centres. In the province of Catania, educationally the most progressive in Sicily, there should according to this rule have been 28 Lancasterian schools: in fact only 11 were active. The regulation remained a dead letter and education remained a luxury available only to a small minority.

The Lancaster system of instruction seemed to offer a solution to the problem of massive illiteracy among the poor in this backward area. It is a further example of unexpected Anglo-Sicilian connections. Joseph Lancaster, born in 1788 in London, had founded a novel type of elementary school in which gifted children became pupil-teachers (monitors) and instructed their less gifted as well as their younger school-mates. This left the teachers free to carry the educational standard somewhat higher than they could otherwise have done. The method was accepted in Sicily as an example of English know-how in solving difficult problems; in England it was, no doubt rightly, regarded as a potentially retrograde step. The opposition to his system made Lancaster leave London and move to another area which had education problems: the United States. There his system proved highly successful in rapidly overcoming illiteracy and became the basis of a good deal of American education.

In Sicily children of Verga's background were taught privately. Young Verga learned readily and his favourite subject was history. A bread-and-butter letter which the 10-year-old Giovanni wrote to his uncle Don Salvatore to thank him for the gift of a book, claims that he had almost finished reading an Italian translation of Rolin's *Histoire Romaine,* a rather forbidding textbook for one of his age group.* The child's reply to his uncle's enquiry as to what other presents might please him was "more books on history, please", and he reported at the same time good progress in the study of Latin.

To write courteously to Don Salvatore was not only good manners; it was good policy as well. This uncle was the wealthy member of the family, the only one who generally had money readily available. He was Lord of the Manor at Tiepidi, where much farmland belonged to him. A forceful personality, who lived in style, with seigneurial appurtenances and practices which had survived from the feudal period. He was not married, but lived with a *femina*.** She had given him a daughter, whom, in sincere attachment to his *femina*, he decided to recognize. In order to have the best of both worlds—he would be expected to give a suitable dowry to his only child, and yet wished that the Tiepidi estate should remain within the family—he decided that she should marry his nephew Mario, Verga's brother. Calogera ("Lidda") Fortunato thus later became Verga's sister-in-law, and Tiepidi eventually the property of his brother. This marriage gave Mario a distinct financial advantage. Remaining childless himself, he used it to help his brothers, who were almost always in need. He eventually adopted his brother Pietro's only surviving child, Giovannino,*** and left the estate to him.

Young Verga, with his keen interest in history, became a first-rate pupil in the rather fanciful private school where Antonio Abate for almost half a century prepared practically all entrants for Catania's University. It was—exceptionally for the period—a lay establishment. Antonio Abate, its founder, came from a well-to-do family which, as the result of an unsuccessful commercial venture, had been suddenly impoverished. The 17-year-old Antonio, hardly out of school himself, founded a new school on his own. He took most of his younger ex-school-mates with him, and made them his own pupils. Moreover, appointing himself headmaster, he employed about a dozen members of his own family, among them his parents, brothers and sisters.

In spite of such unorthodox beginnings the new school

*Charles Rolin (1661-74), Rector of the University of Paris, was held in high regard as humanist and scholar. Young Verga's letter is published in Gino Raya, *Ottocento inedito*, Ciranna, Rome, 1960.

**Femina* was the technical term attached to the "common-law wife" of a person of standing, who—as frequently practised in Sicily—lived with a peasant girl whom, possibly for family reasons, he did not wish to marry.

***The writer of the letter which follows the Preface.

was very successful, and its success was due to the ability and the colourful personality of its headmaster. Within the framework of his own rather limited education, Abate introduced his pupils to a type of knowledge which the old-fashioned religious colleges neither knew how to, nor wished to, provide. The College of Acireale for instance, at that time a famous scholastic institution, still taught that the earth did not move, and condemned Dr. Jenner's method of vaccination as heresy. The prevailing Public School type of education had not progressed from the climate of the 18th century, with its quarrelsome scholasticism, prevalence of Latin over Italian, almost total lack of knowledge of Italian authors and writings, and preoccupation with rhetorical maxims. Instruction in the classical languages followed mechanical and mnemonic methods and required excessive study of Latin grammar. Associated with all this was a complete absence of exercises designed to develop the intellectual potential of the students.

The education provided by Abate was a great improvement on this type of instruction. His pupils were not only introduced to Dante, Petrarch, Tasso and Manzoni, but even to some of Hegel's *Aesthetics*. The headmaster's own knowledge of Italian had remained rather limited. For example, as the best method of solving the Italian equivalent of the English "would" or "should" dilemma, he recommended his pupils "to close the eyes and let the ear decide what sounds more harmonious". He was, however, a gifted writer of historical poetry, some of which, e.g. his *Venerdì Santo a Catania 1849* (Catania's Good Friday of 1849), dealt with events of the very recent past.

When Verga went to Abate's school, he had completed three years of primary education, and was eight years old. He spent ten years with Abate, mostly as a day boy, but became a boarder when the family went to the country during the summer.

Abate took Verga immediately to his heart, possibly as the result of his admiration for Domenico Castorina, the historian-poet already mentioned* as a cousin of Verga's mother. Castorina's cumbersome *I tre alla difesa di Torino nel 1706 (Three Men at the Defence of Turin)* was regarded by Abate as a "perfect work of art", and he forced his pupils to write summaries of all its 68 chapters. He taught history as well as literature, and when he spoke of the 1837 revolt and the revolution of 1848, he tried to instil a spirit of revolutionary

*See p. 1.

fervour into his pupils. It can well be imagined how exciting and interesting such school lessons must have been. Abate had taken part in that "last ditch" stand for Catania's freedom when Bourbon troops were thrown back from the Porta d'Aci with severe losses (see p. 12). In fact, this engagement might well have resulted in a victory—even if only a short-lived one—if, in the evening light of a rainy Good Friday, the defenders had not been attacked by the fresh Swiss mercenaries which the Bourbon commander was able to throw in, and who revived the courage of their faltering comrades and overcame the resistance of the Catanese.

During this heroic fight, that "glorious disaster" as Abate had called it later on, he had, though wounded, fired his blunderbuss up to the last possible moment. This weapon was later kept in a secret place at his school and his pupils, roused to the idea of freedom by his lectures, were made to swear by the blunderbuss to devote their lives to the overthrow of the Bourbon tyranny.

Abate used his own writings, poetry as well as prose, for patriotic purposes, and taking advantage of the "ignorance and stupidity" of the Bourbon provincial prefect to whom he had read it, he managed to get the first chapter of his novel *Il progresso e la morte* (Progress and Death) past the censor and to have it published. However, the prefect soon realized his blunder, turned sour and put Abate under strict police supervision. Abate's name was added to the list of convicted political criminals, and since possession of firearms was punishable by death the blunderbuss had to disappear.

When Abate had fought at the Porta d'Aci, Verga was only nine years old but he also had a personal memory related to the sacking of Catania. When the battle seemed imminent, his family had evacuated themselves to Vizzini. On returning, they found their house plundered to such an extent "that the only place left to sit on was the outside doorstep". When it was Verga's time to take the oath, Abate's blunderbuss had gone, but in its stead he was permitted to touch the Bourbon bullet which had healed in his teacher's abdominal wall.

Abate always remained a Republican. When the might of the Bourbons began to totter, and Sicily was looking towards a different future, he campaigned violently against the "idiotic resolution to replace one monarch by another". The somewhat complicated political situation of this period is best explained by the two alternatives it offered.

The first alternative was a choice between union with the main-land of Italy, and Sicilian independence. Sicilian independence had at first been the accepted ideal of all liberals. However, by the time Bourbon power faded, union with the mainland of Italy became feasible, and this led to the patriotic Sicilians becoming either Union-ists or Separatists. Abate held that declaring Sicily independent of the rest of Italy was a "totally stupid idea", and Verga wholeheartedly agreed. In their attitudes to the second alternative though, whether the new state should take the form of a Republic or that of a Monarchy, master and pupil differed, and Verga never shared his teacher's republican convictions. He had yearned for liberation from the Bourbons and for the unification and independence of Italy. When the miracle happened, and the patriot's dream became reality, he was filled with gratitude and relief: this resulted in a feeling of admiration for the new "national" monarchy.

Abate, on the other hand, remained a Republican to the end of his days, which brought him again and again into conflict with the "establishment" and much affected the later part of his life. After 1860, when all those who rightly or wrongly claimed that they had "made" the new Italy were presenting their well merited, and their less merited bills, and had their honours and sinecures allotted to them, Abate was left out in the cold. He, the man who still carried a Bourbon bullet in his body; he, the man who had been officially described by the Bourbon State Marshal Statella as "a formidable enemy of the Bourbon dynasty, a most intrepid felon, who, although already wounded, had dared to fight against the legitimate troops and had with his blunderbuss on the plain of the Porta d'Aci killed several soldiers", quite rightly regarded this as a severe injustice and he did not hesitate to say so.

In a pamphlet he claimed that the new rulers deserved the name "Italian" as much as the most tempestuous ocean in the world deserved the name "Pacific", and that their government "belonged to the Italian people in the same way that Judas belonged to the Apostles of Jesus Christ". Abate's trait of contrariness became successively more and more unreasonable, and after an astonishing double love-affair with a mother and her daughter—which ended with a pistol shot and an injury to his leg—he eventually manifested symptoms of a paranoid persecution mania.

Verga always remained loyally attached to his old teacher, well aware that Abate had given him much more than just lessons in literature and history. When he lived in Milan he tried, though without success, to find a publisher for him. He also attempted to recommend him for an honorary degree in literature, which might have made him eligible for the post of Director of Education of Catania, which Abate ardently desired.

Towards his contemporaries, Verga's attitude was generally pleasant and natural, and he was a popular companion among friends of his own age. This group of friends enjoyed playing at "The Three Musketeers" in and around Catania so much that even 30 years later they still addressed one another by names from this novel.

In 1854 and 1855, when he was 14, Verga's education was interrupted by a long cholera epidemic during which the family again went to their country home in Tiepidi. During this period, schoolwork was restricted to occasional instruction in a convent where an aunt of his lived and taught; this enforced holiday proved of great importance for his future.

Although he did enjoy companionship, Verga often chose to be alone. This desire became very noticeable during the family's stay at Tiepidi. He was a competent rider, and enjoyed exploring the countryside on horseback. He came to know the district very well, and he met and began to mix with young peasants. Being rather shy himself, it was very acceptable to him to associate with those who, as a result of their own shyness, put him at his ease. He became attracted to his new friends who, on account of the difference in social standing, did not attach themselves too closely to him, and he was astounded to note the difference in their attitude and outlook. The peasant youths for their part responded by telling him freely about their lives, and from the stories he heard at this time derive the "true cores" of some of his best known stories.

To Edouard Rod, his close friend and translator (see p. 64), he thus referred to the stories in the book *Vita dei campi* (see p. 86):

"In my childhood a long cholera epidemic forced my family to seek refuge in the island's interior, at Vizzini, where we owned some land . . . I took part in the life of the peasants and had close companions of my own age, whose background and characters impressed me deeply. I became very fond of those courageous people I used to see every day, and became involved in their dramas of passion and distress. Instinctively, I tried to understand them. Much later, those impressions of my youth returned with tremendous vividness, and I tried to hold them fast."

Although the wish to put the experience connected with his youth down on paper arose in Verga only comparatively late, he was already at the age of 15 encouraged by his headmaster to write his first novel. Abate had always greatly admired the American War of Independence, through which a "handful of exiles", united by their love for freedom, had "transformed themselves into the leading nation of the world". Under this influence Verga wrote *Amore e patria* (*Love and Homeland*), a story of rather unlikely events with a plot in the style of Dumas. The main work of reference which Abate had recommended for this novel, an Italian version of Macaulay's *History of England,* is still in the library at Verga's house. Verga's novel pleased his headmaster so much that he pressed for its publication. However, another of Verga's teachers, Mario Torrisi, whose lectures Verga attended together with his friend and contemporary Mario Rapisardi, strongly advised against this.

Verga's keen interest in writing gradually became evident. Unlike most of the younger writers, including Rapisardi, who all wrote poetry, his bent was entirely for prose.

Prose writing was in the melting-pot. The old rhetorical prose, full of latinisms and worn-out phrases, still survived, and was used for eulogies and panegyrics, for funeral orations and for all ceremonial occasions. Its anachronistic existence was perpetuated by the lack of interest in, and the lack of proper knowledge of, Italian as a spoken language: the majority of educated people, largely as the result of the teaching of the *padri lettori,* the Father Lecturers, regarded Italian merely as a vernacular. Though no minor solecism in the Latin of their students would escape the eyes of those learned clerics, they willingly permitted them to violate elementary rules of Italian composition. As a result, these pupils habitually committed grave errors of grammar and syntax, and acquired and retained a liking for the obsolete terms and stale constructions which delighted their teachers.

Due to their disinclination and inability to understand and teach their own "live" language, these clerics became the cause of surprisingly widespread mistakes: practically all Sicilian writers of the first 70 years of the 19th century substitute, for instance, the imperfect for the present subjunctive,* a "Sicilianism" which stamps their writing like a hallmark—and an error regularly committed by Abate. Verga later learnt to avoid this faulty construction and it does not appear in his works. It recurs, however, together with other "Sicilianisms", in letters he wrote after his return to Catania.

*e.g. *"Chi guerra vuol, guerra si avesse"* (instead of *abbia*), which in translation reads "Whoever wants war *would* have war" (instead of *"may* have war").

This linguistic indifference increased the danger that Italian would permanently divide into two languages: an "educated" one, full of latinisms and worn-out constructions, and a "popular idiom", differently spoken in each region of Italy. If—from the vantage-point of hindsight—this does not appear a serious danger, it is pertinent to recall that this very division occurred in the next peninsula to the east, i.e. in Greece. Here the division into two languages not only occurred, but persists to this very day, and the existence of two separate Greek languages, a purified one (καθαρεύουσα) and a popular one (δημοτική) is without doubt a contributory factor to the discord which recurrently clouds the Greek political horizon. It is easy to realize what sort of spanners are thrown into the works of democracy if the political parties, beyond their legitimate differences, decide for good measure to speak a different language as well.

In Italy the writer Alessandro Manzoni greatly helped to avert this danger, and became filled with enthusiasm for the project of a lively and universal Italian language. After he had published several, mostly poetical, works, the urgent necessity of selecting a definite pattern of spoken Italian as the proper language for writing and speaking Italian throughout the country impressed itself forcibly on him. Intuition made him, a Milanese, decide that the most suitable choice was the language spoken by the intelligent and educated people of Tuscany, i.e. the Italian of the Florentine intellectuals.

In accordance with this idea, he revised the printers' proofs of his novel *I promessi sposi* (*The Betrothed*), and altered all modes of expression which did not fit into the new concept. This proved of great importance for the creation of a universally acceptable modern Italian idiom, and in the history of Italian literature it is referred to as Manzoni's "rinsing of the proofs in the river Arno". It had taken place in the year of Verga's birth, 1840, and its impact made itself felt in Sicily during his youth. It influenced Verga profoundly, particularly as already in his adolescence he was favouring Sicily's total integration with the Italian mainland. He remained so hostile to any sign of the separatism which always smoulders in Sicily and which can readily be set alight by any discontent with the "continental" government, that he repeatedly offended his friends by his unwillingness to criticize publicly any government action even though he might strongly disapprove of it in private.

Parallel with such feelings went Verga's views regarding the use of dialect in literature. Except privately and only occasionally, Verga never wrote in Sicilian dialect, and disapproved of almost every attempt to do so. He adhered strictly to the language based on the Italian of Manzoni, and resolved to use this as his only means of literary expression.

At the age of 18 he enrolled, conforming to his father's wishes, in Catania University's Faculty of Law. It was an act of filial obedience rather than a personal desire, and any flicker of interest in his subject which might have developed was soon extinguished by the Franciscan priest Antonio Maugeri, the Professor of Canon Law. Even before going to university, Verga and his friend Rapisardi had attended this cleric's classes in philosophical propaedeutics. During this instruction Maugeri had set as a theme for an essay the question as to whether language was of human or divine origin. Verga's approach, "The completely human nature of speech", proved unacceptable. Rapisardi referred later to Maugeri's lectures as a "hotchpotch presented as philosophy". Verga quickly lost interest and occupied himself with the writing of an historical novel.

The subject of this novel was the Carbonari movement, a patriotic independence movement of considerable significance. Its members, the *Carbonari*—the name means charcoal burners— belonged to a secret revolutionary society which was organized on the lines of Freemasonry. The movement had its own, rather odd ritual. A lodge was called *vendita* (sale), members called one another *buoni cugini* (good cousins), God was the "Grand Master of the Universe" and Christ the "Honorary Grand Master". Its red, blue and black flag remained the standard of revolution, until replaced by red, white and green in 1831. The movement's spirit continued in the "Young Italy Society" of Mazzini. Verga's paternal grandfather, previously referred to as member of the "British" parliament for Vizzini, had been a *Carbonaro*. Among well known non-Italians who belonged to the *Carbonari* were Lord Byron, and the young Louis Napoleon (Napoleon III).

Verga's novel *I Carbonari della montagna* cannot be called a good book; its plot of complicated adventures still shows the influence of the revered Dumas, to whom Verga had been presented when Dumas visited Catania for three days in July 1860. The historical basis of the book is inaccurate. In Cattaneo's* opinion its political conclusions show immature judgment and misinterpreted patriotic sentiments: not only did Verga transpose the attitudes and outlooks of 1859 into the quite different atmosphere of 1810, but his verdict

*Giulio Cattaneo, *Giovanni Verga* (*La vita socialle della nuova Italia,* vol. vi), UTET, Turin, 1963.

on the 10 years of Napoleonic rule in Naples, the period of "King
Murat", is faulty and unfair. The years from 1805-15 were, as
Benedetto Croce has pointed out, of great importance because they
diminished to a considerable degree the massive backwardness of
Italy's southern regions. Gioacchino Murat had become a popular
national King of Naples, a second "Rinaldo",* and up to 1860 and
beyond "you could meet old men who treasured as a relic a coin of
this period, looked at it with longing, and kissed it with a sigh".

No wonder Verga felt later thoroughly ashamed of this novel,
and it is characteristic that this youthful effort came in for special
praise from biographers of the Fascist era: the book was made use
of to discover an anti-French or "anti-Gallic" sentiment in Verga,
and also to give Fascist views a respectable background by mis-
interpreting Verga's "interesting conclusions of racial and social
character", and to make him a "pre-Fascism Fascist".**

While the 19-year-old was writing his *Carbonari,* war had
broken out again. Garibaldi with his Thousand had landed at
Marsala, and after the short battle at Calatafimi all Sicily was in
arms. The people rose, burned the records and the buildings
associated with the flour tax, freed the detained and raised the
tricolour. Verga did not join the *Garibaldini* but joined instead the
"National Guard", which after the phase of ferocious violence
culminating in the massacres of the gentry had become open to
craftsmen and peasants as well as to the bourgeoisie. In its No. 1
Legion, 2nd Battalion, Company No. 5, Verga served for almost
four years. During this period general national service was introduced
in Sicily for the first time. It proved an extremely unpopular measure,
Sicilians being prone to believe that whoever leaves the island will
never return. After the first drafts of recruits were sent to the mainland, most families tried to evade the call-up laws. This led to
exacting searches for evaders and to severe punishments. These
aggravated the situation because the evaders, too frightened to
return, had to hide in the forest areas, the *macchie,* greatly increasing
brigandage and its accompanying problems.

*One of the bravest Knightly Heroes, as important and well known in Italy
  as are the Knights of the Round Table in England.

**This unfortunate attraction contributed to the eventually realized desire
  of a Fascist Minister of Education to obtain possession of all Verga's manuscripts. It was done for the benefit of a literary-minded lady friend and her
  brother; the ensuing situation—which was not put right when the regime
  fell—still bedevils the position of Verga's manuscripts and delays the long-
  awaited edition of Verga's *opera omnia.*

During his period of active service, Verga was involved in an ugly incident. When the hopes of improving the economic situation after the departure of the Bourbon kings failed to materialize, the repeated outbreaks of violence, and widespread insurrections of disappointed peasantry, created great nervousness. A group of young people, including some local youths of bad repute, gathered one day outside the Tribunal in Catania and shouted "Viva l'Italia, Viva Vittorio Emanuele," and "Morte ai Borboni" (who had already disappeared anyway). The demonstrators were arrested, because cries such as these, as well as "Viva Iddio", "Libertà" and "Madonna Immaculata", had preceded the disturbances which led to the massacres of the gentry. The townspeople demanded the immediate execution of the arrested. The prisoners were held near the statue of the "Elephant" in the Piazza Duomo*, surrounded by guards; any attempt at execution on the spot by shooting them down would have endangered the platoons opposite. A clever young officer had the idea that the men could be safely shot if they were marched to a place where a dip in the road eliminated this danger. Time passed. The officer-in-charge, who went from time to time over to the nearby Caffè Sicilia for a cup of coffee or a glass of wine, finally decided to go home. The crowd's pressure for the executions increased. Eventually, without any question of a trial, the prisoners were tricked into marching to that "safe" spot, and were shot.

Verga's company was not directly implicated in this murder, as they were guarding another group of prisoners in the municipal offices nearby. It is even claimed that Verga's company had refused to take part in the slaughter. However, the deed was done, and contributed to Verga's feeling of disillusionment with military service. He successfully appealed to his father for help, and with the payment of 3,000 lire to the provincial treasury his days of soldiering and military discipline were over.

During his period of service he had finished *I Carbonari della montagna*. Handing his father the completed manuscript, he asked him for permission to become a writer, and to end his studies. His father agreed to this request, and the novel was published in May 1862. In February 1863, Verga's father died. In the same year, a further novel in contemporary patriotic mood, *Sulle lagune,* which dealt with a love affair in Austrian-occupied Venice (a town Verga had never visited), was published. The publication of these early novels was followed by a period of journalism with several newly-

*See illus. 10.

founded literary-political periodicals in Catania.

Not with patriotic novels, nor with political journalism, nor with the French-influenced "erotic novels" which were to follow, did Verga find his true vocation. His greatness arose out of his knowledge and understanding of the Sicilian "primitive", and was the result of an intuitive appreciation of character traits and a compassionate understanding of the common people. Periods of residence at his mother's villa in the Etna countryside, due to outbreaks of cholera in Catania, extended his experience in this field. He became critically aware of the traits which differentiated the peasantry from the Sicilians of his own class, in particular their "family worship" (specifically the "mother worship"), and their impressive resignation in adversity. He realized that their regarding the birth of a girl as a calamity which saddled the home with a new "parasite" was a point of view which was bound to produce repercussions in their attitude to women in general. Girls were generally looked upon as useless and were compared to couch grass ("twitch"), one of the most obnoxious of weeds. He became interested in the peasants' manner of speaking, not in their dialect—which he regarded as unsuitable for literature—but in their characteristic method of expressing thoughts by linking subordinate clauses "chain fashion" in a non-syntactical way. He observed their habit of repeating the verb, or parts of phrases, at the end of the sentence. He was not a social reformer: it was the psychological interest of the writer which attracted him to the "primitives", not the thought of improving their plight. He was capable of deep compassion for a person and for an individual fate, but he was totally lacking in a feeling for their community or "class".

Most of this, however, still lay in the future. He was thirty-four when his story of a girl from near Sant'Agata li Battiati (see p. 71) heralded the "lyrical insurrection of the Sicilian primitives"; he was over 40 before this reached its heights with the stories about the fisherfolk in nearby Acitrezza which he wove into his masterpiece, the novel *I Malavoglia* (*The Malavoglia Family*).

As yet, he was not concerned with all that. His first novel had been reasonably successful. He felt that he might be on the way to literary fame. What was hindering him were the conditions in his home island. In spite of recent developments, in spite of the liberation from the Bourbons, Catania, like the rest of Sicily, was morally still close to the feudal period and geographically isolated from the centres of real culture. Without railways, without schools, without newspapers and almost without books, men of his background generally not only wrote poorly, but also read little and badly—and the women could not even match that! Ships were the only communication with the outside world, and this meant sailing ships rather than steamers.

The resolution that he must leave this difficult and backward island and go to the mainland, became firmly anchored in his mind. Not as an emigrant in search of a better life, but seeking an Italy where he would be nearer the political and literary events that mattered, and where the rhythm of life was more exciting. An Italy where he, so enthusiastic a supporter of the position of Sicily "within Italy", could experience the exhilarating sensation of being a true Italian—rather than an inevitably somewhat backward, provincial and insular Sicilian.

In 1864 Florence had become the capital of Italy. The political importance of its new status, together with the linguistic glory of Manzoni's Tuscan language, proved an irresistible attraction to the young writer. A year later, at the age of twenty-five,* he left his native Sicily for the first time.

---

*According to De Roberto. Other biographers put the event two to three years later.

CHAPTER III

FRIENDS IN FLORENCE AND MILAN

FRIENDS IN FLORENCE AND MILAN

NOT only was Florence a new town for Verga, it signified a new way of life as well. A life which was almost frightening in its elegance, its cosmopolitanism, its advanced views on everything from politics to sex and in the quite different position of women inside and outside the house.

Florence seemed a strange, fascinating town, with its own problems—but how different were her problems from those of Verga's hapless Sicily! Everything here was far more restrained and genteel than in Sicily. During the great revolution which had forced the last Grand Duke of Tuscany to abdicate, no one had been fatally injured. Yet, in 1865, the Florentines seemed to make much of their own problems, such as these were. Three thousand new inhabitants had descended upon them, mostly from Piedmont, introducing rather perturbing new business methods and manners which caused much criticism. More of these strangers were arriving daily.

Thinking of Catania, Verga may well have been amused to read a leading article in Florence's official newspaper *La Nazione*:

"What will Italians from other provinces who arrive at the station of Santa Maria Novella say if they have to argue with the cab driver who asks for more than the official tariff permits, or with the porter who snatches suitcases out of their hand? If they can see at the first cross-roads that the rules of civic cleanliness—well enforced in other places—do not seem to apply here! If their ears are assaulted by the indecent language of ruffians, and if at night the noise of the inconsiderate or intoxicated disturbs the silence and the well-deserved rest of those who work by day? What are they going to say about this Florence, our admirable centre of art and learning, and about that famous gentleness of our Tuscany people which everyone likes to brag about?"

Amid the many differences, there was, however, one feeling that the people of Tuscany fully shared with the Sicilians, and that was a thorough dislike of compulsory military service. The Tuscan people were prepared to fight for their country—if necessary—but they were only prepared to fight of their own free will. In May 1848, at Curtatone, a volunteer corps of students from the University of Pisa successfully repulsed the three times stronger force of Austria's famous Field Marshal Radetzky and, by doing so, they made Carlo Alberto's victory at Goita possible. When they were told a few days later that they were to be conscripted, it completely changed their attitude. Rather than join the regular troops, they gave up every desire to defend a homeland for which they had been prepared to fight as free soldiers. *"La montura è sempre livrea"*, they said: "Call it a uniform if you like: it's still a servant's livery".

Whoever could, tried to evade the call-up, but even this evasion was conducted differently. Sicilians had to take to the woods, and become brigands. In Tuscany there existed the possibility of the "exchange", and for 1,000 or 1,500 lire a man could persuade some desperate fellow to join up in his place for the prescribed period of eight years.

"Those who could not afford such a sum knew of no sacrifice they would not make, no expedient they would not use, no fraud they would not commit in order *not* to become soldiers. The peasants changed houses to conceal their identity, and would even cut off fingers from their right hand to prove their inability to carry arms. There were arrests, prosecutions and severe sentences. But what did that matter? When all was said and done, was it not better to serve ten years in prison than eight in the barracks?"

At the beginning of his stay in Florence, Verga followed the golden rule of all émigrés: he mixed mostly with people from home, and thus he got to know Dr. Mariano Saluzzo, Professor of Hygiene at the Florence Lady Teachers' College. He was a colourful personality whose lectures were rightly popular: vividly interesting, delivered in Sicilian mixed with Italian during his first years, and later in equally entertaining Italian mixed with Sicilian expressions, they never failed to amuse his students. He was a generous man and, after he had inherited a sum of money, he was prepared to help his friends with loans free of interest and without security; provided they paid back on time, he was even prepared to repeat the process.

Verga was for many years one of his regular debtors, and during the period of "continental" acclimatization, Saluzzo and a few other Sicilians formed Verga's intimate circle of friends. The most intimate of them all, and the one who was to remain his greatest friend all his life, was Luigi Capuana.

Verga had known Capuana, who was one year his senior, all his life; Mineo, Capuana's home town, was only a few miles from

Vizzini, and the Verga family possessed an interest there.* Capuana's social and financial background was similar to Verga's. Their ambitions, too, were in harmony. Capuana was an enthusiastic writer, and at the time of Verga's first visit to Florence he was the feared theatre critic of the *Nazione*. This was a position of some importance, though of such poor reward that he was unable to support himself, and felt forced to return to Mineo. He too was an admirer of the new trends which were emerging in French literature, and in particular of Emile Zola.

Verga's Sicilian friends prepared him for his entry into the new world. Much had to be changed: the cut of his trousers, the style of his jackets—everything was wrong. The buttons on his shoes were big—in Florence they now had to be small. Keeping his eyes open for a bargain, Verga made himself presentable, and eventually he felt ready to visit the people to whom he had letters of introduction. A year or so previously, his friend Mario Rapisardi had been warmly received in the house of the writer Dall'Ongaro, and Verga was made equally welcome. He was most impressed by the cultured atmosphere which reigned there, and it was through this home that he quickly widened his social contacts. The Dall'Ongaros were friendly with the Fojanesis, a Tuscan family from Fojana della Chiana, who stayed in Florence because their daughter Giselda was studying at the College where Dr. Saluzzo taught. The mother's good looks had induced the painter Carlo Ademollo to use her as his model for women of beauty and importance in his historical Risorgimento pictures. The father, of Jewish ancestry, had been a small landowner and was now a timber merchant. They were a high-spirited, intelligent and charming family, though living in somewhat restricted circumstances—the timber business had not prospered.

More affluent were other friends of the Dall'Ongaros, the Assing sisters. These two sisters had a splendid villa in Florence, and here Verga came for the first time into contact with a rather elegant custom of the time: the weekly receiving evening or *salon,* to which all friends, once accepted, were not only automatically invited, but were also expected to come regularly unless prevented by valid reasons. At the Assing's one could meet delightful company in the most

*The interest was a 'capellaneria', a piece of land entailed to the church in such a way that the proceeds had to pay in perpetuity for Masses said for its original donor's and the subsequent owners' souls. It therefore presented its owner (Verga inherited it) with all the responsibilities but few rewards of agricultural ownership. Only on payment of a substantial capital sum to the church could the land be freed from its burden (see p. 183).

pleasant surroundings. A retinue of servants offered refreshments; one could listen to music, or converse about literature and politics in another room, or walk or sit in the garden.

The Assings were of German origin, voluntary political exiles of the Bismarck era. Ludmilla Assing was highly literate, and tried with tact and persuasion to promote the understanding of Goethe in Italy. In order to prevent Italian readers of *Werther* from feeling scandalized when Lotte attends a festive occasion alone and unaccompanied, she praised and explained in a well-written article the less restricted life of Germany's young women. Ottilia, Ludmilla's sister, championed the cause of the American Negroes. In the despair of unrequited love for the Negro leader Douglas, she eventually committed suicide. These two sisters had gathered a cosmopolitan set around them, and Verga was charmed to meet in their house people whose attainments and outlook were totally new to him.

Catania, a town always liable to outbreaks of cholera and given to revolutions, was not a place foreigners cared to live in. Florence was so full of them that they almost caused resentment; Giuseppe Giusti (1809-1850) had already satirized the lavish entertainments of the Russian and Polish aristocrats who were buying the palaces of the impoverished Florentine aristocracy. However, people from abroad were not disliked, and were indeed welcomed, particularly if they, too, were animated by that spirit of excitement which the Risorgimento had brought to the town.

Especially imbued with this spirit of the Risorgimento was Evelyn Cattermole, a beautiful girl of English extraction and Italian upbringing, whom Verga met at the house of the Dall'Ongaros. This 17-year-old had surprised Florence by the publication of a book of verse entitled *Canti e Ghirlande* (*Songs and Garlands*). She was as poetically gifted as she was attractive, and had shaped her poetry—some of it in the spirit and in praise of the Risorgimento—on the rhyme and rhythm of Tuscany's popular verse. A good example is her charming *Miraculous Telescope*:

> I wish I had a telescope, with which to see
> The thoughts that others shelter in their heart;
> Then all your secrets I would spy with glee:
> Are you quite true to me? Or full of art?
> I wish I had a telescope, enabling me
> To read the secrets which your heart keeps guarded,
> That hidden secret which I cannot spot:
> Is it "you love me" or "you love me not"?

But afterwards I'll hand the glass to you,
For you to see my feelings, plain and true.

*Se avessi un cannocchial con cui mirare
dentro al cor della gente ogni pensiero,
tutti i segreti tuoi vorrei spiare,
vorrei vedere se tu sei sincero;
se avessi un cannocchial miracoloso,
leggerei ciò che in cor tu tieni ascoso;
leggerei ciò che il cor ascoso tiene,
se male tu mi vuoi, se mi vuoi bene:
ma il cannocchiale poi ti donerei,
chè tu vedessi i sentimenti miei!*

William Cattermole, Evelyn's father, was a kinsman of the well known painter, and himself a gifted amateur. He had come to Florence from Cannes, where he had been British Consul for some years*, and became Professor of English Language at Florence's Technical Institute. The reason for his move was the education of his eldest son, who was a gifted musician and who hoped to study the violin in Florence. Evelyn, born in Florence in 1849, was from her earliest childhood outstandingly beautiful and very graceful in movement and behaviour.

The Cattermoles became friendly with Dall'Ongaro, who encouraged Evelyn to publish her own poetry as well as her translations of Moore's *Here's the Bower* and parts of his *Odes to Nea*. Thomas Moore** particularly appealed to Evelyn on account of his close association with Lord Byron, for whom she felt the greatest admiration and affinity. Evelyn's first book was very successful, and the combination of charm and beauty with so remarkably early a literary success made her a much admired figure in Florentine society.

The longing for love which characterized so much of her poetry was a true reflection of her own feelings. As a 16-year-old she had been infatuated with a young South American who returned home suddenly, and left Evelyn "to ponder sadly in thought and poetry

*The Public Record Office in London can neither confirm nor deny this appointment. The early lists do not contain Mr. Cattermole's name, but these lists are not complete and do not contain appointments which were part-time and had not always carried full official status. Proper lists only began in 1860.

**The *Odes to Nea* (a character in Euripides' *Medea*) were written in 1803-4 while Moore was Admiralty Registrar in Bermuda. None of Moore's poetry had previously been translated into Italian.

about the loyalty of men and the value of their promises".* At least
four of the little poems in her book point to this episode. However,
soon afterwards she met and married an eligible young officer,
Lieutenant Eugenio Mancini, who came from a distinguished family,
had himself written and published verse, and thus shared Evelyn's
leanings. Shortly after their marriage, which took place in Florence
in 1871, he had to move to Naples to join his regiment. The Count
and Countess Mancini (he reassumed a title his father had relinquished
for democratic reasons) soon became a popular young couple in
Naples' military society (illus. 12).

Verga, too, was socially successful in Florence: his good looks,
his elegant bearing with its hint of sadness and his obvious discretion,
greatly appealed to women. He lived as modestly as he could in order
to mitigate the burden which his maintenance imposed on his family.
This did not prevent his enjoying himself, and he felt very happy in
this new environment. As a good son, he frequently wrote to his
mother about his lodgings, food, activities and friends, and from his
vantage-point in the elegant world gave advice to the rest of the
family. "Tell Teresa [the youngest sister] to let her hair grow right
down to her shoulders. All the smart girls here now wear their hair
in that way."

It is uncertain how long Verga's first visit to Florence lasted.
By the early summer of 1867 he had returned to Catania. A new
outbreak of cholera forced the family to move to their villa at Sant'
Agata li Battiati. The spread of the disease continued, and they
moved further away to a *villetta* his mother owned at Trecastagni.

Trecastagni (Three Chestnuts), an attractively situated village,
lies high up on the slopes of Mount Etna, amid extinct volcanic
craters of the headland of an old lava stream. De Roberto describes
it as "covered with a thick carpet of vine, and graced by a tall and
slender campanile, visible for miles around, from the mountain cliffs
of Taormina to the open fields of the lowland". Resuming his old
habits, Verga rode every day towards the craters "which stud the
flanks of the great fire-mountain with independent hillocks, like giant
warts". At the foot of one of these crater hills, in the shade of a group
of ilex (holm oak, a distinctive Mediterranean evergreen), was the
house of the Perrotta family, friends of the Vergas. Giuseppe Perrotta,
his contemporary, was a gifted musician and Verga often enjoyed
listening to music there in the evenings.

*Maria Borgese, *La Contessa Lara*, Treves, Milan, 1936.

Again he made friends with the peasants and the workers of the district. He was later to use a sad incident from the nearby little town of Viagrande for his story *Nedda,* the work which marked the turning-point in his career. An incident underlying another of his stories belong to this period as well. The Etna foreland contains sandpits under the lava streams, and the disappearance of a red-haired boy under those treacherous pits led to Verga's *Rosso Malpelo* (*The Redhead*).

Florence gradually become Verga's second home. He spent the summers in Sicily, but returned there every autumn until 1871, when he was thirty-one years old. On his homeward journey in 1869, he travelled to Sicily in the company of Signora Fojanesi and her daughter Giselda, who was by now a qualified teacher. A convent school in Catania wanted a teacher of Italian, and Giselda had applied for the post. Being a graduate from Florence's famous Teachers' Training College was distinctly in her favour; moreover, Dall'Ongaro had written to Verga's friend Rapisardi asking him to support Giselda's application. Rapisardi had met Giselda's mother in the house of the Dall'Ongaros, and he was in a good position to help, because the president of the college was a friend of his family. In due course Giselda was appointed, and she was to begin her duties in the autumn.

If made in comfort, the journey from Florence to Catania would at that time take three or four days. In Naples they all went sight-seeing, and spent the night in a hotel. The hotelier thought that the double bedroom which had been booked was to be occupied by the young couple, and not by mother and daughter. The error amused them all. Verga's mother, favourably impressed by the attractive and well-mannered girl, welcomed the Fojanesis warmly. Rapisardi, too, came to see them—he had not met Giselda before.

Evelyn Cattermole and Giselda were later to become close friends. To this friendship we owe her description in the sonnet, *Giselda,** which Evelyn had dedicated to her.

> She is so modern. Powdered is her face.
> Her apron round the narrow waist she ties.
> Her hair's in plaits, and heightened is her grace
> By large and dark and sparkling Jewish eyes.

*Published in the volume *Versi,* Sommaruga, Rome, 1883.

Tutto moderna. Il volto incipriato,
I fianchi stretti da un grembiule, i bei
Capelli in treccie, il fascino celato
Ne lo splendor dei neri occhioni ebrei.

Mario Rapisardi was an odd creature. From an early age he was filled with a passion for writing poetry, and he was undoubtedly very gifted. At the age of 24 (in 1868) he had published the poetical work *I Palingenesi*, a huge epos for which his home town awarded him a gold medal. Later he was to have a monument as well (illus. 16) and he was a true poet laureate of Catania. He regarded love as an essential stimulus for the writing of verse, and belonged to "the modern long-haired, poet-prophet tribe". His *Prometeo liberato* is still regarded as a fine translation of his revered Shelley's *Prometheus Unbound*. With all that, he was inordinately vain, and altogether a somewhat ludicrous personality. He accentuated his eccentricity by dressing in an unusual manner, wore a black bow-tie, and usually carried an umbrella, which is a quite unnecessary habit in the climate of Sicily. He immediately fell in love with Giselda, and seems to have already made up his mind to do so before he even set eyes on her. Giselda did not fancy him much at first, but eventually, "as any good 18-year-old would under the circumstances", she was impressed by his outpourings of love poetry (illus. 13 and 14).

Rapisardi was very jealous by nature, and this jealousy led him to request that Giselda should not see Verga again. He did not suspect Verga and Giselda of having a love affair, but as Verga's mother had befriended Giselda, and Giselda had often stayed with the Verga family in the country, he felt that Verga had much easier access to Giselda than he had himself, and this irritated him. Giselda and Verga agreed not to seek each other's company. Eventually, Giselda accepted Rapisardi's proposal, probably influenced by her mother, who was longing to see her engaged to one or the other of the two before she herself had to return to Florence.

It proved fortunate that Signora Fojanesi was friendly with Dall'Ongaro: he was a friend of the Minister of Education, Correnti, who now recommended Rapisardi for the appointment as Professor of Italian literature at Catania University. The salary and security of this appointment made an early marriage possible, and this took place on 12th February, 1872.*

The known facts regarding the friendship between Verga and

*See also p. 118.

Giselda allow the following four conclusions:

It was an innocent friendship, and Giselda was, in fact, a virgin when she married Rapisardi.

Had Verga asked Giselda to marry him, she would have preferred marrying him to marrying Rapisardi.

Not only was Verga not in a financial position to consider marriage, he had—Rapisardi or no Rapisardi—no desire to propose.

Giselda did not really love Rapisardi, but even for girls brought up to independence, and trained for a profession, a marriage proposal can prove an almost irresistible temptation.

Dutifully and loyally, Verga fulfilled his obligation, and did not see Giselda for ten years: in doing so he brought an innocent and enjoyable friendship to a sudden end.

The main literary results of Verga's years in Florence were the two books *Una peccatrice* (*The Girl Sinner*) and *Storia di una Capinera* (*The Blackcap's Story*). *Una peccatrice* reveals Verga's pipedreams, or "forbidden dreams", as they are called in Italian. Pietro Brusio, a young writer, comes from his island home to the big city and meets instant literary success; success with women and money follow readily. In reality this wishful autobiography was never fulfilled, and Verga was never to become a Pietro Brusio. This proved all the more disappointing as many features of the novel fit the successful career of someone else: Gabriele D'Annunzio, whose gift of poetical expression Verga appreciated, but whom he regarded as a *"mistificatore"* (a hoaxer or cheat),* and whom he thoroughly disliked.

Una peccatrice is a book which has few merits. In some parts it is unduly sentimental, in others it emulates French *grand guignol,* with recognizable traces of *La Dame aux camélias.* The women conform to the contemporary desire for sylphide and siren types, elegant, beautifully dressed ladies in whom "the brilliance of the butterfly makes one forget the caterpillar". Its most original aspect is perhaps the surprise ending—a deliberate ironic and cynical tilt akin to some of Heine's poetry.

The story of the *Capinera* is a work of much greater importance, and remained for many years Verga's best known book. The blackcap (*capinera*) is a bird of the tit family, but the name is also used for the members of religious orders. In Sicily, where girls were regarded as

*Though unacceptable to Verga's contemporaries, this assessment is now regarded as in some respects accurate.

parasites, the idea of disposing of them by assigning them to convent life was always tempting; particularly so if they could not be expected to be an asset in the marriage market.

Verga had some knowledge of convent life. His own mother had been educated at the Badia di Santa Chiara, a convent school only a few hundred yards from the family's house in Via S. Anna. She had never concealed that as a result of her own experiences she strongly disapproved of certain hardships connected with monastic education. She was particularly critical of the forced detention in the "mad cell", a form of solitary imprisonment which was used as a disciplinary measure for even minor cases of breaking convent rules.

Verga's *Capinera* has a stepmother and a stepsister. She falls in love with a young man who reciprocates her feelings, but the stepmother covets the young man for her own daughter, and succeeds with her plan. In order to get her out of the way, she forces her stepdaughter to enter a convent. She dies there, tormented by consumption and a breaking heart—while her ex-lover and stepsister "live happily ever after".

The *Capinera's* story is a variation on the Cinderella theme with a different—and perhaps more realistic—outcome, and bereft of Perrault's fairy-tale illusions. Characteristic of Verga is his description of the heroine's imprisonment; she joins the mad cell's inmate, a grossly backward, insensate female. This animal-like creature shows simple, communicable compassion for the heroine, a feeling conspicuously lacking in the sane characters.

The book has many faults; its letter form alone is too obviously contrived. It is, however, not without true feeling, and shows Verga's preoccupation with the accuracy of incidental detail. In a letter from Florence he had requested his mother's advice about a convent custom: in Italy the newly-married are expected to visit their friends and relatives. These duty-visits are referred to as *dar parte*, i.e. "giving part of", or announcing the marriage. He asked:

"What is the present custom in Catania, if a relative of the bride is in a religious order? Who goes to *dar parte* to her? The bride only? Do bridegroom and bride both go? Or do only the bride's parents go? Please write what is the done thing in this respect—and please reply at once."

Requests of this type occur not infrequently in Verga's letters. To his friend Luigi Capuana he wrote:

"Do you remember that spot near the brick-yard on the road down to the plain—we generally walked no further than that—and can one see

12. Evelyn Cattermole—at the time of her marriage

13   Giselda Fojanesi

14   Mario Rapisardi

15   Verga during his
Florence period

16   Rapisardi's monument in the Bellini
Gardens, Catania

the campanile from there, or the windows of the church? Please reply quickly, I need it for *Il marito di Elena"* [*Elena's Husband,* a novel which appeared in 1882].

Capinera reveals Verga's sympathy with the "derelict", the forsaken, to whom he later referred as the *vinti.** The unfortunate novice in the *Capinera* is his first doomed heroine, though her tragedy is still marred by undue sentimentality.

The *Storia di una Capinera* soon became a relatively successful book. This was partly due to the fact that the consigning of unwilling girls to convents had lately come under public criticism, and the subject had thus acquired some news value. The feudal system had, in theory, been abolished fifty years before the book appeared, but in fact many feudal habits persisted. According to De Roberto:

"With every type of deceit and pretence, and every conceivable abuse or substitution of deeds of trust, the firstborn of the aristocratic families usurped all the hereditary estate. The same applied to the bourgeoisie who aped them. For the *cadetti* [the younger sons and the females] there remained nothing but a miserable allowance called the *piatto* (the plate), which was meant to prevent them from dying of hunger. Most of them were therefore forced to enter one of the many rich abbeys where at least a sustenance was assured."

There was therefore much to condemn, and the book was hailed as a criticism of the system. In truth, Verga had possibly only intended to portray its sentimental aspects. Be that as it may, his book, with Dall'Ongaro's introduction in the form of a letter to the writer Caterina Percoto,** who was fighting wholeheartedly against these abuses, became popular and the critics reviewed it favourably. Financial independence seemed at last to be in sight. A writer's rewards were poor enough. Publishers paid from 15 to 30 lire for a *foglio* (i.e. 16 pages) of the first edition. After six months, the writer could dispose of his work again and sell it elsewhere if he desired. To earn the first 100 lire at the age of 31 did not suggest a lucrative profession, but at last one work had produced a revenue,

*This is often translated as "the vanquished", though it seems better to call them "the doomed".

**The Countess Caterina Percoto, nicknamed *"Contessa Contadina"* (the peasant Countess), was a person of some significance in Italian literature. Born in 1812 in the small, attractively named Friul village of S. Lorenzo di Soleschiano sul Natisone, she lived there until her death at the age 75. She wrote both in Friul and in Italian, and her character sketches and stories display the compassion for the humble which was fashionable at the time.

as well as 200 free copies. The first edition was printed by Lampugnani, but the book was reprinted by Fratelli Treves, and thus was founded a lasting association between Verga and the Treves brothers as authors and publishers as well as friends. A payment of 300 lire secured Emilio and Giuseppe Treves the rights for the *Capinera,* together with those for another novel, *Eva,* for five years.

Verga felt later that the success of the book was undeserved. He never repudiated the *Capinera*—as he did some of his other early works—but he did not like to be reminded of it either. Twenty years later when Treves' republished it in an "elegant definitive edition" Verga wrote:

"I think not to let me know about this new edition was the best thing you could do! Had I known of it, I would have had to rewrite the whole thing, and, without doubt and without pity, I would have thrown out those fineries which you so kindly praise. I can assure you that this would have greatly improved the whole story."

In 1872, seven years after Verga had come to Florence, he decided to leave. He had lost some of his best friends: Dall'Ongaro had moved to Naples, where he died in 1873; Ludmilla Assing's home life had come to an end as the result of illness. Florence had ceased to be the capital, and Rome had taken its place.

For patriotic Italians this was the moment of fulfilment. It seemed nothing less than a miracle that the Eternal City should again be the capital of a united Italy—after an interval almost as long as European history itself. However, when the delirious joy had subsided a sense of disappointment, of anticlimax, made itself felt. The holy places of ancient Rome, and the incomparable buildings of its later periods were all there—but too little else. It seemed difficult to invest Rome with anything akin to its ancient importance.*

Verga did not go to Rome: he went to Milan, the city which saw itself as the real capital (*capitale morale,* see p. 202).

It was in the north that the great industrial expansion was taking place, and where material prosperity stimulated all forms of artistic expression and cultural achievement. Lombardy had all the essentials for success; it had an intelligent and easily trained working population which was prepared to work hard for modest rewards, and possessed ingenious industrialists full of new ideas in design and mechanical

*A section of the intelligentsia, realizing that new Rome would never match the ancient city, felt themselves as epigones, living in a "byzantine" town. The derisory name 'città bizantina' led to the name of one of Rome's literary periodicals, the *Cronaca bizantina* (see p. 125).

application. Lombardy's astonishing industrial development brought
Milan prosperity and increasing importance, and its publishers and
printing presses became the most important in Italy. Their success
was not only equalled, but surpassed, by the music publishers who
soon gained world-wide importance.

The music-theatre had always been of great importance for
Milan. During the Austrian period, which ended in 1859, the Scala
continued with its *stagione* type of opera production, in contrast to
other Austrian opera houses which operated on the repertory principle. While the *stagione* method had the disadvantage of greatly
limiting the number of works performed—Milan had to wait a
hundred years to hear *Fidelio* performed at the Scala—it had the
advantage of facilitating performances of unrivalled excellence in
singing and conducting. It was generally admitted that, particularly
when Miss Malibran was singing, no opera house in the world could
match the perfection of La Scala.

An average of 12 to 14 operas, including two or three
new ones, were prepared for each season; the actual number of
performances for each opera was not fixed and depended upon the
success achieved. An opera which failed to please was generally not
repeated. Highly successful operas saw 30 or 40 performances within
one season. This system gave the person who controlled the theatre
great power—and opened up certain temptations, all the more so if
he himself owned the performing rights (see p. 168).

If the Scala was the centre of Milan's musical life, it was not all
of it. Supplementing the Scala and other places of public performance
were an astonishing number of private opera houses in the homes of a
nobility among whom were many first-class singers and instrumen-
talists. An unprecedented desire for opera had developed, and
everything associated with such performances seemed very important
to the city's cultured circles. No wonder the Italian patriot
Massimo d'Azeglio, who visited Milan from Turin to "rouse the
people and make them shake off the Austrian yoke", complained that
the Milanese aristocracy were more concerned with the eternal casting
problems of their private operatic performances than with a desire
to change by violence the existing pattern of Austrian government.

The most important social feature in this artistic scene was the
famous *salon* of the Maffeis. Andrea Maffei, a literary and musically
gifted young nobleman of Italo-Austrian descent, with considerable
artistic achievements to his credit, had in 1834 married the Contessa
Clara Carrara Spinelli. More by accident than by design, their house

became the meeting place for the best known musicians and writers of the day.

Bellini, Rossini and Donizetti belonged to their intimate circle of friends and so did Giulio Carcano, a writer of great importance for Anglo-Italian cultural exchanges, who had translated all Shakespeare's dramas into Italian hendecasyllables.

Honoré de Balzac had visited the Maffeis in 1837. He was a fascinating guest, varying in mood from Rabelaisian humour to melancholy silences. With the Countess and her husband he discussed the possibilities of developing the island of Sardinia on lines not so different from those presently pursued.

Balzac's visit had presented the Countess with a social problem. He had, in writing and in conversation, criticised Alessandro Manzoni's *I promessi sposi,* and thus offended one of her close friends. This induced the Countess to attempt a reconciliation of the two great writers by making them meet in her house, and to her delight the plan succeeded. Her efforts to bring people together deserve posterity's gratitude, for she caused Manzoni to meet Giuseppe Verdi, her most intimate friend, and when the two giants of music and literature got on well together it was she who suggested that they should create a lasting memorial to their friendship. In fulfilment of her wish, Verdi dedicated the Requiem he had composed to commemorate Rossini to the memory of Manzoni, and himself conducted the Requiem at the Church of San Marco on 22nd May, 1874, the first anniversary of Manzoni's death.

Andrea Maffei lacked his wife's energy and charm, but possessed varied literary gifts. He wrote poetry in sonnet, ode and idyll form, and used his profound knowledge of English and German to put into Italian works that had not previously been translated, among them Milton's *Paradise Lost* (*Il paradiso perduto*). He introduced Heinrich Heine to Italy and his translation of *William Ratcliff* inspired the young Mascagni to compose the opera of that name (see p. 141).

Engaged in these cultural activities and filled with cosmopolitan ideas, Andrea Maffei lacked in the eyes of his wife the national zest necessary to free Milan from the Austrians. The Countess's interests had, under the influence of Massimo d'Azeglio and later of Carlo Tenca, veered towards more patriotic work, and the proportion of politicians among her friends had increased significantly. After 1848, her interest in the Risorgimento became passionate and her dislike of Austria led her to play a role in the tragically mismanaged Easter Rising of 1851, when at a signal given from London by Mazzini a dozen or so Austrian soldiers—in fact batmen who were bringing pastries and gateaux to their officers—were ambushed and killed. This led to immediate and energetic counter-measures, and as a result the general atmosphere in Milan badly deteriorated. This deterioration also affected public reaction to works of art, and operatic works were henceforth judged more by their patriotic content—or by the possible imputation of such content—than by their artistic value or the quality of the performance.

The operas which lent themselves most to demonstrations of such political sentiment were Verdi's *Nabuccodonossor* (later generally referred to as *Nabucco*), *Attila* and *Ernani,* and Donizetti's *Belisario.* The trend culminated in the extraordinary incident during the performance of Bellini's *Norma* on the eve of the war of liberation (29th January, 1859) when the whole audience rose and joined the principals and chorus in singing *"Guerra, Guerra, le galliche selve",* the war hymn of this opera. If sung at all correctly, it must have been a difficult feat for them to perform.

Andrea Maffei's lukewarm attitude towards his wife's patriotic activities created friction between them which eventually led to a voluntary separation. The deed of separation, with a loophole for a possible reconciliation, was signed as witnesses by Giuseppe Verdi and the writer Grossi, the author of *Marco Visconti.* Verdi, an agnostic, had no prejudices against the dissolution of a marriage, but in general the separation alienated sympathy and reduced the esteem in which Andrea Maffei was held. One result was that he came wrongly to be regarded as selfish and tyrannical.

The Countess's social activities are now considered to be of such importance by historians that they have been divided into three separate phases. The first, with Donizetti, Bellini and Rossini, was the classical period. The second (or political) period culminated in her contribution to the eventual liberation of Milan from the Austrians in 1859. During the third period (in 1872) Verga became a guest, and soon a friend of the house. He was accepted from the beginning with open arms, as it was remembered that his uncle Domenico Castorina (see p. 31) had been a visitor during the first period. How popular Verga was in these circles is documented in a letter from Ferdinando Martini, the founder of Italy's first literary weekly journal of national importance, who wrote to Verga on 13th March, 1875, from Pisa:

"I am sending you a whole load of requests, all neatly arranged in lines, one after the other. Here they are. Point One: please apologize for me to the Countess Maffei. After my fleeting appearance in her home, I really ought to have gone back—but as usual and in spite of every good intention I just did not have the time. If you are prepared to use with that dear old lady the eloquence which you so expertly employ with the younger (and probably less good) ladies there, you are bound to obtain forgiveness for me."

For Verga, the Countess's salon was the ideal introduction to the high society as well as to the artistic circles of Milan. His link with this society led to his adulterous love affair with the Countess Paolina Greppi, an affair probably connived at by her husband. In his short story *Fantasticheria* (see p. 83), Verga gave the Countess an unusual memorial.

Two of the men who were to become his close friends, Giuseppe Giacosa and Arrigo Boito, Verga met first in the Countess's home. They formed an inseparable trio for many years to come.

Giuseppe Giacosa came from Ivrea, near the Val d'Aosta, an alpine area of great beauty on the borders of France and Italy, and inhabited by a French-speaking community. By vocation a dramatist, he became, from *La Bohème* (1894) onwards, Puccini's foremost librettist. At the beginning of his friendship with Verga, Giacosa was still a struggling playwright. His plays showed undue preoccupation with the mediaeval accoutrements which were favoured at that time, the pages, dames, and minstrels. This led his critics to the bon mot that he was "already in his youth condemned to permanent middle age", though several of Giacosa's well written and well constructed plays have earned a place in Italian theatrical history. They are favourites of Italian amateur dramatic societies, with occasional performances on the Italian radio.

Arrigo Boito was one of those young rebels who turn ultra-conservative in middle age. Born in Padua in 1842, of a Polish mother and an Italian father, he possessed the double gift of musical inventiveness and poetical expression. He was a man of integrity and impartiality whose judgment was always guided by honest feelings. *Mefistofele,* his operatic version of Goethe's *Faust,* was a failure when first performed at the Scala in 1868, but a revised edition later proved successful. His great work, *Nerone,* became something of a byword. Its impending presentation was prematurely announced many times; the eagerly expected work took many years to complete.

Boito was attracted to German 19th century romanticism in music and literature and echoes of the *Freischütz*'s wolf's glen scene appear in his *Mefistofele.* He was a romantic in behaviour as well, and unlike his friend Verga, who never abandoned his aristocratic reserve and remained disinclined to show his feelings (behaviour hardly to be expected in a Sicilian), Boito was prone to sentimental outbursts. On the occasion of a holiday spent at Giacosa's home, Boito felt so overcome by the beauty of the Theodule glacier that he wept from emotion in the much disconcerted Verga's presence.

Boito made two erroneous predictions regarding theatrical fortunes which were much commented upon, and both concerned works of his friends. He wrongly foretold failure for Verga's play *Cavalleria rusticana* and for Puccini's opera *La Bohème*. Both times the error was due to the true romantic's insuperable antagonism to everything connected with *verismo*. His mistake over *La Bohème* so upset Boito that he resolved never to advise on theatrical ventures again. The error had not been caused by a failure to appreciate Puccini's work; on the contrary, Boito had helped to put Puccini on the map, and had given him great support during the Sonzogno scandal of 1884, the year the first "Sonzogno competition" had taken place.

Edoardo Sonzogno was born in 1836. In 1861 he succeeded his father in the management of a successful publishing business. Other interests gradually followed (see p. 168). The wealth of the firm originated from the sale of cheap editions of Italian classical writers, as well as from the type of popular novel once referred to as "servants' hall literature".

In an attempt to improve the firm's standing, Edoardo added in 1874 a music publishing firm to the Sonzogno empire. Competing with the established Milan firms of Lucca and of Ricordi, his firm devised in 1883 the "Sonzogno competition". This was a publicity venture in which the *Teatro illustrato* offered 2,000 lire to young composers as the prize for a popular one-act opera; it was subsequently repeated in 1889, 1893 and finally in 1903.

Puccini had just completed his four years at the College of Music in Milan. During his final year he was the outstanding pupil in Ponchielli's composition master class, and his leaving work, *Capriccio sinfonico,* had not only been praised, but had been printed as well—a memorable achievement for a beginner. Puccini decided to enter his opera *Le Villi* in the Sonzogno competition, for which Boito was one of the judges. Puccini's work was the best entry in the competition, yet the prize did not go to him, but was shared by two now forgotten composers, Luigi Mapelli and Guglielmo Zuelli.

The reason for this extraordinary misjudgment later aroused

considerable curiosity and speculation. It was, for instance, claimed that Puccini's handwriting was so bad that the judges "could not be bothered with it", a contention which is also put forward in Mosco Carner's biography of Puccini.* It is a most unlikely explanation: Puccini's writing was good enough not to have caused serious trouble during his studies, during which the neatness of handwriting must have been judged more severely than in an open competition. It is, therefore, most unlikely that the appearance of his manuscript, however amended or untidy, should have barred him from the prize.

Probing into the rather misty subject of the *Premio Sonzogno* (the firm's archives were destroyed during an air raid in August 1943) suggests that the competition was not only—quite properly—a publicity stunt, but a "fiddle" as well. It seems that Sonzogno imposed the reasonable condition that he should have the casting vote in the case of differences of opinion among the judges. However, he interpreted this in a rather unorthodox manner and presumed that it entitled him to name the winner himself, unless the verdict of the judges was unanimous. On the occasion of the first competition at least two of the judges, Boito one of them, were in Puccini's favour. There was no unanimous verdict, and this gave Sonzogno the opportunity to champion Zuelli and Mapelli.

The two prize-winning operas were performed at Milan's Manzoni Theatre on 4th May, 1884. Carlo Gatti writes:**

"Anna e Gualberto by Luigi Mapelli and *La Fata del Nord* by Guglielmo Zuelli . . . after a few performances, the two prize-winning operas, hardly applauded and damned by faint praise, disappear forever from the operatic repertory. On the other hand, a sensational triumph awaited Puccini's *Le Villi.* Some maintain it did not win the prize because it was unfinished, others assure us that illegible scrawling was the reason. In any case, Puccini's triumph meant at the same time a condemnation of the competition as well as of the jury."

This condemnation of the jury is not justified; it only permits Sonzogno, the real culprit, to escape criticism. In fact, the jury's error was redeemed by Boito's courageous and risky action. He immediately declared that the judgment was wrong and that Puccini's work should be performed publicly. Assisted by Puccini's ex-teacher, Ponchielli, he campaigned with skill and energy towards this aim. They were supported by the writer Ferdinando Fontana,

---

*Mosco Carner, *Puccini,* Duckworth, London, 1958. The name of Puccini's competitor given on p. 38 is wrong: it was Mapelli, not Borelli.

**Carlo Gatti, *Il teatro alla Scala nella storia e nell'arte,* Ricordi, Milan, 1964.

who introduced Puccini to the publisher Ricordi, and a performance of *Le Villi* was arranged at Milan's second opera house, the *Teatro dal Verme*.* It proved a resounding success.

Boito and Ponchielli's enthusiastic recommendation of the work, together with the information that the opera had been entered for the Sonzogno competition without winning prize or recommendation, was used to advertise the performance. The whole affair cast an ambiguous light on this competition.

Verga did not know Sonzogno, but had been in touch with him at the end of his stay in Florence, when he was trying to get the novel *Eva* published. Nothing had come of this, but it had not left a feeling of resentment or hostility. There is no doubt that, through his friend Boito, Verga was very well informed about every detail of the Puccini affair. It is conceivable that it occasioned a feeling of animosity towards Sonzogno in him.

Verga enjoyed his years in Milan, and these years proved the most fruitful period of his life. He continued to visit Sicily most summers, generally staying with his brothers. His standard of living in Milan was higher than that during his stay in Florence. Though he continued to rent furnished rooms he used and travelled with pieces of his own furniture; an iron bedstead, his lectern and one or two chests. He led a busy social life, and often visited the Scala. He had made many new friends.

Most of Verga's works from the publication of the *Capinera's* second edition onwards were published by the brothers Treves. Emilio Treves had used a period of political exile in Paris to acquaint himself thoroughly with the advanced methods of French publishing houses. Returning to Milan he and his brother founded their publishing company** and applied these methods successfully. He was Verga's careful adviser and proved, on the whole, a good friend; he possessed a keen business sense. The failure to recognize Verga's masterpiece when he had it in his hands was something he shared with many others. Verga did not really blame him for it, and bore him no grudge. Treves owned the Villa Cordelia at Pallanza, where he liked to entertain his authors, and Verga was a frequent and welcome guest there (illus. 55).

---

*The theatre later became a cinema; it does not exist any longer.

**The company (Fratelli Treves) existed until 1940 when, under the Nazi rules which were adopted by Fascist Italy it was 'aryanized' and renamed Garzanti.

Another of Verga's Milan friends, though perhaps not quite on as intimate a level, was one of Italy's most gifted journalists. Eugenio Torelli-Viollier, the bilingual son of a French mother and Italian father, was born in Naples in 1861, more than 20 years Verga's junior. Alexandre Dumas had followed Garibaldi to Naples, and Torelli-Viollier became his secretary during Dumas' stay there. After a period with a Naples journal he moved to Milan as editor of one of the Sonzogno papers. Later, he moved to the Treves-owned *Corriere di Milano,* which he converted into the *Corriere della sera.* With the first issue of this paper on 5th March, 1876, he became the founder of modern Italian journalism.*

Torelli-Viollier was an early and sincere admirer of Verga's writings, and the only man in Milan to predict the success of Verga's *Cavalleria* play (see p. 114). He died in 1900, at the early age of forty, and was succeeded as editor by Luigi Albertini, the son-in-law of Giuseppe Giacosa.

To a busy newspaper editor, Verga may well have been at times a source of irritation. Verga encouraged his lady friends with literary leanings to translate successful novels from the French, and then attempted to sell these translations on their behalf to newspaper editors for publication in serial form.

Verga read and spoke French fluently, but never attempted to write in French, or to translate his own works. However, he was not only keenly interested in the translations of his writings, but very anxious to help in a personal way as much as possible. This led to a friendship with the French-Swiss Edouard Rod, a writer with a great interest in Italian literature, who had published a series of articles on Italian writers for the French journal *Parlement.* Originally, he approached Verga with the request for permission to translate one of his less felicitous short stories for the *Nouvelle Revue,* a French literary periodical. Rod's knowledge of Italian was limited, but it was improved somewhat by his engagement to Mademoiselle Gonin, a university student of Italian language and literature. Rod was a prolific writer; he published 50 novels, one of which is dedicated to Verga. His writing shows similarities of expression to several great writers who had successively impressed him,

*It is worth noting that the changes he introduced were based on English rather than on French examples: for instance, the objective presentation of political views without supporting any party (he himself was a moderate liberal). The paper's new obituary column was modelled on that of *The Times.*

initially Flaubert, later Zola, and eventually Anatole France; this last affinity made Léon Daudet refer mockingly to him as "Anatole Suisse" (illus. 27).

To Rod, Verga always wrote in Italian; to Zola, he wrote in somewhat imperfect French. René Ternois has published several of Verga's letters to Zola *"où les phrases sont parfois incorrectes, mais les idées interessantes"*, adding *"j'en respecte les mots, même incorrects, mais je n'ai pas cru devoir respecter les fautes d'orthographe."*

Making new friends did not diminish Verga's affection for his old companions, in particular Luigi Capuana who, after his forced return to Mineo, served for a period as its mayor. In 1877 he followed Verga to Milan, and during the summers in Sicily Verga often stayed with him at Mineo. Capuana was endowed with many gifts. He was keenly interested in psychological problems, was an accomplished engraver, entomologist, archaeologist (he published a paper on Greek vases), photographer, naturalist, and sometimes a spiritualist as well. He shared Verga's views on "true" and "natural" writing, and with Verga is regarded as co-founder of *verismo* in Italy (illus. 19).

Their approach to story writing was somewhat different. Verga's own stories invariably contained a "true core" and, judging Capuana by his own standards, Verga expressed amazement at the effort Capuana must have made to hear and to trace all the Sicilian stories which he published. Capuana replied that the effort had been negligible; the stories had entered his imagination in an inexplicable manner, and came to him in a hallucinatory kind of exultation, mostly in the early hours of the morning, while lying awake.

One of Capuana's most successful books is his collection of Sicilian fables *C'era una volta* (*Once upon a Time*), and every child in Sicily knows *Scurpiddu*, a favourite figure from one of his children's books. His children's stories were so popular that in 1910, encouraged by a newspaper, children from all over Italy sent Capuana many thousands of postcards on the occasion of his seventieth birthday.

Verga always enjoyed reading Capuana's work, and he particularly liked Capuana's *Comparatico*.* This is the story of a husband who, after four years of marriage, realizes for the first time that the man he believes to be his friend, and who is his child's godfather, is in fact his wife's lover—and the real father of his son. On the night of

*Reprinted, with an English translation, in Alfred Alexander's *Luigi Capuana's Comparatico*, Ciranna, Rome, 1970.

a carnival he feigns drunkenness and manages to contrive that all three go to bed together. While his wife and the godfather make love, he stabs them to death.

Capuana's short story has its own history. The Sicilian writer Lionardo Vigo had in 1857 published a selection of Sicilian folklore poetry, the *Canti popolari Siciliani,* and Capuana had upon Vigo's request supplied several items from the Mineo district for this work. Later, Vigo decided to enlarge it and from 1870-74 he collected over 6,000 original pieces of popular poetry for his *Raccolta amplissima di canti populari Siciliani.* For this work Capuana had sent him *Lu cumpari* (see p. 81), a "leggenda" which seemed to Vigo to be so undoubtedly genuine that he unhesitatingly included it in his collection. However, this poem was a practical joke, to which Capuana admitted when he published the same episode in its short story form (*Comparatico*) in his book *Homo,* which appeared in 1883.

Verga—and posterity agrees with him—regarded the novel *Il marchese di Roccaverdina* as Capuana's best work. The setting is Sicilian enough. The Marquess of Roccaverdina has taken Agrippina, a 16-year-old peasant girl, as his mistress. She loves him dearly but circumstances arise which make it advisable for him to marry her off. The Marquess stipulates that the marriage must not be consummated. When the young couple begin to be fond of one another, the jealous Marquess murders Agrippina's husband. Agrippina accepts all this in dutiful love and represses the turmoil in her heart.

The Marquess takes a dislike to her, agrees to her marrying again and sends her away. No reproach leaves her mouth—she obeys her lover, who is God-like to her. The Marquess suffers a stroke and loses his senses; he is haunted by the recollection of his crime. Agrippina returns to him in order to look after him, talks to him as if to a child and comforts him when the memory of his own deeds plagues him. Finally, she has to endure the family's accusation that she had persuaded the Marquess to kill her husband.

Agrippina is the main figure of the novel. In spite of the setting, which in its psychology is somewhat contrived, Capuana has succeeded in overcoming his tendency to cold, experimental story telling. "No longer", says Croce, "is the overwhelming love of Agrippina Solmo mere analysis like so much else in Capuana: it has become true poetry".

The explanation for the particular warmth with which this girl's story is told is supplied by Capuana's own life. In 1875 the 36-year-old Capuana began to live with the servant girl Beppa

17 Arrigo Boito (1842-1918)
at the age of 26

18 Verga at the beginning
of his Milan Period

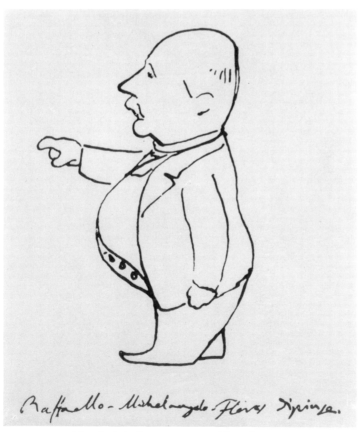

19 Luigi Capuana—a self caricature

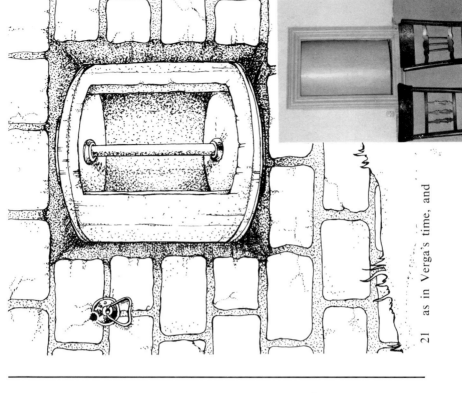

21   as in Verga's time, and

22 (inset)   as used at present in a convent near Catania

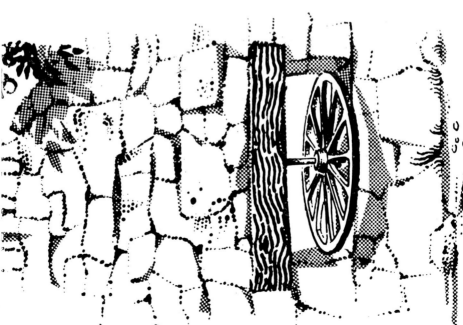

20   in its simplest form

Sansone. She was absolutely devoted to him. In 1877 Capuana went to live in Milan. His departure left Beppa, who believed that he would never return, so heartbroken that she attempted to commit suicide. She drank a phosphorus solution, which she had obtained from match-heads and prepared on the chemical principles learned from her lover and master. Capuana was so touched by this evidence of devotion that he took her with him to Milan in 1879. She continued to address him there in public as *Voscenza* (short for *Vostra Eccellenza*, i.e. "Your Excellency"), a habit which the Milanese found rather unusual. Their relationship caused much adverse comment in Milan as well as in Sicily, where Capuana's family were anxious for it to end, particularly as it resulted in the production of a child every year. The children were, one after the other, put on the wheel* (see p. 73).

Capuana's brother attempted to make him break off the relationship by accusing Beppa of infidelity. The almost certainly innocent girl denied the accusation and, in order to arrive at the truth, Capuana hypnotized the girl and submitted her to various spiritualist tests, all of which she passed successfully.

Capuana's liaison with Beppa Sansone, which had lasted 15 years, ended in 1890 in Sicilian fashion when Capuana, under increasing pressure from his family, married Beppa off to one Mario Speranza. In the *Marchese di Roccaverdina* Capuana represents himself; even in the nightmare of the Marquess's jealousy the book contains much autobiographical material. Beppa was his great love.

In his letters to Capuana, Verga is more open about himself than to anyone else, and the feeling of sincere contact was mutual. Many years later, when Verga attended a meeting at Catania University in Capuana's honour, he referred to their "brotherly communion of literary sympathies and intentions".

Surrounded by interesting friends, and stimulated by pleasant surroundings, Verga continued to write insipid novels, novels of his "erotica among the well-to-do" phase, novels which had Florence or Milan as background, and which somehow gave the impression that they had been translated from the French. Their names, too, were characteristic—*Eva, Eros, Tigre Reale* (*Royal Tigress*).

*In this respect Capuana compares very unfavourably with Emile Zola, of whom Gino Raya reports in a delightful article (I fagiani di Emilio Zola, *Nuova Antologia* n. 2009, 1968) that he was so fond of his illegitimate children that he had them walk to and fro under his window, just in order to be able to see them. Eventually his wife, herself childless and appreciating his affection for the children, one day simply put her arm on his shoulder while he looked out of the window, and said: *"Fais-les monter"*.

In 1874, at the age of 34, ten years after he had left Sicily, Verga suddenly wrote an altogether different story. It was the first story in which he used a Sicilian rural setting with the desperately poor of his island home as background. In the words of Luigi Capuana, this story opened up "a new seam in the mine of Italian literature".

The title of the story was *Nedda, bozzetto siciliano* (*Nedda, a sketch from Sicily*).

CHAPTER IV

TRUE WRITING AND VERISMO

TRUE WRITING AND VERISMO

INAUSPICIOUSLY enough, *Nedda* begins with a hackneyed introduction, but it soon becomes clear that this story of the pathetically poor girl who scratches a meagre living out of harvesting olives is written with real psychological understanding. In every respect it presents a great improvement on anything Verga had written before. Nedda herself is one of Verga's "doomed", those unfortunate people who, once they have committed their "tragic error", take one blow after another in pathetic resignation, unable to escape from their fate. As nearly always in Verga's writing, the story is based on a true core, an incident which had occurred in the little town of Viagrande on the slopes of Etna, when one of the periodic cholera epidemics of Catania had driven the Verga family to the nearby Sant'Agata li Battiati.

Nedda's* character is drawn with precision. She is, according to Benedetto Croce:

"animated by a feeling of justice at the bottom of which lies a respect for personal property, as well as a certain restraint resulting from the resignation of those who cannot imagine that things could be different from the way they are".

For olive-picking from daybreak to nightfall a girl would at that time earn somewhat less than one lira. Correctly adjusted to purchasing power, this represents less than one tenth of the value of the present daily wage for a 9-hour day. In *Nedda* everything is described realistically, and the black and white division into good and bad is gone. Even the "torturers" of the doomed are reasonable people, and at times are even kind. Bad weather had caused loss of working hours, and Nedda has earned very little. She does not dare to complain, but when she goes to collect her pittance her eyes are filled with tears.

"Are you complaining?" growls the factor.

"No", says Nedda timidly, "it was the fault of the weather that I only earned half of what I should have had."

*Nedda is the Sicilian diminutive of Sebastiana, short for SebastiaNedda. Janu is the corresponding male name, short for SebastJanu.

" Pay the poor girl her full week," says the owner's young son to the factor. "It is so little that the whole thing doesn't matter."

"But I must only give her what's due to her."

"And if I say that you should?"

"All your neighbours will be up in arms against us if we do that sort of thing."

The rain makes the olives from the fruit-laden trees fall into the mud—but no one must attempt to pick up a single olive to eat with his dry bread! The olives must rot: for fear of the factor no one dares touch them.

"That's only right," says one woman, "because the olives are not ours."

"Quite," replies another, "but they do not belong to the ground either, and it eats them up!"

"But the ground belongs to the landlord, too," says Nedda, with triumphant logic and expressive eyes.

"That's true," agrees the woman, who does not know what else to say.

Nedda's mother is dying, and after her death Nedda's loneliness is relieved through the love she and Janu have for each other. In a scene described with realism and tenderness, the barriers fall and they become lovers.

When she realizes that she is pregnant, they decide to marry after the olive harvest. In order to increase his earnings, Janu works in a malaria-infested area where danger money is added. When she sees him again, Nedda notices with distress that he is ill.

"I can still work on most days," he affirms. "The fever only comes every third day."*

He tries to work as hard as possible, but in an attack of weakness he falls from a tree and dies as the result of his injuries. On the morning after his death Nedda goes to pray. When she enters the church she meets the priest who knows of her condition, and turns back. She is alone and forsaken. Her savings are gone, and when she tries to find work, people just laugh because she is quite obviously not capable of strenuous physical work.

After several experiences of this kind she shuts herself up in her hut, like an injured bird in its nest. A rickety and stunted child is born. When she realizes that it is a girl, she cries, but she does not wish to give it to "the wheel" and prays that her poor infant may not have to suffer too early in its life. When the other women realize that she intends to keep her child, they regard her as a brazen and

*Malaria in Sicily was typically of the "tertian" type, with fever occurring every third day. The disease is now eradicated.

unrepentant sinner. The child misses the mother's milk as much as
the mother misses her own bread, and on a winter's night the baby
dies of cold and hunger. "Blessed are you who are dead," says Nedda
at the end of the story. "Blessed are you, holy Virgin, who have
taken my little creature away from me so that she should be spared
that suffering which I have to endure."

Nedda's desire to keep her child is caused by her "being neither
a hypocrite, nor wanting to act contrary to nature", but it antagonizes
the women around her. What was Nedda, according to Sicilian
custom, meant to do?

For the poor, the obvious means of disposal was "the wheel" of
the orphanage, which institution was generally attached to a convent.
The stone walls of the convents had, at some distance from the gates,
a rectangular opening in a convenient place in which a wheel could
rotate horizontally (illus. 20). Nearby was a bell handle. The unwanted
child, wrapped in its swaddling clothes and accompanied by anything the mother could spare, was placed on the wheel, and the
bell was rung. The nun on duty would hear the bell, walk within
the convent towards the wheel, and in turning it admit the infant
into the convent. The mother could feel assured that it would be
taken care of, and that her own anonymity remained safeguarded:
there were neither doors nor windows nearby, and the nun could see
as little of her as she could see of the nun.

The children were then reared and brought up in the orphanage.
However, as the convent's means were limited and the unwanted
children many, these children were, as soon as they were capable
of doing some work, handed over to whoever wanted them for
help in the house or on the land. Their future was therefore uncertain,
and their prospects generally poor.*

*This unfavourable outlook made the procedure unacceptable to the rich,
who preferred a different method of disposal: by paying a sum of money to
a willing family they had their unwanted children brought up under some
supervision and control. When this was not desirable, "Angel Makers" were
resorted to: these were people who lived in places difficult of access, often
in mountainous regions, whose task was the speedy conversion of the child
into an angel. (The child's innocence automatically assured the status of
"angel" once death had occurred.) Death was caused by slow starvation,
and a wasting illness was blamed. This foul murder was hard to prove, and
the ghastly system difficult to eradicate. In some districts of Bavaria and
Austria the loathsome practice persisted until late in the 19th century and
ended only after a number of executions of Angel Makers on the gallows.

The final disappearance of the system was probably due less to prosecutions and punishments than to the advent of "criminal" abortion.

Nedda marks a turning-point in Verga's work. It is the first story of his that we regard as belonging to *verismo,* the Italian literary movement which had links with French realism and naturalism. French prose writers had a large public in Italy; any Italian not wishing for a steady diet of poetry (little good Italian prose was being written) was able to augment this with liberal helpings of prose in French, which was widely understood in Italy. Several Italian writers could write in either language. Among Verga's friends, Luigi Gualdo (1847-1898) made it his habit to alternate between writing novels in French and Italian (he translated Verga's story *La lupa* into French); Giuseppe Giacosa, too, wrote French sufficiently well to use it as a second creative language.

In the 19th century French novel writing underwent great expansion and great change. It was a case of development rather than of new departures. Stendhal, George Sand, Balzac and Mérimée had turned to a painstaking observation of reality. Earlier writers had, of course, not ignored this completely, but only permitted themselves a partial view of it; the great 19th century novelists now wanted to reproduce reality *in toto.* Every side of human nature, pleasant or unpleasant, was to be shown; no wonder that the warts became at times unduly prominent.

In 1857 Flaubert's *Madame Bovary* dealt romanticism its final blow and opened the way for the realist novel. Emile Zola (born in 1840, the same year as Verga) at first followed Flaubert, but soon branched out into naturalism, the theory of which he expressed in 1880 in his *Roman expérimental.* Realism intended to give a faithful, documented picture of reality; naturalism now claimed a scientific basis. For the realist writers it had been sufficient to observe and to document: Zola claimed that "the novelist is both observer and experimenter."

Zola had embraced this view as the result of the new trends in physiology, particularly Claude Bernard's *Introduction à la médecine expérimentale* (1865). This rational guide to the assessment of experimental studies was not only an advance in method and interpretation, it had literary side effects as well.

"I shall only have to make an adaptation," wrote Zola, "as the experimental method itself has been established by Claude Bernard. The scientist provides me with a solid basis; he deals with the whole problem and I can limit myself to quoting his irrefutable arguments wherever necessary. In every respect I shall keep behind Claude Bernard. My work is nothing but compilation; more often than not, it will be sufficient to substitute the word 'novelist' for 'doctor' to make my thoughts clearer, and to give them the power of scientific truth."

Verga found the new French literary trends much to his taste, and admired Flaubert, Maupassant and Zola. Zola, the Italian* who had become a Frenchman, was a natural subject of affection for francophile Italians, a symbol of Italo-French friendship. Italy's cultural, social and political structures, however, made Italian writers apply the naturalist principles rather differently. The most significant difference, perhaps, was that the French realist and naturalist writers had concentrated their attention upon bourgeois town-dwellers, while the Italian *veristi* highlighted the lowest rung of the social ladder, the poor peasants of their individual country regions.

Verga's respect for French writing can be readily proved. Edouard Rod (see p. 64) was interested in contemporary Italian literature, and a mutual friend, the journalist and writer Felice Cameroni, had drawn his attention to Verga. At Rod's request Verga sent two of his books to him which Rod intended to review. In his first letter (March 1881) to the man who later became his translator and friend, Verga wrote, "I should be very pleased if you would be kind enough to send me your article about my work. Among you, there are so many valiant captains in this battle of the arts, that we private soldiers over here are most anxious to know what you think of us." To Verga's delight, Rod translated *Nedda* for the *Revue Littéraire* of April 1881.

Together with Rod, a friend of Zola's, Verga visited Zola in Médan in 1882. A short while after he again wrote to Rod: "One of the biggest debts I owe you is for introducing me to the writer whom I esteem highest of all." When he later sent Rod *I Malavoglia*, with the request to hand it to Zola (he was too shy to send it direct), Verga asked Rod to convey that this was a token of respect "to the genius, to whom all of us who try to describe life in its real state owe so much".

As not infrequently happens in cases of long-distance admiration, the actual personal contact proved disappointing. In 1894 Zola was working on his novel *Rome,* and visited the town in order to obtain circumstantial detail. In his systematic and meticulous manner, Zola had prepared lists of questions on oddly assorted topics. As an acknowledged expert on the subject, Luigi Capuana volunteered to

*The Zola family originated from Venice and after a period spent in Austria, had settled in France.

supply information about the women of Rome. Zola had requested well-documented notes, in telegraphic style, and these were discussed between them at Rome's Grand Hotel, where Zola was staying. Shortly afterwards, Zola returned the visit at Capuana's fourth-floor flat in the Via Arcione. Verga was present, and so was a young journalist, Lucio D'Ambra, a friend of Capuana's who had been asked to manipulate the photo-camera's shutter for the portrait group of the three "realist" writers which Capuana intended to take.

D'Ambra had the good sense to make notes when he got home, and his account of the tea-party in Capuana's flat is amusing. However, his notes were published 35 years after the party had taken place, and all other participants had died. It seems likely that he added a considerable number of embellishments. According to Ternois,* Verga's name does not appear in Zola's notebook which only mentions the meeting with Capuana at his (Zola's) hotel. René Ternois therefore contends that the *"récit de Lucio D'Ambra"* is *"de pure fantaisie"*.

Everything Ternois writes, but not all of what Lucio D'Ambra writes, deserves to be taken seriously. Nonetheless, it seems unlikely that there was only one meeting, and that Zola *did* visit Capuana's flat is proved by a photograph Capuana took there (illus. 23).

This is how D'Ambra described the occasion:**

Both Capuana and Verga addressed Zola as *maestro,* and Zola responded with *chers confrères.*

Zola looked around Capuana's very simply furnished lodgings, which were cheered up by a few of his own pieces and pictures. The cooking facilities were rather primitive but Capuana explained that his group of friends from Sicily often had their evening meal there to save restaurant expenses. So popular had these functions become that they were referred to as "Sicilian vespers" (the name given to the wholesale slaughter of the French in Sicily in 1282).

"I hope pro-French ones, though," said Zola with feigned apprehension.

The conversation centred around literature and, as expected, Capuana did most of the talking. Cultural movements, new methods of novel writing, naturalism and *verismo* were discussed. Verga spoke little, and when he did so, used the word *vérité* (or *verità*), i.e. truth,

---

*René Ternois, *Zola et ses amis italiens,* Publications de L'Université de Dijon XXXVIII, Société les Belles Lettres, Paris, 1967.

**Incontro di Verga con Zola, *Studi verghiani* (ed. Lina Perroni) (2 vols.), Editioni del sud, Palermo, 1929.

in preference to *verismo* (akin to truth). This seemed to irritate Zola. Verga gave his aim as "true" writing and said that he disliked all -isms. This annoyed Zola too. They discussed their individual methods of writing: Zola liked to write methodically, three pages every morning, a hundred lines; Capuana worked "in principle from morning till night, interrupted by a series of disturbances". Verga said he wrote when he felt like it—often at night, sometimes every night for a week. He preferred to write while standing up at his lectern (illus. 24).

Zola obviously felt that he had more in common with Capuana than with that odd Verga, who did not speak much, was none too easy to understand, and who could take a discussion completely to pieces with a dry comment. After Verga left, Zola said to Capuana that Verga's ideas were not convincing. What were these ideas?

Verga's ambition was natural, true story-telling. After *Nedda*, he had come to the conclusion that this "true" writing rests on two conditions: firstly, the author must "disappear" so that the described incidents can give the impression of actual happenings and the story tell itself, without any evidence of an author's hand. Secondly, the language which is being used must fit and characterize the individuals. This second postulate led to Verga's most important stylistic innovation. Without resorting to dialect or to ungrammatical writing, he distinguished his characters by the *cantilena* of the spoken words of the simple folk, whether they were syntactically correct or not. By the simplest stylistic means, and generally within the boundaries of correct Italian, he echoed their manner of speaking and their mannerisms mainly by an asyntactical arrangement of the subordinate clauses. These were strung one after the other, a feature as characteristic of the speech of the Sicilian peasant as the repetition of the verb at the end of the sentence:

A te non ti fanno nulla tre o quattro soldi, non ti fanno!
(To you, a few coppers just don't matter, no they don't.)

(Nedda)

or

Per voi tirerei tutta la casa, tirerei.
(For you I would lift the whole house up, I really would.)

(Cavalleria rusticana)

This construction became a feature of Verga's writing and was later used by his imitators*—among them D'Annunzio, who wrote

*See also p. 184.

in 1882 in a book of short stories:

> *Una sera, proprio l'ultima di Luglio, una sera si vide davvero se*
> *il sangue era rosso si vide ...*

(One evening, the last July evening in fact—an evening which
really makes one see whether there is red blood in one's veins,
it makes one see it . . . . . .)   (*Terra Vergine*)

What made Verga develop this idea of "true" writing as he per-
ceived it, and what led him to the impersonality of style and the
"natural syntax" of his characters, are questions which cannot be
answered with accuracy. French writing certainly influenced him,
though he neither copied Zola nor tried to adapt him to Italian needs.
The frequently stressed Zola-Verga influence was, as Ternois has
recently pointed out, not a one-way traffic either; if Zola's *La
fortune des Rougon* consciously or unconsciously served as the model
for the *Ciclo dei vinti,* Verga's *I Malavoglia* acted as eliciting agent
for Zola's *Joie de vivre.*

Verga was always guided by his artistic intuition; once he felt
convinced that his new method of writing reflected actual happenings
in the truest way possible for him, he continued on this path in spite
of lack of success, vilification and hostile criticism.

When he was more than 70 years old, and had eventually
met with public success, interest arose in the origins of Verga's
innovations. Journalists and fellow writers asked Verga for the
reasons for his style and how it all began. By this time Verga was
taciturn, depressed, and disinclined to talk, particularly to people he
did not know.

Nevertheless, an interview which he gave to a young journalist
seemed to produce all the answers: in the *Tribuna* of 2nd February,
1910, Riccardo Artuffo was able to publish, as a real literary scoop,
the story of how *verismo* had begun in Italy, and the reasons leading
up to it. The story became widely known and the subject of much
comment. It was included in practically every account of Verga
published not only in Italy but in other countries as well.

D. H. Lawrence quotes it in the preface to a collection of Verga's
stories which he had translated: *

"He (Verga) tells us himself how he came across his new style:
'I had published several of my first novels. They went well: I was
preparing others. One day, I don't know how, there came into my hands
a sort of broadside, a halfpenny sheet, sufficiently ungrammatical and
disconnected, in which a sea-captain succinctly related all the vicissitudes

---

Cavalleria rusticana and other stories, Jonathan Cape, 1928 (see also p. 81).

through which his sailing-ship has passed. Seaman's language, short, without an unnecessary phrase. It struck me and I read it again, it was just what I was looking for, without definitely knowing it. Sometimes you know, just a sign, an indication is enough. It is a revelation . . .' This passage explains all we need to know about Verga's style. . . ."

. It is a good story, interesting enough to be reprinted whenever Verga's work is discussed, and informative enough to have found its way into all literary assessments of *verismo*.

The story has only one defect. It is quite untrue. The credit for the unmasking of the falsified interview goes to Gino Raya who, when editing Verga's letters,* came across a letter dated 18th February, 1911, 16 days after the first publication of the *Tribuna* interview, which reads:

". . . I had already received the interview in the *Tribuna*. I am afraid I have now reached the stage when I become gloomy whenever I see a new face. How can they possibly do to an innocent conversation such a . . . Talking to them [the journalists] recalls, as indeed I said to that gentleman, the good intentions with which the way to hell is paved. The whole affair only serves as publicity for those who like that type of stuff, and to make copy for the interviewer."

The whole log-book incident must be rejected as a fabrication. However, an important reference to his own style is contained in a letter Verga wrote to Rod. Rod had used the word *verismo* in the preface of a French translation and, anxious to correct it, Verga wrote on 14th July, 1899:

"I have never taken part in literary criticism. All these so-called 'schools' which we have here, and you have as well, are only classifications made by critics. I think that in an original writer his own method is of supreme importance and that his so-called school matters very little, and then only by reflection. If I were to make a 'literary confession' to you, as a friend (not to the public!), I would say that I tried to put myself under the skin of my characters, tried to see things with their eyes, and express things with their words—that's all. This is what I did with *I Malavoglia*, and I am trying to do the same—in different surroundings—with the *Duchessa*.**

"But here one has to add what Goncourt has expressed—that the background as well as the personalities of ordinary people are much easier to handle, because they are more characteristic, and simpler. The 'upper classes' express themselves by implications; this complicates matters, and

*Lettere a Dina (ed. Gino Raya), Ciranna, Rome, 1962.
**The Duchess of Leyra (see also p. 83).

then one must also consider that type of mask and damper which education imparts to the expression of feelings. A certain stratum of society is almost internationally identical, due to the nearly universal varnish which usages, fashions and the idioms of speech provide. All of this affects my method very much, and may the Lord help me with that Duchess of mine!"

Verga meant all this very sincerely, but it does not give a full answer, nor does it indicate the conscious or subconscious reasons which had made him alter his style so suddenly and change his whole approach to writing. Benedetto Croce, that wise literary critic, saw the situation perhaps more clearly. He wrote:

"This formula of *verismo* has helped him in a different way: it has helped him in the need to improve and to perfect his art. We have seen all that which was conventional and somehow provisional in Verga's previous work, and we have also seen the signs of his discontent with himself. In fighting his own defects, he agreed with the theoreticians of *verismo* that a work of art must be 'impersonal', and must not 'preserve in its living form any imprint of the mind in which it germinated, nor a shadow of the ear which overheard it, nor a trace of the lips which murmured its first words, those words which are akin to the Creator's *fiat.*'

"And following the theoretical rules of *verismo,* he now believes he must proceed with the objectivity of the historian or the naturalist, and apply to the art of writing the methods of history and the natural disciplines; i.e. 'human documentation' and strict scientific observation.

"All these ideas are clearly erroneous. Art always remains personal. Impersonality is a confused concept for asserting a correct need, i.e. that the work of art must have an inner logic or necessity and can tolerate neither arbitrariness nor whims.

"However erroneous these veristic formulas may be, impossible and artistically monstrous as it may be to throw out one's own personality with a pitchfork,* they undoubtedly acted beneficially for Verga—as well as for others—because they converted themselves into a stimulus for great scrupulousness in artistic workmanship."

Croce then proceeds to quote several passages of Verga's writings, showing his very personal and compassionate attitude to human problems, and concludes: "This is what the so-called 'impersonality' of Giovanni Verga is like! And it is just because it is like that, that we love his work."

It is therefore legitimate to assume that Verga—opposed as he was to the fashions of literature—accepted the rules of *verismo* because he felt that those new standards improved the quality of his

*Croce uses the quotation from Horace: expellere furca. Benedetto Croce, *Giovanni Verga,* La letteratura della Nuova Italia, III, Laterza, Bari, 1964.

writing. If we then seek that piece of writing which more than any other set Verga off on his lonely and difficult path to his own style and finally to fame, we can accept Corrado Di Blasi's* evidence and find it in Capuana's story *Comparatico* (see p. 65). Verga wrote to its author about it on 24th September, 1882: "This is a little masterpiece and I freely admit that I owe to you my first inspiration for that plainly popular form which I have tried to give to my stories."

Gino Raya** has summed up the situation accurately as well as poetically:

"The log-book fathered Verga's style as much as Mars fathered Romulus . . . that Capuana's seed should have ripened better in Verga than in Capuana himself was due to the interaction between seed and soil. That the seed was *Lu cumpari* [see p. 66] is proved by the subsequent literary efforts of Capuana in praise of Verga. Of Capuana, who saw in Verga his own issue; of Capuana, who, in Verga, glorifies himself."

Nedda is important because it constituted Verga's first attempt to put the new principles into effect. The very turning-point is there. In the introduction, the writer sits by the fire, watches the smoke of his cigar drift away, and lets the drifting smoke lead him into the story proper. His thoughts roam away to "that other fire" around which the olive pickers gathered on a wet day, and where the real story begins. This shallow contrivance is incompatible with *verismo*; only with the story itself begins that "discovery of the new seam" which Capuana had hailed.

At the time of its publication, *Nedda* was not thought a work of any importance. However, it was translated into German and its appearance in a German periodical made Verga become interested in the rights of authors. When Verga's writings aroused interest abroad he was always delighted. The mere fact that the translation of *Nedda* was unauthorized*** would not necessarily have affected his welcome for it; what infuriated him was that the story had been cut.

*Corrado Di Blasi, L'avvio della lingua del Verga tra storia e leggenda, *Narrativa*, VII, I, Rome, 1962.

**Raya, *La lingua del Verga*, Le Monnier, Florence, 1962, p. 17.

***In his *"Vita di Giovanni Verga"* (Le Monnier, Florence, 1940, p. 344) Nino Capellani makes the astonishing allegation that D. H. Lawrence's publication of *Cavalleria rusticana and other stories*, a book published simultaneously in 1928 by MacVeagh of New York, by Longmans Green & Co. of Toronto and by Jonathan Cape of London, was unauthorized and indeed improper, as Lawrence "never took the trouble to request permission, nor paid for copyright".

"How can they possibly do such things," he wrote to Capuana, "in view of our own laws, as well as all those international agreements about authors' rights? . . ." His experience made Verga interested in the "Society of Authors" which was just being founded in Italy, on the pattern of its British precursor. He became a founder member and henceforward followed the problems of national and international copyright with keen interest.

After *Nedda*, Verga did not consistently follow his new method, and from time to time fell back into his previous manner. However, *Nedda* had not only given him a new method. It gave him a new plan as well which, vague at first, gradually became more clearly defined as time went on. He wanted to write a cycle of novels about people who, in different strata of society, fail as the result of a "tragic error" in their struggle. In five separate, though interconnected works, this new cycle was meant to embrace the whole of Italy's social structure, each volume dealing with a different section.

The first person to whom he mentioned this ambitious plan was the solicitor Salvatore Paola, a childhood friend. Born in 1837, Verga's senior by three years, he was the son of the legal adviser of Verga's mother's family, the de Mauros, and had helped them during a prolonged inheritance dispute, the "Barbagallo case". The families' friendship extended to the next generation, to Verga as well as his brothers; Salvatore Paola was later to act for Verga professionally. The fact that he was the first to hear of the literary plans* for *La marea* (*The Tide*), a title later changed to the *Ciclo dei vinti* (*Cycle of the Doomed*), testifies to the intimacy of their friendship, as this plan was at that time still treated with great secrecy (illus. 37).

Beginning with the simple fisherfolk, the *gente del mare,* a particular section of the Sicilian poor, he intended to portray the misfortunes of the family of Antonio Malavoglia, a fisherman from Acitrezza who had a small boat, a house and a family. The ownership of the boat entitled him to be called "Padron" Antonio, and *Padron 'Ntoni* was to be the title of the first book.

It was to be followed by a second novel. Gesualdo Motta, its protagonist, was a craftsman builder, referred to as "Mastro Gesualdo". Hard work, good fortune and successful speculations enabled him to raise himself to the ranks of the bourgeoisie, and this upgrading entitled him to the prefix "Don". To remind him of his humble background, he was mockingly referred to as "Mastro-Don" Gesualdo, a paradoxical combination of two incompatible pre-

*In a letter of April 1878.

fixes. *Mastro-Don Gesualdo* was to be the title of the second volume of the series.

The third novel, still with a Sicilian background, was to feature the Palermo aristocracy. Its central figure was Mastro-Don Gesualdo's daughter. Verga originally intended to call her, as well as the book, the *Duchess of Gargantàs*, but later he altered this title to the *Duchess of Leyra*.

The fourth volume, *L'onorevole Scipioni,** was to use Rome's political scene as its setting; the fifth and last, *L'uomo di lusso* (*The Man of Luxury*), was to have its action among the wealthy industrialists of Florence and Milan.

The Tide (later the *Cycle of the Doomed*) according to Verga's plan of 1878.

1. *Padron 'Ntoni* (later *I Malavoglia*, published 1881).

2. *Mastro-Don Gesualdo* (published 1889).

3. *La Duchessa della Gargantàs* (later *La Duchessa di Leyra*, only one chapter completed).

4. *L'onorevole Scipioni*
5. *L'uomo di lusso* (*The Man of Luxury*) } never begun.

Deeply committed to this programme—which was never to be completed—Verga set to work with energy and meticulous care,** fully aware that this was to be his most important work. The outline of the plan for the first volume, *Padron 'Ntoni*, was ready in his mind, but the writing itself failed again and again to please him. He revised, he altered, he changed and rewrote. The title underwent changes, too, and when the book was eventually published, its title was *I Malavoglia* (*The Malavoglia Family*).

In order to introduce the characters of this book to the public, Verga made use of an odd expedient: he published in a literary journal a short story, *Fantasticheria* (*Daydream*, see p. 60) which is really an open letter to a past mistress, the Countess Greppi (her

---

L'onorevole means "The Honourable", a mode of address granted to Members of Parliament (*Deputati*).

**Verga's painstaking method, with its chronological listing of events, and files for each character was not at all unlike Zola's. It is documented in L. Perroni, *Preparazione dei Malavoglia, Studi verghiani* (see p. 76), and L. & V. Perroni Storia dei Malavoglia, carteggio con l'editore e con L. Capuana (The history of the novel *I Malavoglia*, correspondence with the publisher and with Capuana), *Nuova Antalogia*, Rome, March, 1940.

name is not mentioned, but the attribution is generally accepted). They had spent a few days together in Sicily, and on the return journey, they were both looking out of the window while the train passed the picturesque fishing village of Acitrezza. She had cried out:

"How I would love to spend a month there!"

"We did return, you and I, and your big suitcases made the people there think that you had come to stay for good. But already on the morning of the third day you had tired of seeing nothing but green and blue all day long, and had gone to the station, impatiently waiting for the train. In 48 hours we had done in Acitrezza all one can do there, and you said, 'I completely fail to understand how anyone can live here all his life.'

"And yet, you know, it's simpler than it seems. To start with it is only necessary not to have 100,000 lire, and to share instead the toil and drudgery of those people, among those enormous rocks in that sea so blue that it made you raise your hands in admiration. This may well be enough; the poor devils who sleepily waited for us in their boat, *do* find in their ramshackle and picturesque huts all that you so anxiously search for in Paris and Nice and Naples.

"I thought of you when I saw that poor woman whom you had helped when you bought some of the oranges, neatly laid out on the little table in front of her door. The little table is no more. The tree in the small garden has been cut down, and the house has a new window.

"Do you remember the old boy who stood at the helm of our boat, and who at least ten times prevented your stockings from getting soaked? He died in the hospital of the town, the poor chap, in a white ward, between white sheets, chewing white bread and cared for by the white hands of the Sisters of Charity. They could hardly understand what the wretched old fellow groaned about in his semi-barbaric dialect, but it was not their fault. Had he been able to have his own way, he would have chosen to die under his own roof, in that dark corner next to the fireplace where he had slept for so many years. That's why he cried, and whimpered, as the old often do, when they carried him away.

"The son—you know, the fellow who hardly dared to touch your foot to help you out of the rabbit snare you got caught in—was lost at sea. He was out at sea, alone, on a dark winter's night, amidst wild and unbridled waves. Seventy miles of darkness and storm were between his boat and the shore, where his people were waiting for him, running to and fro, and almost out of their minds!

"And yet it is better to be dead than to eat 'the king's bread' like the other boy does, in the prison of Pantelleria, or like his sister, who lives by the grace of God—meagre enough a grace it is at Acitrezza I can assure you!"

A depressing law of destiny is put forward in conclusion.

"If one of those poor chaps, either because he is weaker, or less careful, or more egotistical, wishes to detach himself from the others— whether he does this out of desire for the unknown, or for betterment, or just out of curiosity for the world, does not matter—the world, which always behaves like a greedy fish, will swallow him up, and with him those nearest and dearest to him."

Thus Verga introduced the novel he was about to publish. The foreword to the novel itself states his artistic intentions. Verga wishes to be a hidden observer, and not a participant. In order to remain accurate he intends to use those words which are most suited to the characters:

"Under the subtle influence which education exercises upon character, people show less originality and more curiosity. Even their language undergoes change. We must stay sincere in our wish to show the truth. Form is just as important for its subject as the subject in all its parts is necessary for the unfolding of the tale."

The words "even their language" now sound surprising, accustomed as we are to the idea that individuality of style and choice of language are highly desirable and must certainly not be discouraged. In Verga's time—and the problem has not completely disappeared even now—any acceptable Italian prose was meant to follow the tradition which Manzoni had set in *I promessi sposi*. Because Verga used the words which were natural to his characters, because he used a language restricted in vocabulary, frequently incorrect in syntax, and sometimes even in grammar, the critics as well as the public found it difficult to accept his innovations.*

Another significant passage in this introduction states that:

"Only the observer who looks around has the right to interest himself in the weak who remain behind on the road, in the weary who, in order to drown the more quickly, let themselves sink under the waves, in the doomed who raise their arms in despair . . . And the man who observes all this has no right to judge . . . it is to be studied without passion, the scene is to be rendered in its true colours. It must give a representation of reality and reveal everything just as it has been."

All this shows that Verga, while he had much in common with the French writers in their pursuit of truth and its expression in an impersonal manner, was not a follower only: in writing about the

---

*Italo Svevo, who was unpopular with the critics for some of the same reasons as Verga, said scornfully that "Italians never write without a dictionary in their hand".

weak and unsuccessful without any attempt to judge them he is an
innovator.

The tragic error of the Malavoglia family is a speculation in a
cargo of lupins,* a cargo to be paid for out of the profits yet to
be made. The boat is lost in a storm, and a son is drowned. The debt
has to be paid. A daughter's reputation and hopes of marriage are
sacrificed by their lawyer who, in order to hide her brother's smuggling
activities, has to pretend that his knifing of a customs official
was justifiable family vengeance. The house has eventually to be sold
and the family falls apart.

The whole book breathes an underlying and deep sadness, and
yet it has become an outstanding novel of Italian literature. Its
importance lies in the poetical, but still lifelike, description of the
psychology of those "primitives", their moral values and family bonds
and their obedience to those laws of conduct which are of their own
making. In their simple way they display—more clearly than their
sophisticated brethren—the combination of the two qualities so often
praised in the dog and in the cat; the loyalty of the dog to the master
of the family, and the firm attachment of the cat to the house.

As a token of their friendship, Verga later gave Capuana the
final manuscript of *I Malavoglia* as a present. The great Milan
Exhibition of 1881 had included a lottery for 100,000 lire, and
Capuana had sent Verga two lire to buy tickets. The two friends
often spoke of the "dream room" (the *salottino dei sogni*) which they
intended to build with the money they were going to win. In the mood
of their "dream room", Capuana told Verga that this manuscript of
Italy's most important novel "would be worth millions". "Perhaps in
time", was Verga's reply, "but much too late for us to enjoy them".

While *I Malavoglia* was in preparation, the short story *Cavalleria
rusticana* appeared in March, and further short stories in May and
July 1880. At the end of the same year, the Treves Brothers collected
these short stories in a volume entitled *Vita dei campi* (*Life in the
Fields*). This book had a modicum of success with the public as well
as with the critics, but nothing Verga's contemporaries had to say
suggested that 80 years later they would be counted amid the best
short stories of Italian literature.

*Not the flower but a legume, a forage crop which grows well on the acid
soil of the island. Its seed, when dried, serves as winter feed for animals.
Its high protein content gives it a value comparable to that of linseed or
groundnut cake for the agriculture of Great Britain. It was also used for
human consumption among the poor.

Rosso Malpelo is the pathetic story of an ill-treated, derided and rejected red-headed boy who meets his death in the sandpits which occur under the lava in the Etna district, the same sandpits which had already caused the death of his father. Written in impersonal prose, it anticipates in its psychological understanding of the reactions to oppression some of the analytical psychology of Freud and Adler; contemporaries suspected atheism in the story.

Ieli Pastore is a story with autobiographical connotations, dating from the 15-year-old Verga's friendship with "the boy who looked after the horses".

La Lupa is a dramatic story of incest, written about an actual occurrence of which Capuana had told Verga. It is a story whose later fortunes were in some respects similar to those of *Cavalleria rusticana* (pp. 191-193).

L'Amante di Gramigna (*Gramigna's Lover*, i.e. *The Twitch-boy's Lover**), another of the stories in the same volume, is prefaced by an open letter to the writer Salvatore Farina, which expresses Verga's view that a true incident is the essential ingredient of a story. The story itself concerns the compulsive action of a girl who abandons the man who loves her, and to whom she is betrothed. She does that in order to throw herself into the arms of a hunted outlaw, whose adventures she has heard of, but whom she has never seen before. She joins him in his hideout: he is wounded, apprehended by soldiers, and she follows him to the town where he is imprisoned. It is a "Flying Dutchman" type of situation based on a true happening. Peppa, the main figure, is clearly portrayed, in her pathological, rather than normal, psychology: the resulting picture is more lifelike than that of her famous "sister", Senta.

Already before he wrote *I Malavoglia,* sadness and disappointment had affected Verga from time to time. His youthful conviction that the mainland of Italy was going to welcome him triumphantly was fading, and no longer did he see himself as Pietro Brusio, his autobiographical hero of the *Peccatrice* (see p. 53). His first doubts about success appear in a letter he wrote to Luigi Capuana before his arrival in Milan in November 1872.

". . . If you are able to give me a letter of introduction to a newspaper editor or a proprietor I should appreciate it very much; and if through your help I can obtain a very modest post on a paper I shall be most grateful."

Gramigna means twitch or couch, a weed as antisocial as an outlaw.

Clearer signs of frustration appear in a letter of February 1873:
February 1873:

". . . you know as I do, that we have to stay in this *via crucis* of
ours, beset with vexations and publishers, and that we have to try to
march forward with empty pockets and aching feet . . . that those who
are absent are wrong, and that politics and industry sweep the road at
the end of the year without counting the wounded or missing . . .

"I finished my novel *Eva*; my enthusiasm evaporated when a
publisher offered me 800 lire and thought he was paying handsomely!
True enough, I still have faith in myself, but how do I know that this is
not vanity, too, and will disappear as well?

"When my book is published, I shall send it to you. Meanwhile, do
send me all your work, always so beautiful and full of life. At least one
luxury we can afford—that of creating!—even if no other. As far as
pleasures are concerned, I almost forgot that we have another one, too:
those praises from the Countesses and Marchionesses who do us the
honour of asking us to send them our books! Bound in leather,* of
course, and at our own expense!"

Bitterness and disappointment became more marked after the
publication of *I Malavoglia*. Its shipwreck episode had appeared in
January 1881, in the *Nuova Antologia* under the title *Poveri
pescatori (Ill-fated Fishermen)*. The book itself went on sale in
February 1881, and Verga waited impatiently for the reactions.
Milan was full of intelligent people, many of them intensely interested
in, and appreciative of, contemporary art and letters. How did they
react to the new book?

Tullio Masserani, a writer and friend, wrote an enthusiastic
letter. Another friend, Luigi Gualdo, came to see Verga to say how
enormously he appreciated it. A letter from Luigi Capuana, full of
praise and congratulations, arrived the same evening. But that, and
a congratulatory message from the Countess Maffei, was all. Only
four people greeted the greatest work of Italian prose, and this at a
time when the people of Milan seemed more conscious of new
artistic achievements than at any time in their history!

In April 1881, Verga wrote a sad letter to Capuana:

"My *Malavoglia* is a failure, a total and complete fiasco. Only Boito
and Gualdo had anything good to say about the book. Many people,
in particular Treves [Verga's publisher] said outright that it was bad, and
those who do not directly say so, avoid me as if I had committed a sin.

"As far as the papers are concerned, no one, apart from a very few,

*Italian books were generally paperbacks. Only presentation copies were
(individually) bound.

took any notice, not even those who are supposed to be well disposed towards me: obviously, they did not want to spell the De Profundis* out to me.

"But the worst of it is that it all fails to convince me—and if I were to write my book all over again I would do it in exactly the same way.

"I am afraid pure analysis without the pepper of dramatization does not work in Italy. I need all the strength of my convictions to refrain from writing those silly niceties which please the public—and to laugh behind their backs afterwards.

"Torelli told me that he himself was going to write in the *Corriere*; I should have welcomed this after the general silence . . . but I heard nothing further. I do not know whether this is the result of forgetfulness, or the usual 'lack of space', or if it is a friendly critic's reticence in order to spare my feelings. Treves wants to arrange for your article to appear in the *Nazione* or *Antologia*, but I can assure you that he does it only for business reasons, and not out of literary interest.

"Luigi, I can tell you that the indifference with which the so-called 'literary public' here in Italy looks upon our efforts absolutely nauseates me.

"From what I understand, it seems quite possible that the first proper criticism will appear in France, by Rod, a friend of Zola's, in the *Parlement* or *National*. A nice state of affairs when one has to wait to hear something about an Italian book until they say it from the other side of the Fréjus! Oh, if only there was not that accursed mania for writing!"

Even in the expected French interest, Verga was to be disappointed. After many difficulties, the *Malavoglia* translation eventually appeared in France after a five years delay (in 1886**)—without the introduction which Zola had promised—and met complete silence there as well.

The mood of impending despair which Verga expressed in his letters to Luigi Capuana remained as yet only a passing sentiment. His wish to write was not affected, and no sooner had *I Malavoglia* appeared in print, than he was at work on the next book of the cycle, *Mastro-Don Gesualdo*. This book took the tragic error and its consequences a rung up the ladder of the social scale. Gesualdo Motta, a skilled bricklayer and therefore "Mastro" Gesualdo, made a good deal of money by energy and hard work, and the use of his consider-

---

*The first words of the Psalm 130, in Latin, used as a prayer for the dead; "a cry from the depth of sorrow".

**Les Malavoglia, mœurs siciliennes, translated by Rod: with the date 1887, published by Hachette, Paris.

able intelligence. His progress culminates in his marriage to Bianca Trao, offspring of an ancient and aristocratic, though impoverished and genetically enfeebled family. All his efforts are of no avail: neither his friends of humble origin, nor the new relations and their own social set, fully accept him. Despised and forgotten, he eventually dies a lonely death in the palace of the Duchess of Leyra, whom he wrongly believes to be his own daughter.

Apart from telling its own story, the book contains the key to the next volumes as well. The Duchess of Leyra becomes the protagonist of the third volume. Her own son, begotten before her marriage to the Duke of Leyra, by the penniless poetaster Corrado La Gurna, and put on "the wheel" at Palermo, was to become the Hon. Scipioni, the politician-hero of the fourth volume of the cycle, "a man with his head in the clouds and his feet in the mud".

While he was working on the *Mastro,* another volume of short stories was in the making as well. This volume of 12 stories, *Novelle rusticane (Country Short Stories),* contains the story *Libertà* (see p. 15) as well as *Pane nero (Hard-earned Bread).*

This latter story reveals a further shift of psychological emphasis in Verga's writing. The impressive idealism of the characters in *I Malavoglia* had already given way to a more ironical or sarcastic description of events in *Mastro-Don Gesualdo.* This progresses in *Pane nero* to near cynicism. The story deals with the habit among Sicily's rich of disposing of past mistresses by giving them a tempting dowry and marrying them off to a fitting suitor. With great artistry a case of wholehearted acceptance of this reprehensible practice is presented in *Pane nero.* A proper dowry is provided and everyone is pleased. Even the souls of the dead become implicated in this cynicism, the story ending with this reference to the dead mother: "She is in paradise", says Rossa [the sister-in-law], "and prays to God for us sinners. She knows about this splendid dowry, and she is pleased, the poor old thing: Mastro Brasi is bound to marry you now."

All Verga's masterpieces fall within the period 1880-1890, and to write stories and novels of such quality and importance within comparatively so short a time was—apart from anything else—a sign of great determination and capacity for work.

Neither financially nor morally did it produce any worthwhile return for him. Verga's language, now regarded as a pearl of Italian prose, left the critics cold. The mastery of expression with which he sketches his characters so that the reader has the impression that he is living among them and hears them speak, did not excite his readers. His contemporaries were not thrilled by his masterly use of words and phrases in order to characterize the individual, nor pleased with his shunning of artifice and absence of mannerism.

In his recent book, *La lingua del Verga* (*The Language of Verga*), Gino Raya concludes that "if the language of the *Promessi sposi* is an Italian rinsed in the Arno, the language of *I Malavoglia* is steeped in, and permeated by, the Ionian Sea".

Verga's use of language is very important now. It is taught to children at school, explained to students of literature, discussed by literary historians and critics, and supplied with extensive commentaries by scholars. It is the subject of many monographs and many courses of lectures. In Verga's time it was different. One of the main objections of most critics was that Verga was "making a language of his own brand". They would have preferred it if he had used dialect, at least for the direct speech of his characters; others suggested that the stories should have been written entirely in Sicilian. These were practices which Verga deprecated and strictly wished to avoid.

One of the most influential literary critics of the period was Edoardo Scarfoglio. He was a man of striking personality, who regarded himself as born

"to hunt elephants on the banks of the Omo, or to steer a ship through the cracks of the polar icepack, but this idiotic Italy mercilessly closed all the roads along which my own impulses would have led me, and compels me to do the forced and thankless task of the hack writer, to the despair of myself, and the annoyance of many others".

About Verga he had the following to say:

"One day we talked together at length . . . and eventually we went to eat anchovies on board a boat from Messina, which was anchored at Ripa Grande. Verga soon started to speak Sicilian to the sailors, and he spoke with such delightful fluency of expression, that I said to myself: 'Why the hell does that chap not make the Sicilians in his stories speak in Sicilian?' "

Verga had considered all these possibilities for a long time, but he had rejected them as essentially wrong. To Luigi Capuana he had written that:

"Local dialects differ from place to place . . . and all of us, if we want to write dialect, have to translate our thoughts into it. And as the thought in our mind is undoubtedly born in Italian, no one, neither you, nor I, nor the Patriarch St. Joseph, can possibly succeed in translating

a phrase which quite clearly was born in another form, into *pure* dialect.
And, after all, what for? Only to decrease our potential appeal, and to
create divisions among ourselves? By all means, let's use local colour and
flavour, as you are doing so masterfully, and as I attempt to do as a
pupil, but otherwise let's be understood right through the length of our
country."*

Occasional words in Sicilian dialect appear in *Nedda* and also in
Cavalleria rusticana, but with *I Malavoglia* all use of dialect** in
Verga's writing ceases. Once he had decided to abstain from the
use of dialect, adverse criticism would certainly not induce him to
alter a decision which he had firmly made, believing it to be the right
one.

The impasse was therefore complete.

On the one side Verga, who regarded his stories as true, or
almost true, incidents whose artistic value lay entirely in the new
method of their presentation; on the other side the critics who, while
they appreciated his stories, disliked the way in which they were told.
Not only did they dislike the language, they also disliked Verga's
pessimism and the harshness of the reality he described. Manzoni,
too, had of course described situations of harshness, but there was a
fundamental difference in their respective attitudes towards it.
Manzoni's harshness is invariably mitigated by his deeply religious
feeling, a feeling totally lacking in Verga, who was an atheist and
who had stated: "God does not exist, or is cruel: that's all there is to
be said about it."***

Such characteristics set Verga too far apart from Manzoni to
become acceptable to critics or public; his total rejection could, in
turn, not fail to leave its mark on Verga's general attitude, and
eventually on his determination to continue with his work as a
writer.

*The Italian phrase Verga uses, *pulmoni larghi,* means large lungs. The
image conveyed is that Italy is a long peninsula. To breathe right down
its length, requires big lungs.

**Verga's decision to avoid even the occasional use of dialect was, according
to an anecdote, strengthened when a Milan friend who had read *Nedda*
drew his attention to a pretty girl and said: "Look, a '*Varannisa!*' " Verga
looked surprised; the friend explained that he knew from Verga's *Nedda*
that *varannisa* in Sicilian must mean "a pretty girl". However, *varannisa* means in Sicilian a person from Viagrande Etnea (*Varanni* in dialect),
Nedda's home town. Whether the anecdote is true or not, it shows how
readily the use of dialect can lend itself to misinterpretation.

***Verga: *Lettere d'Amore,* ed. Gino Raya, Tindalo, Rome, p. 230.

Verga's claim to fame is based on four volumes, all written within the span of a few years: the collection of short stories *Vita dei campi* (1880), the novel *I Malavoglia* (1881), the *Novelle rusticane*, a volume of short stories (1883), and the novel *Mastro-Don Gesualdo*, eventually published in 1889.

None of those books, which now guarantee his immortality, made any impression at the time of their publication. The readers of *I Malavoglia* could not hear the *cantilena* of the simple people of Sicily echoing poetically in this great work.

CHAPTER V

CAVALLERIA RUSTICANA

CAVALLERIA RUSTICANA

SOME of the material which had formed part of earlier versions of *I Malavoglia* was, as often happens, eliminated during revisions. This included an incident which, developed into a self-contained story, became the short story *Cavalleria rusticana*. Verga never expressed any special fondness for it (see p. 213), but the belief that he eliminated it from the novel because he regarded it as not good enough is unfounded.

Influenced by *verismo* principles, it was written in strictly factual, almost sketchy style; not only was the author's hand purposely concealed, but a good deal of the in-between information was left unsaid, for the reader to supply. The story still retained certain names* and characteristics from the original *Malavoglia* setting. Like much of Verga's work, it is based on a true incident.

The enormous popularity this story subsequently achieved, first as a play and then as the highly successful opera, led later to considerable curiosity about the facts on which it was based.

Verga never gave any indication about its source; it is therefore not surprising that different and contradictory versions of what were supposed to be the true facts should exist. Practically every Verga chronicler had his own view. It is generally accepted that the story is derived from an incident in the "black chronicle" of Vizzini which had occurred in 1865 outside the gates of the Palazzo Verga. The following account, based chiefly on Giuseppe Paternò (see p. 6), whose father was schoolmaster in Vizzini at the crucial time and remembered the affair, probably comes near the truth.

National Service had been introduced into Sicily in 1860. The old belief that he who leaves the island is unlikely to return had cast its shadow upon a young man who had left Vizzini to serve in an infantry regiment. When the girl he had wished to marry did not hear from him for several months, her parents persuaded her to accept the rival proposal of the head of the Vizzini horse-cab drivers,

*e.g. *Compare* Alfio Mosca, who is a carrier in *I Malavoglia*.

altogether a better proposition than the impecunious and absent soldier. In due course the marriage took place. The couple had remained childless for over four years when, to everyone's surprise, the ex-fiancé returned, his military service completed.

The childlessness of their only daughter had been a cause of concern to the young woman's parents. It was not only a stigma, but there was some property to inherit, for which a grandson was highly desirable. The young wife's mother had the idea of attempting to remedy the situation by facilitating meetings between her married daughter and the strapping, fit ex-fiancé who was quite obviously still attracted to her. The encounters took place in her parent's house, on occasions when the husband was away on longer journeys.

The young ex-soldier, too, was an only child. His mother kept a wine shop in the Piazzetta Santa Teresa (illus. 25), behind the Palazzo Verga. When her son left for the army, she was in dire need of help in the house and, as was the custom, took a waif of twelve years or so from the local convent's orphanage into her house. The girl got to know of the meetings and divulged them to the husband. Most probably she acted in childish innocence but may have been influenced by jealousy resulting from an infatuation with the handsome soldier.

Shortly afterwards, he was found stabbed to death in one of those half-wild plantations near some tanneries in the valley below Vizzini, where prickly pears (*Fichi d'India*) are grown. The murder remained unpunished.

At the time of this event, the 25-year-old Verga was working as a literary journalist in Catania. About 15 years later he used the story as an episode in his *Padron 'Ntoni*, but by the time this had become *I Malavoglia*, he had eliminated it.

In view of its subsequent history, it is interesting to examine how Verga came to publish this episode on its own, and to explain the curious name of the journal, *Il Fanfulla*, in which it first appeared.

Italian interest in short story writing was greatly stimulated by the success of Guy de Maupassant's stories; a new French challenge had emerged, and Verga accepted this challenge with pleasure. Maupassant's three principles,

1. Scientific exactness (the "photography of reality"),
2. Impersonality and impassiveness of the writer,
3. "Cult of form", that is, style and form must correspond to their "sacred function" and express reality,

were in full agreement with Verga's idea of true writing. A mutual respect and appreciation developed between the two writers, culminating in Maupassant's willing, though never fulfilled, offer to write a foreword to the French translation of the *Novelle rusticane*.

To take up the literary challenge of the French was the avowed purpose of the Italian newspaper *Il Fanfulla*. Its very name proclaimed this purpose: it recalled the famous challenge of Barletta, the *Disfida di Barletta*, of 13th February, 1503, a favourite episode in Italian history. Locked in siege and countersiege near Barletta, in the province of Apulia, were three armies, a French, a Spanish and an Italian. A French knight by the name of De la Motte, who had been taken prisoner, made a disparaging remark about the valour of the Italian knights; the slight led to a challenge, and thirteen chosen Italian knights met their French counterparts in a combat which ended with the victory of the Italians.*

In the mood of the Risorgimento, the story of this challenge was eagerly revived. In 1833, Massimo d'Azeglio had written a novel entitled *Ettore Fieramosca*, and the *Disfida di Barletta* became a fashionable subject in literature and painting.

One of the Italian knights in Fieramosca's team was a certain Fanfulla, from Lodi, whose name lent itself better than Fieramosca's as a name for a newspaper.** It intended to challenge the supremacy of *Le Figaro* of Paris, a paper which in dignity of presentation as well as in accuracy of contents had by then established itself as the leading daily paper of the continent of Europe.

Following its French example, a weekly literary edition, the *Fanfulla della Domenica* (*The Sunday Fanfulla*) was founded in 1879. It was Italy's first literary weekly of a national character. Its new editor was Ferdinando Martini, a friend of Verga's, who approached him with the request for short stories, and Verga was one of the earliest contributors to the new journal. *Fantasticheria* (*Daydream*, see p. 83) appeared on 24th August, 1879, to be followed on 14th March, 1880, by *Cavalleria rusticana*.

*Their leader, Ettore Fieramosca, survived. He died 22 years later, in 1525, after being thrown off his horse.

**It first appeared, as a daily paper, in Florence in 1870 and transferred together with the new government in 1871 to Rome, the new capital. It was the official paper of Italy from 1870 until 1876, when it became the journal of the opposition. It continued in existence until 1919. A paper by the name of *Fieramosca* also existed in Florence for a few years from 1881 onwards.

Cavalleria rusticana has repeatedly been translated into English. The translations have all become affected by translation's blight: its liability to date. Writing and translating are very different activities. Good writing is a work of art, and like all true art, remains timeless. Translating is not art; it is expert craftsmanship, and therefore echoes its own period and is bound to lose its flavour. Translations have to fulfil two different requirements: to render the original author's sentiments clearly and correctly, and to be readable. These two requirements eventually conflict, and for this reason new translations become necessary from time to time.

In appreciation of this need, a new translation of the story is here presented, followed by the necessary notes on pp. 105 and 106.

CAVALLERIA RUSTICANA
A Rural Code of Honour
by
GIOVANNI VERGA

Ever since his return from military service, Nunzia Macca's son Turiddu[1] liked to strut around the piazza on Sundays, wearing his regimental uniform with the red beret: the beret that looks like the fez of those itinerant fortune-tellers, who set up their stall anywhere, complete with bird-cages and canaries which pick the predictions out of a box.[2]

The girls on their way to Mass, with their faces tucked coyly up to the nose in their mantillas, could hardly take their eyes off him. The boys swarmed around him like flies. He smoked a pipe decorated with a carving of the King on horseback, and when he struck his matches on his trouser-seat he raised his leg as if he wanted to kick someone.

In spite of all this, Lola, the daughter of farm manager Angelo, neither appeared at church nor did she show herself on the *ballatoio*.[3] She had recently become engaged to a man from Licodia, a well-to-do carrier with four good Sortino mules in his stable.

When Turiddu first heard of the engagement, "Holy smoke", he swore; he was going to tear this Licodia chap's guts out, he really was. But he never did anything of the sort and only let off steam by singing all the disdainful songs he knew under Lola's window.

The neighbours wondered; had Mrs. Macca's Turiddu nothing

better to do than to spend his nights chirping like a solitary sparrow?[4]

Eventually he ran into Lola. She was returning from a barefooted walk, which she had vowed to do, to the "Madonna of the Dangers". When she saw him, she turned neither white nor red; it was just as if it had nothing to do with her.

He said, "Well, I think I'm lucky even just to *see* you!"

"O *Compare*[5] Turiddu," she said, "I have heard that you came back at the beginning of the month."

"I have heard other things as well!" he replied. "Is it true that you are going to marry Alfio?"

"Well, yes, if it is God's will, I shall," replied Lola, adjusting the ends of her headscarf over her chin.

"Do you think that your chopping and changing from one to the other is God's will? That it is God's will that I had to come back from afar to hear such stories, Miss Lola?"

The poor chap tried to continue his remonstrations, but his voice failed him. He walked behind the girl, sadly shaking his head, and the tassel of his red beret swayed from one shoulder to the other. Lola felt genuinely sorry to see him so sad, but she did not really wish to encourage him by being kind.

"Listen, Turiddu," she said in the end, "let me join the other girls. What are people going to say if they see me with you?"

"That's right," answered Turiddu. "Now that you're going to marry that rich Alfio, with all his mules and everything, you mustn't cause any gossip! When I was in the Army, Mother had to sell our only mule, that nice bay one, as well as that little piece of vineyard close by the road which we used to own. Yes, times have changed! You don't remember now how we used to talk to one another through the window in the yard, and how you gave me that handkerchief before I left! God knows how many tears I cried into it while I was so far away that the very name of our town seemed strange. Anyway, that's that. Goodbye then, Lola, and let's forget all about it."

So Lola married her carrier man and the following Sunday she stood on the *ballatoio*, holding her hands well up so that everyone could see the heavy golden rings her husband had given her. Turiddu walked with assumed indifference up and down the little street, a pipe in his mouth and his hands in his pockets, and looked with feigned interest at the girls who passed by. But within himself he was furious that Lola's husband was so rich, and that she pretended not to notice him.

"The bitch," he muttered, "how I'd love to teach her a lesson!"

Opposite Alfio's was the house of Nicola, the wine grower, who was believed to be very rich, and who had an only daughter. By making himself pleasant in word and in deed, Turiddu managed to be given a job as a farm worker, and soon he started to go to the house and make flattering remarks to the girl.

"Why don't you go and tell Lola all that stuff of yours?" asked Santuzza.[6]

"Lola is a great lady now," he said, "and married to a rich man."

"I don't think I shall get a rich man," said Santuzza.

"You are worth a hundred Lolas. I know a chap who wouldn't look at her, or her patron saint either, while you are about! Lola is nothing; she's not even fit to clean your shoes."

"I see," said Santuzza. "When the fox could not reach the grapes. . . ."

"He said how pretty you are, you sweet little thing."

"Keep your hands off, *Compare*."

"Are you afraid that I'll eat you?"

"I'm not afraid of you, nor of anyone else."

"I know you're not; with a mother from Licodia, you're bound to be full of pride. Still—I really could eat you with my eyes."

"All right, then, eat me with your eyes—that won't hurt me. But meanwhile go and lift that bundle up for me."

"For you I'd lift the whole house up, I really would!"

She didn't want him to see her blush, took a piece of wood that lay handy, and threw it at him, just missing him.

"Come on, Turiddu, let's get on with it. Talking won't tie these prunings up for us."

"If I were rich, I would look for a wife just like you."

"I don't want to marry a rich man, like Lola. Thank the Lord, I have a good dowry myself, and am ready for the day when He sends me someone."

"We all know you have lots of money. . . ."

"Well, if you do know it, then hurry up. Father will be back any moment now, and I don't want him to find me in the yard!"

Her father began to look disgruntled, but the girl pretended not to notice it. The tassel of the *bersagliere's* beret had touched her heart; all day long it danced in front of her eyes. Eventually her father forbade him the house; however, she opened her window and chatted with him night after night. The whole neighbourhood began to talk about it.

"I'm so much in love with you," said Turiddu, "that I can't sleep and can't eat."

"What nonsense."

"I wish I were the King's son, just so that you would marry me!"

"Nonsense."

"I could eat you."

"Nonsense."

"But I swear to you it's true."

"Do you really mean it?"

Well concealed behind a big pot of basil,[7] Lola listened night after night to their talk. She went pale and red in turn. One day she called Turiddu.

"Well, Turiddu, don't old friends know each other any more these days?"

"Well," sighed the young man. "I'm lucky even to have a chance to say hello to you nowadays."

"Well," replied Lola, "if you really want to see me, surely you know where I live!"

Whereupon Turiddu went to see her so frequently that Santuzza noticed it, and shut the window in his face. The neighbours grinned, or nodded to one another whenever the *bersagliere* passed. Lola's husband was away, travelling with his team of mules from one fair to the other.

One day Lola said to Turiddu, "Next Saturday I must go to confession—I had a terrible dream last night; I dreamed of black grapes."[8]

"No, no," he begged. "Wait."

"I can't wait. It'll soon be Easter and Alfio is bound to want to know why I didn't go to confession."

Kneeling in front of the confessional, Santuzza was waiting for her turn, while Lola attended to the washing of her sins. "If I had my way," muttered Santuzza, "it isn't to Rome that I'd send her for a penance!"

At last, Alfio returned with his mules, and with his pockets full of money. He had bought his wife a lovely new Easter dress as a present.

"You have good reason to bring your wife a present," said his neighbour Santuzza to him, "because while you are away, she cuckolds you in your own home."

Alfio was one of those swaggering fellows who wear their caps right over their ear, and when he heard his wife spoken of in that way his face changed as if he had been knifed.

"By the Devil," he shouted, "if that's a lie I'll tear your and all your kin's eyes out, and you won't even have anything left to cry with!"

"I am not the crying type," said Santuzza. "I didn't even cry when with my own eyes I saw Turiddu go into your wife's house at night."

"Very well, then," replied Alfio. "Thank you very much."

Since the cat had come home, Turiddu no longer walked up and down the little street, but whiled away the time at the inn in the company of his pals. One evening before Easter they all had a plateful of sausages on the table. When Alfio entered, Turiddu at once realized what he had come for by the way he looked at him, and he put his fork on the plate.

"Anything to say to me, Alfio?" he asked.

"Nothing special. We have not met for a while and I just wanted to see you about that matter you know all about."

When Alfio had first come in, Turiddu had offered him a glass of wine, but Alfio raised his hand in refusal. Turiddu got up and said:

"Well, I'm ready."

Alfio put both his arms around Turiddu's neck.

"If you want to come tomorrow morning to the cactus grove by the tannery, we can talk that matter over, *Compare* Turiddu."

"If you wait for me at dawn on the main road, we can walk along together," he replied.

They exchanged the kiss of challenge. Turiddu pressed his teeth into Alfio's ear, and this signified a solemn promise to be there.

Turiddu's friends got up quietly, left the sausages on their plates and walked back with him to the house.

Poor old mother Nunzia waited up late for him every night. "Mother," said Turiddu. "Can you remember how you thought that I wouldn't come back any more when I was called up? Give me a big kiss, just as you did then. I've got to go a long way away tomorrow."

Before daybreak, he took the clasp knife out of the hay where he had hidden it[9] when he was called up, and started to walk towards the prickly pear grove by the tannery.

Lola saw her husband getting ready to leave, and asked in tears and terror, "Holy Jesus and Mary, where are you going to in such a fury?"

"I'm not going far away," replied Alfio, "but it'd be better for you if I didn't come back at all."

Lola began to pray at the foot of her bed, still in her nightgown, and pressed the rosary which Brother Bernard had brought her from the Holy Land against her lips. She was saying one Ave Maria after the other.

The two men walked quietly along the road, Alfio with his cap over his eyes.

Turiddu said, "By God, Alfio, I know I was wrong, and I really ought to let myself be killed. But before leaving, I saw my mother; she must have sensed what it was all about, and got up early just to see me leave, and pretended that she had to feed the chickens. And, by God, so that the poor old girl won't have to cry her eyes out, I shall kill you like a dog."

"That's all right," said Alfio, removing his waistcoat. "So we'll set to, both of us."

They were both skilful fighters. When the first blow came Turiddu was ready to fend it off with his arm and when he struck back he aimed well and stabbed Alfio in the groin.

"So you mean to kill me," said Alfio.

"I told you so, and I told you why. Since I saw my mother in the chicken-run I see her all the time before my eyes."

"Keep your eyes well open then," yelled Alfio, "because I'm going to pay you back now."

In order to hold his left arm over the wound which was hurting him, Alfio was crouching, and kept his left arm so low that his elbow almost trailed the ground. He quickly managed to collect a handful of dust with his left hand and threw it into Turiddu's eyes.

Turiddu was blinded, and let out an agonised scream. He tried to save himself, jumping desperately backwards, but Alfio reached him with a second stab in the stomach, and a third in the throat.

" That's three," he yelled. "That one was for cuckolding me in my own house. Now your mother can leave the chickens alone."

Turiddu staggered for a few moments among the cactus plants and then fell like a stone. Blood gurgled out of his throat. Not another word did he manage to utter.[10]

NOTES

(1) Turiddu is the diminutive of Turi, which is an abbreviation of Sarvaturi, the Sicilian form of Salvatore.

(2) The words "which pick predictions out of a box" are added to explain the otherwise now obscure reference to the canaries.

(3) The terrace-like landing of the outside staircase.

(4) The expression used in the original, *passera solitaria*, refers to the blue rock thrush (*monticula solitarius*), a bird of solitary habits which lives in mountain regions and sings with drooped wings, perched on rocks or the roof of towers.

(5) Literally translated, *Compare* means Co-father, a term originally used for the *Compare d'anello* or "Ring Co-father" (the marriage-witness who signs the church register) and the *Compare di battesimo* or "Baptism Co-father", the child's godfather in his relationship to the parents of the child (not in his relationship to his godchild, to whom he is *padrino* or godfather). Gradually the word assumed a different and wider meaning, indicating that the person thus addressed was, in the opinion of the speaker, respectable enough to be a godfather. This was eventually even further attenuated, and *Compare* became a general mode of address.

(6) Verga used the name "Santa" in the short story, but changed it to "Santuzza" in the play. "Santa" sounds equivocal in English, and "Santuzza" appears preferable.

(7) Kept in every household. Its leaves are used as flavouring for sauces.

(8) In Sicilian dreamlore, black grapes signify tears of sorrow.

(9) It was a forbidden weapon.

(10) The original gives the words that he was unable to utter as "Ah, mamma mia!"

23 Emile Zola in Luigi Capuana's flat in Rome, 1894. With Capuana's dedication to Verga on the back, it is in the possession of Verga's nephew, who is sure that Verga and Zola met in Rome (p. 76)

24   Verga's lectern—in the library at Via S. Anna

CHAPTER VI

CAVALLERIA URBANA

CAVALLERIA URBANA

VERGA regarded himself as essentially a story-teller. Almost ironically, the only great success in his life was the result of an activity which was for him merely a side-line; that of the playwright.

Verga's interest in the theatre is well documented. Already in Florence he had been working on a play, of which we only know that Dall'Ongaro had praised it, and that Verga hoped that it would be performed in Catania. Several of his short stories, as well as episodes from *Mastro-Don Gesualdo,* reveal his familiarity with the backstage world and the atmosphere of the dressing-rooms.

Two of his Milan friends, Arrigo Boito and Giuseppe Giacosa, were essentially men of the theatre. Both were associated with his theatrical venture (illus. 26).

As can happen in the theatre, Eleonora Duse, a most attractive 19-year-old, had become famous overnight as the result of a sudden indisposition of a colleague. A year later, in January 1880, she renewed her success in Naples' *Teatro dei Fiorentini* with a brilliant performance of Zola's *Thérèse Raquin.* She was named a "Diva", i.e. a Goddess, and was invited to join the company of Cesare Rossi, the best known actor-manager of his time.

Eleonora Duse came from a family of travelling actors, and her education was therefore rather sketchy, and certainly not equal to her intelligence and her thirst for literary knowledge. No one could have been better qualified to guide her intellectual appetite than Arrigo Boito, who was her senior by 17 years, and became her tutor and intimate friend. He greatly influenced her, and he introduced her to the fascinating world of European literature.

She met his friends, among them Giuseppe Giacosa, who hoped that she would act in his new short play in verse, *Sirena,* which was to have its first night in Rome in the autumn of 1883. She agreed.

Duse's principle of acting, "to portray realism devoid of any excess", put her in artistic communion with Verga. They had met, and liked one another. She had read the *Vita dei Campi* stories and, always on the lookout for possible new rôles, had told him that his *Cavalleria* story could well be dramatized, as it possessed great theatrical potential. This suggestion was not wasted on Verga. At the beginning of the summer he returned to Catania, and immediately set to work. It is said that he transformed the story into a play within two days and nights.

From Catania he wrote to Giacosa to enquire whether Duse would be able to act in November in Rome:

"If so, when would I have to be in Rome with the script? You see, I have become ambitious and want to throw myself into the fray, on the condition that you, my brother-in-arms,* act as godfather."

Giacosa replied with an encouraging letter:

"I am sorry that I possess only one pair of hands to applaud you with! I'm simply thrilled to attract you to the theatre. I promise you, with an actress like Duse one can achieve wonders. Her company (the Rossi) are in Rome throughout October and go to Turin in November, where they will stay for six months. If you come soon, and if your play has not more than two acts, one can produce it quite quickly. The Turin public is not very fond of new ideas, but something new from you should please even there—always provided that it has a first-class rôle for Duse. . . ."

This stipulation made it essential to dramatize Santuzza's rôle. The childishly infatuated Santuzza of the "true core" had already been changed into the rather insipid Santuzza of the short story, whose importance lies only in her exposure of the adultery. Now she had to be converted into a tragic heroine in order to give Eleonora Duse the opportunity to show her art. Other changes had to be made and the dramatic impact of the entire work had to be heightened.

In the short story, Santuzza's innocence and virginity are not in question; in tragic, but pure, jealousy she destroys Turiddu's life together with her own future happiness. In the play, her innocent association with Turiddu becomes a guilty one, and the fear of being abandoned, with its disgrace and dishonour, adds to her jealousy. Hand in hand with this change goes a change in Turiddu's emotional attachment. In the short story, he goes to his fate with the thought of his mother—as the intensely family-conscious peasant of Sicily. In spite of his adultery, he appears, in some way, rather innocent, one of Verga's "doomed" who destroy themselves in their folly. In the play, his final concern is for his mistress, and the social preoccupation of

*An allusion to Giacosa's own play of 1878, *Il fratello d'armi* (*The Brother-in-Arms*).

25   The Piazzetta S. Teresa in Vizzini (from an old picture postcard)

27   Edouard Rod
(1857-1910)

26   Giacosa and Boito

28   Eleonora Duse

the gentleman replaces the mother-worship of the Sicilian primitive.

Luigi Russo* claims that this change lessens the tragic quality and finds the story artistically superior to the play. This view is not shared by Benedetto Croce, who feels that Verga's preoccupation with the wilful impersonality of the author causes aridity in the story, whereas the exigencies of the theatre forced him to abandon this impersonality and this makes the play superior.

The final scene of the play differs substantially from the end of the short story. The gory fight disappears altogether, and the play ends—like the opera—with Pippuzza's outcry: *"Hanno ammazzato compare Turiddu"* (They have murdered Turiddu!), followed by the appearance of two *carabinieri* who stride across to arrest Alfio. Replacing the unattractive knife-fight by a dramatically effective scream is certainly a desirable change; but why are the two *carabinieri* necessary?

The need for the appearance of the *carabinieri* is linked to the incident of the bitten ear, a detail which although undoubtedly authentic, has been criticized by Russo as an unnecessary "curio" without tragic meaning. In fact, it signifies the solemnization of a contract by the drawing of blood and can therefore quite legitimately be likened to the incident in the second scene of the first act of *Götterdämmerung* where the blood is drawn by swords. To carry knives was forbidden in Sicily, but the lobe of the ear readily bleeds even if pricked only lightly (a fact made use of for blood tests).

Verga, always happy to incorporate bits of folklore and touches of local colour in his stories, had in his childhood witnessed such an incident himself. The porter's lodge at the house in Via S. Anna was occupied by a family from Palermo. One day young Verga saw from the balcony of his house the porter's son starting an argument with another fellow, and threatening sounds were followed by threatening gestures. Suddenly he opened his arms to his adversary and pressed him to his chest, giving him what young Verga interpreted as a kiss. He concluded, to his pleasure, that the enemies had decided to make peace. An older boy put him right and explained that this had not been a kiss and that the bitten ear meant that they had now challenged each other to mortal combat. There is good reason to believe that no further blood was shed in this case as, according to De Roberto, a policeman arrived in time on the scene, said "come with me", and made the two would-be combatants follow him meekly.

The incident must have made a lasting impression on Verga for

Giovanni Verga, Laterza, Bari, 1966.

him to embody it so long afterwards in his story. He could not possibly have foreseen what results this would have, and to what an incredible extent this particular gesture would come to intrigue the whole world! It still attracts curiosity and attention, and tourists in Sicily not infrequently ask guides or hotel porters whether and where the biting of ears may be observed—enquiring with that half-guilty curiosity which can be compared to the quest for cock-fighting of some visitors to Ireland.

International reactions to the biting of the earlobe were soon forthcoming. A few months after the first performance of *Cavalleria rusticana,* a French translation was sent to Zola for his views on a Paris production. Zola felt that certain changes were necessary in order to make the play acceptable to Parisian tastes, and wrote to Verga on 3rd June, 1884:

"Voici mes craintes: d'abord, le titre qui ne serait pas compris et qu'il faudrait absolument changer . . . également . . . les traits de mœurs, comme l'oreille mordue, devant lesquels nos bourgeois resteraient béants." (Herewith my fears: first of all the title which will not be understood and simply must be changed . . . Likewise . . . the customs, e.g. the bitten ear, which will leave our people open-mouthed).

Zola's apprehensions were quite justified. He had persuaded a famous producer, Antoine, to stage the play in the translation by Paul Solanges at the Menus-Plaisirs on 19th October, 1888. No one in the audience, or hardly anyone, knew of Verga. Some critics* in the next morning's newspapers called him Berga, others Varga, and others confused Sicily and Sardinia. Henri Fouquier wrote in the *XIXe Siècle*: "The action takes place in Sardinia . . . If we try very hard to find interest in this drama without a subject, we have to fall back on the picture of the habits à la Mérimée, on the mixture of religiosity and savagery of the Sardinians, on the way they challenge one another by biting their ears. But it really amounts to too little." Frimousse, *Le Gaulois'* theatre critic, wrote that "you cannot really prevent Parisians from showing surprise if they see people biting one another's ear before fighting a duel"; *La Lanterne* referred to "the picturesque scene in which the lover bites the husband's ear, which means that he is ready to play at knives".

By contrast, the Italian critics took hardly any notice of the ear-biting, though the *Illustrazione Italiana,* in the picture page commemorating the play, includes the incident (illus. 31).

Mascagni's opera faithfully preserves Verga's detail of the bitten

*The Paris reviews are quoted from René Ternois (see p. 76).

ear, thus not only perpetuating, but greatly extending its popularity. When Gustav Mahler, before one of the early performances of *Cavalleria rusticana* at the Vienna Opera, made the conductor's customary "visit of encouragement" to the principal singers in their dressing-rooms, he is reported as having left the tenor's room with the words, "Well, good luck—and good appetite".

The programme notes of the 1957 production of the opera at Sadler's Wells Theatre in London condense the whole action of *Cavalleria* into a mere five lines of print — but the bitten ear is retained! "Later Alfio picks a quarrel with Turiddu and Turiddu challenges him in the Sicilian fashion by biting his ear."*

Is biting an ear a "Sicilian fashion"? It is not. It is a "mafiosity", and may well have occurred in the actual incident which underlies the story. Giuseppe Paternò (see p. 97) confirmed that Alfio was a *"Mafioso"*. Verga alludes to Alfio in the story as well as in the play in words which characterize the *tipo mafioso*: "One of those who wear their cap pulled right over the ear." The elimination of the duel from play and opera raises Alfio's stature, but the incident of the challenge retains Mafia colouring. Verga makes Alfio say: "I can look after my own affairs, I don't need those chaps with their plumes [police] and, thank God, everyone here knows it." This directly refers to the Mafia rule of *omertà* (see p. 23): problems of honour must be solved without invoking the law's authority.

Verga brings the *carabinieri* on to the stage in order to show his own rejection of the *omertà* principle, and this may well have been a desirable move, for Northern Italian audiences are inclined to regard any Sicilian as a probable Mafia sympathizer.

How strongly the Mafia element of *Cavalleria* impressed contemporaries is proved by an amusing letter of Giacosa's to Boito. During the previous summer, Boito, Gualdo and Verga had been Giacosa's guests in the Val d'Aosta, and had much enjoyed their walks and talks. Regretfully, Verga now declined an invitation to repeat this 'peripatetic quartet'. In mock annoyance Giacosa wrote to Boito asking him to tell Verga that:

"After the discovery of the plagiarism he committed by copying his *Cavalleria* from Mafia records, it was more than forgiving of us to be prepared to have him again! By rights, he should have thanked us for this invitation on his bended knees and with folded hands."

The production of the new play encountered unexpected difficulties. Giacosa's play *Sirena* had failed in Rome on its first night (24th

*Sadler's Wells programme of 22nd January, 1957.

October, 1883) in spite of Duse's efforts. This not only left Rossi considerably out of pocket but was a most unfavourable portent as well. In order to assess the situation Verga went to Milan and submitted his Cavalleria to the judgment of a "reading committee" of four friends: Boito, Treves, the writer Gualdo, and Torelli-Viollier, editor of the *Corriere della sera.*

Boito praised the work in general terms but considered it unsuitable for the theatre. The publisher Treves, who had already found little of interest in *I Malavoglia,* was, as far as his taste in the theatre was concerned, even more conservative and did not hesitate to voice a very unfavourable view. Gualdo seemed uncertain and said that he did not wish to commit himself: "a perplexity which seemed a polite disguise of a negative view". The only one of the four who without hesitation predicted a success was Eugenio Torelli-Viollier.

Giuseppe Giacosa, too, had read the play. Although his own plays were of a very different type, he had sympathy with the new trends. This made him feel sure that the play could well be theatrically very effective and he sent it to Eleonora Duse and Cesare Rossi recommending an immediate production. Rossi took a poor view of it and did not really want to proceed with the project, thus creating a difficult situation. Giacosa reported the impasse to Verga as follows:

"I spoke to Rossi, who does not believe in the success of your play. I personally don't agree with him, but Duse is of course influenced by her actor-manager and she, too, now predicts failure. What can we do? The main difficulty is that Rossi is not prepared to incur any expense. I shall certainly go on trying; Rossi is a ham routinier, and Duse's views I don't take seriously. She has tremendous ability and, as an actress, she is certainly courageous—but she is extremely timid in judging anything before it is performed, and is, moreover, frightened that by encouraging you she may incur a responsibility towards Rossi and eventually be blamed. I feel sure that she is at heart still convinced that it will be a success, but if it isn't, it wouldn't suit her at all having to admit that she has made a mistake. The more I think about it myself, the more I am convinced that the play will please—and if it doesn't, so much the worse for the public!"

Verga felt disappointed. He replied to Giacosa on November 18th that he wished to withdraw the play, and that he considered the whole affair "dead and buried."

Giacosa did not accept this suggestion and by telegram requested Verga to come to Turin at once. Upon arrival he was to join him for lunch. The Sicilian actor Flavio Andò, a member of the Rossi group, and a fellow guest, explained that Rossi's reluctance was entirely due to the question of costs. The conversation across the host's dining table resolved the problem; Andò made it clear that Rossi, in spite of expecting failure, was nevertheless quite prepared to stage the play, partly because Duse (illus. 28) "already heard Santuzza's screams of despair within her breast". An essential condition was that Verga and his friends should pay for the scenery and costumes; the proceeds of what was bound to remain a single performance would in Rossi's judgment not cover these expenses.

The whole dispute was thus reduced to a question of costs and Verga at once agreed not only to provide the costumes, but to forgo his author's fees as well. This was accepted by Rossi. He remained however so convinced of failure that he requested Tebaldo Checchi to play the role of Alfio and for himself only took the small part of one of the peasants.

Verga took Duse's measurements and wrote to his brother Mario in Vizzini,* asking for the costumes to be put in hand at once. He gave exact orders for them:

Turiddu Macca: *bersagliere* uniform, beret and trousers. Jacket and waistcoat of olive coloured velvet, red woollen scarf around the neck.

Compare Alfio: leather cap, long sports jacket with many pockets, of chick-pea coloured fustian. Olive coloured velvet trousers, a sporting type of waistcoat with buttons at the back. One earring, nothing around the neck.

Santuzza: white *mantellina,* spencer of yellow and chocolate striped muslin, with flower pattern. Turquoise coloured skirt. Cotton kerchief across the chest, coloured cotton kerchief for the head—the two kerchiefs to be of contrasting colours.

Lola: blue *mantellina,* chequered flannel spencer, light-coloured muslin skirt, striped, with flowers and dark and light stripes. White cotton kerchief for the chest, flowered silk kerchief for the head.

Duse's measurements were: from the hip to the foot, 100 cm. Waist, 58-59 cm. Length of sleeves from the shoulder to the wrist, 36 or 37 cm. All of which adds up to size 12. A replica of the original dress is shown in illus. 29.

*His brother's wife, Lidda Fortunato, was now a lady of such proportions that she had to have a permanent dressmaker on her staff. Later on, in order to accommodate her figure, even her chairs had to be made specially.

The cost of Santuzza's dress was 26 lire. The price for all the costumes together was 160 lire. Everything was to be ready for the first night of the play, to take place in Turin, early in January 1884.

Verga himself returned to Catania to spend a quiet Christmas there, and at the same time to supervise the making of the costumes. Five days before Christmas Eve, in the late morning of 19th December, 1883, news of a practically unprecedented scandal suddenly spread through the town.

Catania's poet laureate, Mario Rapisardi, was a migraine sufferer. Early in the morning of the 19th, he had one of his attacks, and paced the rooms of his house in pain and distress. During these attacks, the whole house had to go into a state of mourning. No one dared to move and, for fear of irritating the bard, his mother and sister did not even dare to wash or to comb their hair; subdued and dishevelled, they would wait for his pain to cease. On this occasion, Giselda, Rapisardi's wife, had taken a bath, an activity regarded as unnecessary by her mother-in-law, who claimed that during her whole life she had never needed one.

At this juncture a woman who used to help in the Rapisardi household in the morning, arrived. She carried a bundle of journals which Giselda had lent to a friend,* and intended to hand them to Giselda.

Wandering from one room to another, Rapisardi saw the woman with her papers, and took the bundle away from her. To his wife's utter consternation, a letter fell out. He picked it up, opened it and turned deathly pale. The letter was in Verga's handwriting and read as follows:

"To Mrs. G.   by hand   Friday 14th

"I received your dear letter yesterday and the only reason for not replying at once was that I wished to avoid having to write that unlucky date! But today, my first thought is for you. Your words are in my heart and I read and reread your letter many times. My dear, my dear, my dear, you are the woman I dream of, my friend, my sister, and my beloved all together (though not my wife, I'm afraid).

"How many vivid and thrilling memories you bring to my eyes! How much I want at least to *see* you. I shall go to the Piazzolis, and if it makes it too obvious to meet you there, I shall at least see you in the street! I feel I just have to write to you, at least once a week, but I fear to become a nuisance to that kind soul who helps us.

"So you liked the little seal? I am delighted! And don't fear to 'ruin'

*Maria Aradas Bruno, headmistress of a private girls' school.

me with your little wishes, beloved; do tell me of all of them, openly: the greatest pleasure for me is to do something with thoughts of you. Before I leave, I shall pass your house— and at least I shall see you from afar.

"What are your plans for the summer? As you know, in January I am off to Turin. How I am longing for your judgment and your companionship there, during this battle for which I am preparing myself calmly, almost indifferently, as if I were only a spectator. What will be, will be—but I feel it's going to be something unusual!

"Will you do what I say? Will you listen to me? Write some more of your sketches from Tuscany for me, some of those true stories from Tuscany. You possess wonderful gifts, and should write more stories like that little gem! [See p. 184]. Send them straight to *Il Fanfulla*, without asking: I promise you that they will be accepted with open arms and will be appreciated, and you will be put on a pedestal and the editors will run after you. Work, work, and work devotedly. Don't let yourself be overcome by depression; if it is nothing else, work is a wonderful hobby and a great comfort. If only I could be near to you, or at least walk under your window, and ask you what you are doing. . . .

"Keep on writing, and when you have ten or 12 stories in the Sunday *Fanfulla* they will make a volume on their own. I guarantee the result.

"Addio, I kiss your face, your eyes, and your mouth, like this, a long, long kiss. All my soul is yours.

"Your. . . ."

A Verga biographer of the Fascist era, Capellani, has calculated that the whole letter amounts to 65 lines of print, of which only ten have a "love content"; the rest, he states, refer to the exigencies of life and to the dignity of work. Quite rightly Cattaneo has remarked that such calculations would hardly have consoled Rapisardi; for a husband, and particularly for a Sicilian husband, there was quite enough in this letter!

In fact, Rapisardi requested his wife to leave immediately—a request Giselda agreed to at once. She started to get herself ready, while her husband collapsed in an armchair and sobbed. Her mother-in-law yelled, "Quick, quick, get out of my sight—quick, quick", and kept on repeating these works like a *ritornello*.*

Within a couple of hours Giselda was ready. She left all her husband's gifts behind, among them the gold medal, mounted as a brooch, which Catania had given Rapisardi for his *Palingenesi* in

---

*As not only the people concerned in this famous adultery, but also many of their friends were gifted writers, its details were incorporated in several theatrical and fictional works of Italian literature. The scene described above was used by Giacosa for his play *Tristi amori* (*Sad Love Affairs*).

1868. Her husband gave her 150 lire in cash and 150 lire in revenue coupons (*tagliande di rendita*). From that time onwards Giselda did not receive another penny from him and one must admit, comments Cattaneo, "that to get rid of a wife—even a disloyal one—for a thousand lire* was undoubtedly very cheap indeed, even in the 1880's".

When Giselda was ready to leave, her husband's behaviour verged on insanity. Three times he got hold of her arm and tried to hold her back. Each time Giselda managed to free herself.** The mother-in-law urged her son to let her go, assuring him that within a week she would be knocking on his door.

The great poet was crying and kicking. Outside it was raining heavily. Giselda took one of the umbrellas from the stand in the hall. Her mother-in-law tore it out of her hand and screamed: "You can't take *everything* with you!"

Mario roused himself. He staggered towards his mother, took the umbrella out of her hand, and handed it to his wife, who left the house and walked away without turning round.

What could have led up to all this?

Loyal to his promise, Verga had not seen Giselda for ten years after her wedding. On her very wedding day, Giselda became aware of her mistake. Maria Borgese thus describes the occasion: ***

"The marriage took place on 12th February, 1872, in Messina. Giselda and her mother had arrived by boat from Naples, and Mario Rapisardi had met them with his brother-in-law Giuseppe Barbagallo, who was to be a witness.

"As second witness, Rapisardi simply selected a porter from the piazza. His vile face disturbed Giselda, but Rapisardi thought this was great fun. After the ceremony they proceeded to Catania; Giselda had not met her mother-in-law before, nor Rapisardi's sister who, with her husband and two children, shared the flat since the death of Mario's father. This was an arrangement designed for her mother's comfort and company.

"The room in which old Rapisardi had died was kept permanently locked. To make room for the newly-weds, Mrs. Rapisardi had vacated her own room, and her own bed had been put in a passage. Giselda was

*Cattaneo's figure is erroneous. According to Maria Borgese, it was only 300 lire.

**This phase of the proceedings, too, was used for a scene in a play by Giacosa, *I diritti dell'anima* (*The Rights of the Soul*).

***Maria Borgese, Anime scompagnate, *Nuova Antologia*, Nov.-Dec., 1937, Rome.

aghast to find no toilet facilities whatsoever: everyone had to use a pot. The washing facilities consisted of a small jug of blue glass and basin to match in the bedroom.

"The wedding meal was a sad affair. The table was carelessly laid in the passage, beside the unmade bed. Giselda's mother-in-law's brother, a tailor by the name of Vincenzo Patti, had been invited, together with his son, who later aped his cousin's long hair and black bow tie. Father and son ate their meal with their hats on. The brother-in-law wore the red fez of the *bersaglieri,* the groom himself wore a woollen cap.

"People from Tuscany were inclined to regard Sicily as mysterious, rather primitive and somewhat paradoxical. Mother and daughter looked furtively at one another, convinced that this was true. The mother-in-law sat sideways at the table, as she usually did, and did not eat. When the cassata* was served, she said in a loud voice, as if continuing a thought : *'Di luni arruzuloni'*, and explained this proverb to the ladies from Tuscany as best she could: Monday marriages are unlucky. Giselda was in tears. Her mother and Mario tried to turn the situation with a joke, but the others remained silent, looking down at their plates.

"Another upset was caused by Giselda having to spend the first night of her marriage in closest proximity to the two mothers. Signora Fojanesi slept next door in Mario's studio and his mother just outside in the passage. Her moaning and sobbing could plainly be heard through the thin wall. Before the young couple could close the door of their room, she came in to help her son undress and to arrange the yellow maroon-dotted cotton handkerchief which kept his hair tidy. When Giselda politely gave her to understand that she could very well have done this herself, her mother-in-law left, and began to cry behind the closed door."

Immediately after the wedding, Giselda was forced to wear mourning, because her father-in-law, whom she had never known, had died half a year before. Even a white collar gave offence, and she had to discard it. Sicilians kept the sad custom of five years' mourning, and in larger families cases of females who had to wear mourning without a break from childhood to old age were not at all uncommon. The mother-in-law remained unremittingly hostile to the *continentale,* the "girl from the mainland". Giselda's hair was brown and, according to her mother-in-law, there were "enough girls with dark hair in Sicily without having to go and look for one elsewhere . . ." In Florence, Giselda had been accustomed to going out alone. Now she found herself completely locked up, apart from rare evening-walks with her husband along a quiet road.

---

*A Sicilian dessert which had, in its original form, curd cheese ("caseus") as its basic ingredient. "*Caseata*" became "*casciata*" and, eventually, "*cassata*".

The years went by. The mother-in-law complained continuously about her son's hasty marriage and the absence of a dowry. Giselda's marriage suffered from her husband's scenes of jealousy, and his various oddities and whims. Whenever the "Bard from Etna" walked in poetic inspiration from one end of his room to the other, his wife had to sit quietly in a corner in order not to disturb the divine inspiration. She had, however, always to be ready to give linguistic advice, which was very necessary owing to the great poet's poor schooling in Italian. Rapisardi did not always like his wife's suggestions, particularly if they differed from his own ideas, and veered from a feeling of inadequacy to the "vexed arrogance of Lucifer".

The account which Maria Borgese gives of Rapisardi's odd traits, of his capriciousness, arrogance, cruelty and violence, suggests that they may well have been due to sexual impotence, and as Maria Borgese was intimately acquainted with Giselda, this assumption is most likely correct. It certainly did not help to improve Giselda's plight.

In order to be more comfortable the Bard slept during the hot season alone in his room: Giselda was forced to move into a dirty study which was alive with cockroaches, as no one was allowed to dust the poet's papers.

Only the male members of the household had the right to open their own letters: Giselda did not see hers until they had passed her husband's scrutiny. When anyone came to see Giselda in the absence of her husband, her small nephew, Pietrino, was encouraged to be present and to report the gist of the conversation to his grandmother, Giselda's mother-in-law.

On the only occasion that they had gone to the theatre together, Rapisardi had forced his wife to leave their box and to return home before the performance had begun, because people had pointed their opera glasses at them. When Giselda burst into tears afterwards, her husband kicked her in the face because he "could not tolerate scenes." After this outburst he begged on his knees for forgiveness.

The Bard himself fell continually in love with other women, among them friends of Giselda; his lack of success in these amorous episodes was compensated for by a prolific production of new verse.

In September, 1880, the Rapisardis were staying with Signora Fojanesi in Florence. One evening, when they were all going to the Arena Nazionale, and Giselda was getting herself ready, her husband suddenly changed his mind and forbade her to go out. When she remonstrated, he hit her repeatedly, using a whip, which at that time formed part of his eccentric armamentarium.

The next morning Giselda went out on her own (in Florence she was permitted to do so) and met Verga quite unexpectedly in the Via Rondinelli. "Oh, you are in Florence!" she said. "Yes, I'm on my way to Milan," replied Verga. She looked into his eyes and began to cry. "My poor dear girl," said Verga, "so it is true that you are unhappy." Giselda could not speak, but nodded her head. Then she asked, "Are you going to stay here for a while?" "Certainly," said Verga, "if you want me to!" Everything was explained to him, and he put himself at her disposal. The "Bard" had his reward.

During the whole of the year 1881, Verga and Giselda managed to talk to one another only on a single occasion, a Sunday reception at Signora Piazzoli's, a lady from Milan who had come to live in Catania. There were many people there and Giselda was accompanied by her 12-year-old nephew: this had been their only chance, as the Rapisardis did not go to Florence that year.

Altogether, it was a most difficult relationship to maintain. Letters were exchanged with the help of a cousin of Giselda's, Linda Fojanesi, who had been appointed headmistress of the College of the Verginelle, a girls' school in Catania. These were carefully written letters, generally containing only literary advice and without any personal remarks. Giselda had become keen on writing and Verga was anxious to help to the best of his ability. In this connection Verga committed the only indiscretion of his life; he told a third person of his relationship with Giselda. This person was Matilde Serao,* 17 years his junior, and one of the few female writers whom Verga, generally not impressed by Italy's literary ladies, much appreciated as an original artist.

Verga had been anxious to obtain permission for Giselda to translate a novel by Edmond de Goncourt, and Edouard Rod had offered to help with this project. A letter about it was discovered by her husband looking into his wife's desk. He recognized Verga's handwriting, took Giselda by the throat, and threatened to strangle her. Giselda managed to free herself, and escaped to her cousin at the College of the Verginelle, but next day her brother-in-law persuaded

*She had begun to write stories with a Neapolitan background in 1878 and later married the critic and writer Scarfoglio. It is possible that she was infatuated with Verga, and was not content to play the literary go-between rôle that Verga may have had in mind for her in order to help Giselda to get her stories published. It is probable that this episode, often commented upon in Italian literary history, contributed to the harsh attitude which her husband Scarfoglio adopted towards Verga. (See also p. 91).

her to return. The news of Giselda's flight had spread rapidly through Catania, which upset Rapisardi so much that he forced his wife to spend almost the whole of the next day with him on the balcony, like a royal couple, so as to demonstrate their reconciliation publicly. This amused the Catanese, and a procession of curious and inquisitive people continued all day long in front of the house.

Verga's letter had not been compromising: the magnanimous Bard eventually forgave his wife, but ordered her strictly to abstain from any further contact. They both had subsequently tried to violate this order as best they could with the aid of various subterfuges and intermediaries, until the disaster of December 1883.

That it was a disaster, considering the social, moral and financial prejudice* which confronted an adulteress at that period, cannot be doubted. However, as soon as she had left the house, Giselda felt immense relief at the break-up of her marriage. In the street, she took a cab and went to Verga's house. She stayed in the hall while he was summoned. She told him what had happened, and explained that she wished to leave for Florence at once. Verga approved, but maintained that he would be unable to travel with her, as he had to keep himself at the disposal of Rapisardi.

What was Verga thinking of at that moment? For once, this question which so often puzzles the biographer can be readily answered. There can be but little doubt that he was thinking of Evelyn Cattermole, and that his thoughts were not pleasant.

After their marriage, the Count and Countess Mancini remained for two years in Naples. A new posting as Captain in the Eighth Bersagliere Regiment forced the young couple to move to Milan, where they went to live at 12 Via S. Simone.** The beautiful Countess "light in step, as slender as a sylph, magnetic in her look, and bewitching in her smile"*** was welcomed with open arms to Milan's artistic society. "When she visits a church, this goddess on earth makes heads turn to profane thoughts. When she entered the Countess Maffei's salon in her gown of transparent red voile, all gossiping

*Left to fight her own battles, and having suffered enough from the indissolubility of Italian marriages, she eventually enjoyed one advantage: after her husband's death she became entitled to a widow's pension (see p. 183). This was 29 years after the 'disaster', when Giselda was 61 years old: even then many voices were raised, and articles written, disapproving of her acceptance of it.

**Now Via Cesare Correnti.

***Raffaello Barbiera, *Il salotto della Contessa Maffei*, Treves, Milan, 1895.

ceased and everyone admired her. When she went to the Scala all glasses pointed towards her."

Her husband developed a taste for military society and its gambling parties, and they began to give such parties at home. He and the rich young Swedish military attaché Alex Wimnel often went out together, and the affairs of the two young captains soon were being talked about. The beautiful young Countess, frequently finding herself alone, began to feel neglected, and eventually consoled herself with her husband's best friend, Lieutenant Giuseppe Bennati di Beylon.

These two made a fairly safe arrangement for their encounters. Mancini used to sleep every afternoon for several hours, partly on account of his late nights gambling, and partly because he had to be on parade at five a.m.

In addition to his own lodgings in Via Solferino, Bennati took a flat in a house only a few paces from the Mancini's (at No. 1 Via Unione), and Evelyn would join him there as soon as her husband was asleep. A stratagem was arranged in case Mancini woke up before his wife returned, and this necessitated the complicity of Evelyn's devoted maid, Giuseppina Dones. She would say that the Countess had gone out for a walk, run across to the flat in Via Unione, knock three times in an agreed manner, and tell her mistress that her husband was awake. Evelyn would then return at once.

All this had worked well for some time. On 22nd May, 1875, however, Giuseppina, possibly because she felt herself to be in love with the good-looking Bennati, replied to Mancini's question as to his wife's whereabouts in a different way; she informed him of his wife's association with Bennati, and encouraged him to go himself to the flat and to give the appropriate signal. He did so, and his wife, clad in a dressing-gown, opened the door. The inevitable result of this discovery was a challenge and a duel.

While the necessary arrangements were being made, Mancini was in a state of hysteria and several times tried to throw himself out of the window. The Countess refused to see anyone. Bennati was the most composed of the three, and declared that he was prepared to accept any conditions for the duel which his friend and his seconds proposed. The duel took place five days later, on 27th May, 1875, at 6.45 p.m., in a pine wood outside Milan at Senaghino, near Bollate. The weapons were pistols of duelling size.

The agreed distance was of 30 metres, with a barrier in the middle and markings spaced out at 10 metres. After the signal was given, the adversaries looked at one another for over a minute. As permitted, Mancini advanced twice, covering five metres each time. Bennati had not fired, and his pistol was pointing downwards, when Mancini slowly aimed, and shot him. He hit Bennati between the sixth and seventh ribs, the bullet injuring his liver. In agony Bennati turned a half circle, bent at the knees and fell on his injured side. With great difficulty (it was not easy to get the horses through the wood to the clearing), Bennati was taken to Bollate, and later transferred to Milan where ten days later he died in the arms of his grief-stricken mother. At his funeral, Giuseppina Dones drank sulphuric acid; she eventually ended up in a mental home.

Before the duel, Bennati had written a letter to the King's Procurator in Milan, stating that he intended to commit suicide. In spite of this letter Mancini was charged with "homicide committed in a duel", according to the penal code, articles 588 and 589. Bail was granted. The proceedings took place at the *Tribunale Correzionale* on July 30th, behind closed doors. The public was admitted on July 31st to hear the Attorney General Cav. Sighele sum up, in the style of a third-rate novel. According to the report in the *Lombardia,* he said:

"Captain Mancini had a friend. His friend betrayed him, and made his wife soil her white bridal gown. On the 22nd the accused surprised his wife in flagrant adultery, and I accept in every respect the accused's account of the happening."

The Attorney General then made two statements which were quite wrong. He said, "I wish to rectify two erroneous beliefs by declaring that, firstly, the doctors gave the injured man all possible help"—in fact there was a good deal of delay and mismanagement—"and secondly, that Bennati had every intention of fighting seriously" —this is not corroborated by the eye-witnesses' account, nor by Bennati's letter to the King's Procurator.

He continued by saying that "men like Mancini who have their chests decorated with medals for military valour cannot be accused of cowardice".

Photographs show Mancini decorated with at least three medals but, in view of his age and the relevant military history, it does not seem likely that they were received for services in the field.

The Attorney General then accepted all extenuating circumstances and requested a punishment of three months' detention and the payment of a fine of 51 lire.

The court pronounced an absolute discharge, a verdict which "was received with great applause by a very large crowd".

Four days after the duel, on 1st June, 1875, the heartbroken Evelyn was ordered to attend the Civil and Correctional Court, and to accept a separation on the following terms:

(1) She had to leave Milan at once, go to Florence to stay with her father, and to arrange for herself a fixed residence there.

(2) If she left Florence, she was not to go to Rome nor to any other place where "her appearance might cause unpleasantness".

(3) She was not to use the name Mancini, and was to be of "honourable conduct".

(4) In compensation, Captain Mancini renounced his rights to her dowry.

(5) Mancini consented to augment her income by 300 lire, payable quarterly in advance, the first payment to be made at once.

The same evening Evelyn left for Florence. Giselda subsequently saw a good deal of Evelyn during her stays in Florence and they became firm friends. Rapisardi, true to his habits, fell in love with Evelyn, but she tactfully converted this into a friendship maintained with both, though particularly with Giselda.

There can be little doubt that when Giselda told Verga of the discovery of the letter he must have had Bennati in mind. When she now expressed the wish to go to Florence, he approved and suggested that she should stay with Evelyn to begin with. He promised to join her later.

His staying behind proved unnecessary. The expected challenge never came, even though at that time this was required by etiquette, and duels were very frequently fought. They were, in fact, so accepted a feature that when a Member of Parliament, Morelli, drew the Minister's (Ricotti) attention to the unsatisfactory disciplinary regulations for army officers regarding adultery, the Minister replied that these did not matter anyway, as the disciplinary measures existed only for the chicken-hearted.

Even outside military circles, duels were often fought for very minor reasons. When Angelo Sommaruga was editor of the Rome literary journal *Cronaca bizantina* (see p. 56), an article in his journal about the ladies of Messina, the *"Donne Peloritane"*, described them as somewhat unrefined in manner, cliquish and not very elegant, loving flowers, music, birds, the theatre, and quails with peas, but "most of all quails with peas". Although Sommaruga had not written the piece himself, he received challenges from three aggrieved husbands of Messina. Fortunately, a minor injury he received in the first encounter saved honour all round.

Rapisardi did not feel inclined to act like the husbands of Messina, even if he had a more valid reason. His behaviour, as can be imagined, caused a good deal of criticism and various explanations for it, ranging from cowardice to indifference, were suggested.

That Verga would have accepted a challenge is beyond doubt. Throughout his life he was a confirmed adulterer who knew what risks he was running; a pair of duelling pistols formed a regular part of his travelling equipment.

The correct explanation of what did, or rather did not, happen is probably that both Rapisardi and Verga sincerely appreciated one another. Though Verga never hesitated to criticize Rapisardi's more obtuse traits, the two had been good friends for a long time. They were aware of the link between them and, to Rapisardi's credit, Verga's betrayal did not totally destroy their esteem for each other; Rapisardi must have thought that the affair was not worth their trying to murder one another.

The survival of an underlying feeling of friendship—even if all personal contacts had ceased—is corroborated by Verga's attitude during the Rapisardi-Carducci polemic. (See p. 189).

Within a year of Giselda's leaving, Rapisardi was joined by a young secretary from Florence, a girl he had selected from photographs which had been supplied to him in answer to an advertisement. Amelia Poniatowski Sabernich lived with him until his death in 1912, and a few months after his death married Alfio Tomaselli, Rapisardi's most intimate friend. She herself died in 1914. After her death her husband published Rapisardi's letters,* among them Verga's letter to Giselda. (See p. 237).

Having waited a few days, Verga left for Florence to join Giselda. He could not stay for any length of time, as the first night of *Cavalleria rusticana* in Turin had been fixed for 14th January.

The play was not long enough to provide a full evening's entertainment. It was therefore to be preceded by a short piece, *Tredici a tavola* (Thirteen for Dinner), a farce written, or rather adapted from the Spanish, by Giovanni Salvestri. Salvestri was a mediocre actor who appeared in second-rate companies and eked out his living by journalism. He could write pleasingly fluent dialogue, and became

---

*Alfio Tomaselli, *Epistolario di Mario Rapisardi*, Battiato, Catania, 1922. Errors contained in the reproduction of the letter were later corrected by Maria Borgese's account in *Nuova Antologia*, see p. 118.

a professional adaptor for all types of stagework; he had dramatized a number of novels for theatrical presentation.

The first performance was awaited with much interest and curiosity. Word had got around that a completely new type of play was in the offing. The feeling of expectancy was increased by an article of Giacosa's in the Turin daily paper, the *Gazzetta Piemontese,* which appeared on the day before the first performance on 13th January, 1884.

"A new dramatic work by Giovanni Verga will be performed at the Carignano tomorrow night. This is an event of great importance, and the eyes of the whole of Italy will be focused upon us. In general, the public have a totally wrong notion of what is new in the theatre: almost invariably it expects the *new* to consist in new *facts.* Whoever finds a combination of happenings which has not been seen before is regarded as a true innovator and the most sought-after artistic effect is the surprise.

"Verga regards this as quite wrong and I agree with him. A theatre which aims at *surprises* first and foremost is decadent theatre. All this coarsening of events, of language, and of voice for the sake of stage effects only opens the door to mediocrity . . . Neither the unexpected theatre coups nor the stage tirades have anything to do with real life: the great tragedies of life occur with terrifying simplicity.

"We are now going to see a work that may give less occasion for applause but might make us think the more.

"I am saying all this so that my fellow citizens, who have heard about this new play, should not hastily pass judgment if they do not find it to be that usual type of new play they are expecting. Verga's newness does not consist of doing *more,* but rather in doing *less,* and certainly in doing it all in a completely new way. I don't attempt to predict the result. It is possible that Verga may be wrong: and if so, he is not the man to take offence if a conscientious public tells him so.

"Whatever may be in store, I feel that tomorrow's date will not only be an important date for Verga, but will be a date to remember for all of us."

If Verga's expectations were high, he certainly did not admit to them in a letter he wrote to Edouard Rod four days before the first performance:

"Can you imagine how much pleasure it would give me to have you here to review my *Cavalleria rusticana*? My play (or rather, sketch of a play) is of a very risky type, quite at odds with the present taste of the public. Here in Italy it is not going to be taken note of, and most people will shrug their shoulders as if the whole idea were wrong. I had, it's true enough, the same hesitations and misgivings before publishing my

Vita dei campi stories, which afterwards their success belied. But with those stories—my first experiment with this new artistic method—I was on different ground: with a book one is face to face with one's reader, and what on first impact may seem too harsh has time to weather. Here, my ideas have to be put across by interpreters, who quite possibly are neither as convinced, nor as daring, as I am. Anyway, we'll see what's going to happen. I am sure it is going to be a flop. The only thing which really matters to me is to assert the principle. The rest will come later, and others will take it up."

For once, Verga's forebodings were wrong. It was not a flop, it was a great success—the only real success throughout his life.

Right from the beginning, there was excited anticipation. When the curtain rose, the scene, painted by Fontana, was brilliantly lit. There was the little square, the church, the road, the wall of the garden, and the cactus hedge. "The first impressions were favourable, and an 'immense' silence isolated the voices of the few chatterers, until the house was 'religiously quiet'." Torelli-Viollier, the *Corriere della's sera's* editor, wrote the story of the evening himself:

"The Carignano was absolutely packed last night. Every single seat was occupied; by 7.45 you could not move in the pit. There were lots of students present. From the moment the curtain rose, the public followed the play with rapt attention up to the scene of the dialogue, during which applause began to burst out. From then onwards, roaring applause marked every scene.

"The fall of the curtain brought a tremendous ovation. The public yelled for the author, and shouted 'Viva Verga! Let's have the author'.

"Amid this enthusiasm, Cesare Rossi eventually appeared at the footlights and announced that the author was not present. His mind had been assailed by doubts about the result, and he had gone to the nearby Alfieri theatre to see an operetta. Some friends, who had come over from Milan for this historic first night, managed to locate him, and brought him the news of his unexpected triumph.

"I am—with legitimate gratification—able to say that I was the only man in the whole of Milan who predicted this triumphal result."

After the performance Verga went to the Caffè della Meridiana, where he was surrounded for hours by writers, critics and playwrights. Turin's artistic set was enthusiastic. Molineri, the *Gazzetta Piemontese's* critic, wrote the next day that with his *Cavalleria* Verga had reached the "summit of artistic expression".

Anticipating total failure, Arrigo Boito had stayed in Milan. He now sent a telegram: "I confess I made a big blunder—and am delighted about it—affectionate congratulations."

It was not the fear of failure which was responsible for Verga's absence from the first night, it was his convictions, and his nature. He held the view that, once completed, the work of art must make its own way, without the help of the author. Furthermore, he was by nature shy, and did not like to exhibit himself in any way. Giacosa persuaded him to attend the second, again highly successful, performance and, in order not to give the impression that he was "too proud to appear in the company of actors", he came on the stage and acknowledged the cheering of the crowd. (See p. 233).

The Turin performances were followed by a triumphal tour of Italy. When *Cavalleria* was performed in Florence, Verga went there, but stayed behind in Giselda's company and did not attend the performance. When friends joined them and brought the news of renewed success, he kissed Giselda's hand and called her his *"mascotte"*.

In order to show his appreciation of Giacosa's help, Verga dedicated his play to him, although he opposed on principle any dedication of works of art as senseless humbug.

Luigi Russo who maintained (see p. 111) that the short story is superior to the play, quotes as an example Santuzza's disclosure of the adultery which, in the story's four short sentences, seems far more effective than its rather lengthy counterpart in the play. Be that as it may, the play shows authentic force in the swiftness of its action. Cattaneo stresses that, especially in those scenes which Verga did not have to "remake" (the play corresponds only to the last three pages of the story), he achieved remarkable effects, particularly in the dialogue between Turiddu and Santuzza, which later became the duet in the opera.

This dialogue and its ensuing scene are given here, in a new translation.

SCENE II

Turiddu Macca returns in haste from the path on the back left, Santuzza leaps to her feet upon seeing him.

Turiddu: Santuzza! What are you doing here?

Santuzza: I have been waiting for you.

Turiddu: Where is my mother?

Santuzza: She has gone to Church.

Turiddu: You should go as well. I can look after the place here myself.

Santuzza: No, I am not going to Church.

Turiddu: On Easter Day?

Santuzza: You know I can't go.

Turiddu: Then what do you want to do?

Santuzza: Talk to you.

Turiddu: Here? In the middle of the road?

Santuzza: I don't care.

Turiddu: But people can see us.

Santuzza: I don't care.

Turiddu: What's wrong with you?

Santuzza: Tell me where you've come from?

Turiddu: What do you mean by that?

Santuzza: Where were you last night?

Turiddu: Have I got to say where I have been?

Santuzza: Why get in a rage when I ask where you have been? Can't you tell me?

Turiddu: I had to go to Francofonte, that's where I was.

Santuzza: It is not true. At two o'clock in the morning you were still here.

Turiddu: Well, then I was where I jolly well wanted to be.

Santuzza: (*letting the mantellina fall on her shoulders*) Turiddu, why are you treating me like this? Why can't you look me in the face? Can't you see that this suffering is killing me?

Turiddu: It's your own fault. I don't know what ideas you get into your head—you accuse me of all sorts of things to upset me—and you try to spy on me to find out what I am doing as if I was a boy—don't you think I am man enough to do what I want?

Santuzza: That's not true: I have never asked anyone about anything to do with you—but I couldn't help hearing, just now, that you have been seen at Lola's door at daybreak.

Turiddu: Who said that?

Santuzza: Alfio said it. Her husband.

Turiddu: Him! So that is what your great love for me means! You go and put such fleas in that fellow Alfio's ear? And put me in danger of getting a knife stuck into me?

Santuzza: (*falling on her knees with her hands clasped*) Turiddu— how can you say such a thing?

Turiddu: Get up—don't you dare to make a scene here. Get up or I shall go.

Santuzza: (*rising slowly*) You want to go now? You want to leave me now?

Turiddu: What do you want me to do if you won't believe what

I say? You only believe what other people say. I tell you again. It's quite untrue. Alfio was mistaken; I was out on my own business. Can't you see how stupid you are to get such ideas about Lola into your head while her husband is at home!

Santuzza: But her husband only came back this morning!

Turiddu: Ah—that you know too—do you? Quite some little spy, aren't you. Haven't I got a right to be my own master?

Santuzza: Yes, Turiddu, yes you have, and you have the right to cut my throat and kill me like a lamb with your own hands if you want to. And if you want me to, I shall lick your hands like a dog.

Turiddu: So what is it then?

Santuzza: But not Lola. Never! That woman only wants my damnation.

Turiddu: Leave Lola in peace. She has enough to do with minding her own affairs.

Santuzza: Then why doesn't she leave me in peace? Why does she want to take you away from me. I haven't got anyone else!

Turiddu: Be careful, Santuzza! You are wrong!

Santuzza: No, I am not. Didn't you run after her before you left for the army?

Turiddu: A lot of water has passed under the bridge since then. Anyway she is married now and she has her own home.

Santuzza: Does that make any difference? I'm sure you are still in love with her even if she is married. And hasn't she stolen you from me out of sheer spite? Can't you see that I am full of fury against you for betraying me like this?

Turiddu: Be quiet, be quiet.

Santuzza: I can't be quiet. My heart is on fire and I feel I'm going mad. And what am I to do if you leave me?

Turiddu: I will never abandon you unless you drive me to it. But I tell you: I must be my own master and free to do what I want to do. As yet, thank heavens, I have not got a chain around my neck.

Santuzza: What do you mean by that?

Turiddu: I mean that you are crazy, with your perpetual groundless jealousy.

Santuzza: It is not my fault. You can see how humiliated I am. I know she is better than I am. Weighed down with chains round her neck, and her gold rings. Her husband sees to it that she is not in want of anything. He hangs jewels on her like on the

Madonna on the altar—that sinful creature.

Turiddu: Leave her alone.

Santuzza: See how you defend her?

Turiddu: I am not defending her. I don't care whether her husband keeps her like a Madonna on the altar or not. What matters to me is that I shan't be taken for one who is not free to do as he likes. That—no!

SCENE III

Lola enters from the lane on the left.

Lola: Turiddu, you don't by any chance know, do you, whether my husband has already gone to church?

Turiddu: I don't know, Lola. I've only just got here myself.

Lola: He told me that he had to go to the blacksmith's because the bay mule has lost a shoe, and that he would join me in church soon. And what about you two? Are you going to listen to the Easter service from outside, and stand here talking?

Turiddu: Well, Santuzza was just telling me . . . . .

Santuzza: I told him that to-day is a very special day. And that the Lord God from above can see everything that is going on.

Lola: Including the two of you who are not going to church?

Santuzza: Church is a place for people who have a clear conscience.

Lola: The Lord be praised and I kiss the ground (*she bows down, touches the ground with the tip of the finger which she afterwards brings to her lips*).

Santuzza: You ought to be pleased if you can say that! Because people in your position should really feel ashamed to show their faces!

Turiddu: Come on, Lola, let's go, we have nothing to do here.

Lola: Don't put yourself out for me, Turiddu, I know my way, and I don't want to interrupt your conversation.

Turiddu: But I told you we haven't got anything to say!

Santuzza: (*holding him by the jacket*) No—we still have to talk to one another.

Lola: Best of luck to you, Turiddu. Go on with whatever you were doing and I'll go on my own. (*Exit towards church*).

SCENE IV

Turiddu: (*furious*) Ah! See what you have done.

Santuzza: Yes, I see.

Turiddu: Did you do that on purpose?
Santuzza: Yes, I did it on purpose.
Turiddu: By the blood of Judas!
Santuzza: Well, go on; kill me!
Turiddu: You did it on purpose! You did it on purpose!
Santuzza: Go on, kill me—I don't mind.
Turiddu: I don't even want to kill you now!

He turns to go.

Santuzza: You are leaving me?
Turiddu: Yes, that's what you deserve.

The elevation bell sounds from the church.

Santuzza: Don't leave me, Turiddu! Can't you hear that bell ringing?
Turiddu: I don't want to be led by the nose. Do you understand?
Santuzza: Do what you like with me, beat me, kick me. I'll take
anything from you. But not from her.
Turiddu: Let's finish. I'm having no more of these scenes. I'm going.
Santuzza: Where are you going?
Turiddu: Where I want to—to Mass.
Santuzza: No, you just go to church to show Lola that you have
left me for her sake. To show her that I don't matter to you.
Turiddu: You are mad.
Santuzza: You must not go, Turiddu. You must not go to church
to-day in order to commit a sin. Don't insult me like that in front
of that woman.
Turiddu: It's you who do the insulting. You want to show everybody
that I mustn't go anywhere without you—that you keep me tied
to your apron strings like a little boy.
Santuzza: What does it matter to you, what she says? Do you really
want me to die in despair?
Turiddu: You are mad.
Santuzza: Yes—it's true—I am mad. But don't leave me alone with
this madness in my head.
Turiddu: (*tearing himself away from her*) Let's finish it all. To hell
with it.
Santuzza: Turiddu—for the sake of our Lord—who now descends
into the consecrated host—you must not leave me for her.

Turiddu goes.

Ah! Curse your Easter!

CAVALLERIA MUSICATA

CAVALLERIA MUSICATA

ALTHOUGH there was always a piano in his *salotto,* music did not play an important role in Verga's home life nor did he play a musical instrument. The first musical influence of any importance reached him through the composer Giuseppe Perrotta, whose parents owned a villa at Sant'Agata li Battiati, and had become friends of the family (see p. 51).

Verga's novels contain many references to music. The heroine of the *Peccatrice,* for example, is an accomplished pianist who at night plays the "Kiss" waltz by Arditi "deliriously". In the drawing-rooms of Florence, Verga's musical education progressed appreciably. He attended musical soirées in the houses of friends, where Mozart, Beethoven and Chopin, as well as the romantic music of Germany could be heard: when he wrote *Eros* in 1874 his piano-playing heroines no longer played Arditi's *Il Bacio,* but Schubert and Liszt.

In Milan, he could often be seen at La Scala, immaculately attired in his *marsina,* the morning coat, and in the company of his elegant friends. His musical understanding had by that time progressed so far that he became a convinced Wagnerian. He attended Milan's disastrous *Lohengrin* première, and the bon mot is attributed to him that *Lohengrin* "in disclosing where he came from, also told the musicians of Italy where to go to". By the time, therefore, that he expressed his wishes for music for *Cavalleria rusticana* he must at least have been a very interested and well-educated listener.

Verga expressed these wishes in a letter to his friend Perrotta two months after its first performance. His ideas were surprisingly predictive. He asked for:

"a piece for small orchestra to introduce the play, a sort of short overture and musical recapitulation of its contents, to be played before the curtain rises. It should be simple, clear and effective, well attuned to the subject without being too intricate or difficult, and should breathe the true spirit of Sicily and of rural life.

"The sound of a love song in the night, the longing of Turiddu singing under Lola's window, and the lament of Santuzza who waits in

vain for him. Life in the village coming awake, the church bells which
summon to the mass. A note of jealousy, and of that love which returns
and persists and forms the basis of it all. Finally the frantic outburst of
jealous fury, the scream for help, and the outcry of the mother and the
beloved."

Perrotta composed the overture as requested and Verga liked it.
However, it was considered too difficult for the public to understand,
and for the available orchestra to play, and so was not used. This
rejection hurt the over-sensitive composer, to whom Capuana had
once felt compelled to write:

"You really ought to learn a lesson from Giovanni [i.e. Verga]
and me: if the two of us had been discouraged by every difficulty in our
way, we would by now have forgotten how to read and write! The future
belongs to those who persevere!"

The advice had had no effect, and, to Verga's regret, Perrotta
remained so discouraged that he abandoned the idea of writing any
further pieces of operatic music for *Cavalleria.**

A different possibility soon presented itself. The composer
Stanislao Gastaldon approached Verga for permission to use *Caval-
leria* for an opera with a libretto to be written by Bartocci Fontana.
Before giving his permission. Verga asked to see the libretto. It was
not to his liking but nevertheless on 3rd June, 1888, he wrote to
Bartocci Fontana as follows:

"I welcome your desire to use my *Cavalleria rusticana* as basis
for an operatic libretto. I must, however, tell you—in absolute frankness—
that in the way you have used it, this subject does not seem to me to lend
itself to musical drama. However, I do not want to make my own view
a reason for a refusal, and I am quite willing to let you use my play, and
shall be pleased if you find within it what you hope to achieve. Yours
sincerely, G.V."

The opera was published by Ricordi and performed in 1888
under the title *Mala Pasqua* (*A Bad Easter*). It was not a success, but
the opera's failure** in no way affected the fortunes of Verga's play,
which was continuously performed for several years, and given in
practically every town in Italy. Generally it was very successful,
though it failed in (Austrian) Trieste. It significantly influenced Italian

*Perrotta's *Cavalleria* overture was first performed in Catania in 1906. In
1910 he committed suicide during a phase of deep depression (see p. 225).

**Its only surviving piece is a serenade, later revived by the tenor Benjamino
Gigli under the title of *Musica proibita* (*Forbidden Music*).

theatrical writing and acting, and its title became a household word.

On 19th February, 1890, Verga received a letter:

"Milan, 15th February

"Three or four years ago—I cannot really remember—I approached you with the request to grant permission to a composer, a friend of mine, to set your wonderful *Cavalleria rusticana* to music, and with great courtesy you granted this request.

"However, the composer—I do not know why, but rather believe for reasons of health—gave up the idea. Now another friend of mine, a young man of great promise, who is competing for the current Sonzogno prize, has asked me for the same favour.

"I replied that I felt as if I already had your permission, as I was sure that you would grant it to me again.

"Afterwards, plagued by various vicissitudes, among them a long and grave illness, I forgot about writing to you until my friend a few days ago wrote that he was in fact competing with an opera on the subject of *Cavalleria* and that your formal permission was therefore urgently required. I now appeal to you on his behalf to be kind enough to grant him this great desire—a desire in which I sincerely join him.

"The name of my friend is Pietro Mascagni and he is conducting in Cerignola. If you—to save time—could write to him direct, I would be very grateful.

"With the expression of sincere gratitude and respect,

I am yours, etc.,

Gni. Salvestri."

Quite justifiably Verga regarded this letter as an impertinence. Verga had known Salvestri, rather vaguely, in Turin in 1884 (see p. 126). He had spoken to him once or twice, but had no recollection whatsoever of ever having seriously discussed with him, not to mention consented to, a musical adaptation of *Cavalleria rusticana*. His annoyance increased greatly when, three days later, on 22nd February, he learned from the newspapers that an opera entitled *Cavalleria rusticana*, shortlisted from 73 entries, was to be played (see p. 148) within the framework of the Sonzogno competition in Rome, on 25th February. Apart from Salvestri's letter, Verga knew nothing about this work. He had heard neither from the composer, nor from the man who had adapted the words.

How could such an extraordinary situation have arisen?

Pietro Mascagni, born in Livorno on 7th December, 1863, was Verga's junior by 23 years. His father, Domenico, was a baker.*

---

*He came from S. Miniato al Tedesco, 25 miles from Livorno on the road to Florence. The mother, Emilia, née Rebua, was Livornese.

Pietro's great musical gifts became obvious early on, while he was a choir-boy at the church of S. Luigi Gonzaga.

His story follows a familiar pattern: father's unwillingness to let young Pietro take up music; intercession by a local nobleman, Count Florestan de Larderel (to whom the composer later dedicated *Cavalleria*); the interest of a generous uncle, Stefano Mascagni, who made himself responsible for the costs of his nephew's musical education.

The first compositions of the 15-year-old Mascagni were pieces of church music. A symphony for piano and orchestra followed a year later. At 18, he wrote *In Filanda (In the Spinning Mill)* for chorus and orchestra, and submitted the work to the musical competition connected with the 1881 Exhibition in Milan. Wisely as well as characteristically, he dedicated the work to the composer Amilcare Ponchielli, head of the Milan Conservatoire, where he hoped to study. The work won an honourable mention, first class. A later composition also deserves mention. His cantata *Alla Gioia* (1882) resulted from a performance of Beethoven's Ninth Symphony (the choral) which he attended in Livorno. Exhilarated by the great work, he sat down when he returned home and composed his own version of Schiller's *Ode an die Freude*.

Later in the same year (12th October, 1882) he successfully passed the difficult entrance examination to the Conservatoire of Milan. This was the examination Verdi had failed, and by doing so has made the "Conservatorio Giuseppe Verdi" the only scholastic institution in the world which is named after a would-be pupil who failed to gain admission.*

The course at the Conservatoire was exacting: it lasted four years, and was interspersed with stiff examinations. The successful graduate won the right to use the title *Maestro*.

At the Conservatoire, Mascagni met Puccini, who was his senior by five years. They soon struck up a friendship and even shared a room for a while. Mascagni was a competent double-bass player, an accomplishment he had acquired in record time, and which he put to use by playing in the orchestra of the *Teatro dal Verme* for three lire a night. It is said that Puccini's and Mascagni's style of

---

*Carlo Gatti (see p. 62) claims that Verdi was a pupil of the Conservatoire after all, and bases this claim on the following extraordinary reasoning: as he was not accepted, Verdi was forced to take private lessons. Among his teachers was one Vincenzo Lavigna, who also taught at the Conservatoire, and *"La questione delle mura non ha importanza sostanziale"*: "the question of the walls has no real importance".

living and their resourcefulness in dealing with creditors is echoed in the first act of *La Bohème*.*

Between the two friends there was, however, one fundamental difference. Puccini was a first-class pupil, and in every respect a serious student who, during his final year, was not only the star pupil of Ponchielli's composition class (see p. 61), but of the whole institution. Mascagni too possessed without any doubt whatsoever the musical gifts necessary to stay the course, but lacked the application to do so. He attended the Conservatoire for little more than the academic year of 1882/3. Early in his second year, in February 1884, he suddenly left, apparently of his own accord, and joined a touring company which was performing operetta in Cremona.

Several years later, in December 1892, after his great success with *Cavalleria*, he was questioned about this defection in an interview. His answer was defensive: **

"In what little experience I have of life it seems to me that the tale of other people's troubles must be much more amusing than that of their pleasures. I do not think this is due to malice—if you understand what I mean—but rather because happiness, fame, and perhaps good fortune as well, always carry something within them which causes dislike, and makes other people turn their noses up.

"Searching my notes and my memory for the years of my wanderings brings my most difficult years back to me. I was a nobody, and the vainglorious dreams of the 22-year-old had to yield to the demands of my appetite—a formidable appetite which gave me as much to think of as lack of appetite or indigestion can possibly give a millionaire.

"I studied at the Milan Conservatoire from 1882 to 1884. I cannot complain of my teachers, who with gentle persuasion encouraged me to work, nor of my fellow students, who almost all liked me. I was there for about a year, when I happened to read a translation of Heine's *Guglielmo Ratcliff*.*** I found Maffei's verses beautiful and, based on my

*The need to deal with creditors was a favourite conceit of the *"Scapiglia-tura"* (Milan's 'Chelsea set' of the period). The founder of the movement, Giuseppe Rovani, left a coffee-house without paying for what he had consumed and wrote on the white marble table-top four lines which later became famous.

Non è credibile	It's quite incredible
Com' è terribile	How it's so terrible
La vista orribile	To see a horrible
d'un creditor.	Creditor's face.

**Daniele Cellamare, *Pietro Mascagni*, Flli Palombi, Rome, 1965.

***William Ratcliff, a tragedy by Heinrich Heine, published in 1823, when he was 26 years old.

school knowledge, I judged them most harmonious. I could not rest until I had written three pieces of what should have been my first opera. I sketched part of the duet in Livorno during the summer holidays of 1882, and completed it in Milan the following year.

"All this did not prevent me from being very lazy and from feeling at the same time a yearning for independence and for freedom to roam the world.

"Living so close to the art which I had only caught a glimpse of, made me concoct all sorts of plans, each one sillier than the other—and seeing so many nobodies above me—and how conceited those people were!—induced me to leave the Conservatoire and to accept an engagement as deputy conductor of an operetta company which was giving a short series of performances in Cremona."

This marked the beginning of Mascagni's wanderings. He started with the Forlì company, but soon changed to the company of the actor-manager Luigi Maresca. The reason for the change was the attractive soubrette of the new company, Argenide Carbognani. For nearly three years they toured together, mostly performing in the smaller places. Rewards fluctuated between scanty and very poor; and in order to buy his "mouthful of bread" he had to sell small possessions. The termination of his studies had at first irritated, and later alienated his father, who did not wish to have anything to do with a son living "a vagabond's life", and who refused to help financially. During his journeys Mascagni continued to work rather spasmodically on his *Ratcliff*, and in a letter to a friend in Livorno he requested information about London (which he required for the first act) and about Douglas' journey.

He became increasingly unhappy and irritable. By August 1886, if not sooner, he had realized that he had made a mistake, and he began to speak of his "disgrace". The financial difficulties of the company, and Mascagni's state of nerves led to friction with Maresca. After several altercations they even came to blows during a performance in Foggia. On the morning of his departure from Foggia, on 28th December, 1886, Mascagni fell down a staircase after some further fisticuffs, and injured his right foot. More trouble was ahead: Miss Carbognani was four months pregnant.

The next town to be visited was Cerignola, about 20 miles from Foggia on the road to Barletta, near the Ofanto River. Many small southern Italian towns contain unexpected delights. Not so Cerignola which the 1887 Baedeker dismisses in three words: 26,000 inhabitants, uninteresting. The company was booked to present operettas for six weeks at its *Teatro Mercadante*, Mascagni playing the piano accompaniments. By the time he arrived there, he had made up his mind that he could continue his itinerant life no longer.

His plans for escape ripened. The most important requirement seemed local help and sympathy. Aided by his youthful good looks, and a personality which enabled him to charm at will, he set out to look for them.

The long winter evenings posed at that time a considerable problem for the inhabitants of a town like Cerignola. Without radio or cinema, with a single theatre which gave only occasional performances, time must have hung heavily on their hands: any entertainment offered was more than welcome.

The town's social club, the *Circolo Ofanto,* possessed a piano, and the musically interested Mayor, Giuseppe Cannone, together with his family, encouraged and supported musical evenings. This club seemed to offer Mascagni the chance to make himself popular.

Mascagni was, of course, a first-rate musician and an excellent pianist. Three years of touring with an operetta company had made him familiar with all the current and past popular tunes. To the members of the *Circolo Ofanto* he could offer heaven-sent entertainment; soon he had made himself indispensable there.

A number of difficulties remained. Mascagni was under contract to Maresca, who was not prepared to release him. His immediate need was money. Towards the end of the company's stay in Cerignola he asked Maresca for what was due to him. This started a row which continued after the beginning of the last performance on the night of 17th February, 1887. The two came to blows, and the audience could see Maresca slapping Mascagni's face. They liked the good-looking Mascagni and sympathized with him.

While the performance was going on, Mascagni's few belongings, including his *Ratcliff* sketches, were packed into a large suitcase by some friends and whisked away from the lodgings which he shared with Argenide Carbognani. Immediately after the performance, Mascagni and Signorina Carbognani left the theatre, unrecognizable and heavily cloaked, and walked in the cold night across the town towards the road to Foggia. A vehicle was waiting to take them to an isolated farmhouse at Stornarella, four miles along this road. Two Albanians who lived nearby helped to make a fire and produced something to eat. It had turned three o'clock in the morning, and the fugitives had to sleep on sacks of seeds. The next day they ventured into Stornarella. The few inhabitants of the village were friendly; they took them for an eloping couple, one of those frequent abduction stories. Anxiously the couple waited for news from Cerignola.

Maresca had obtained the help of the police in his search for Mascagni as some box-office takings were missing. The police forced the door to Mascagni's old room but could find no clue to his whereabouts. Questions put to neighbours produced no result either. Maresca's company was due to perform in Sicily and had to leave. Maresca stayed behind for three days but, as the searches proved fruitless, he, too, left to rejoin his company. The news of his departure was relayed to Stornarella and Mascagni returned to Cerignola.

The first part of the plan was thus successfully accomplished. The second was to secure a living at Cerignola. The day before his escape, on 16th February, Mascagni had written to his father in Livorno:

"My dear Father,

"I have not written to you for a long time, because I wanted to wait until I could give you some good news. I have finally decided to quit my life of a nomad and mountebank, and to settle as a teacher of music here in Cerignola.

"At a meeting which will take place tomorrow, I hope to be appointed municipal conductor here. For the moment, I shall teach singing and piano, but soon I shall conduct my opera at the municipal theatre here and enlarge the music school. I am very satisfied—and besides, it is better to earn five lire this way than twenty with a touring company.

"Furthermore, I shall have ten or so private pupils. Cerignola is a somewhat backward place, but they do like me here, and it should not be too difficult to borrow sufficient money to set myself up decently.

"Could you possibly write to Messrs V. . . . and tell them that I will send them all I owe them soon. Please try to recover my big case from them because of some papers I need, as I must give the mayor here certain documents. It is also essential that you do as follows: please ask Maestro Soffredini to give me a certificate stating that I have studied at his Institute, that I am capable of giving lessons of every type, etc.; make him say as much as possible! The more documents there are, the better for me; and could you, perhaps, through Soffredini,* also get a certificate from Maestro Menichetti of Pisa, and one from Cav. Magroni, the inspector of the Institute? Maestro Luigi Pratesi, too, could be asked to give me a testimonial stating that I am competent to teach music, piano, etc. Also do please ask all these people to write their titles,

---

*Alfredo Soffredini (1854-1923), a Livornese composer who later became a music critic in Milan.

appointments, Civil Orders, etc., below their signatures. That sort of thing makes it more impressive, and is very effective!

"I am very pleased with developments. Meanwhile, I am working seriously at my opera, which will soon be finished. You will see that I will make good after all. I beg you to do all the things I ask for as quickly as possible: my life may well depend on it."

Some of the facts of this letter were anticipatory, some not strictly accurate. However, on 25th March, 1887, 21 members of the town council of Cerignola met under the chairmanship of the Mayor. On the agenda was the proposed appointment of a teacher of singing and music, and the Mayor supported Mascagni's application. Counsellor Chiomento spoke in opposition to the appointment, which he regarded as an unnecessary luxury. The result of the vote was seven against and 14 in favour of Mascagni, who was therefore duly appointed, with a stipend of 100 lire per month and the obligation to be available for the establishment of the "Philharmonia" and of the school of singing, and for the instruction of individual pupils, without further payment. The Philharmonia became an orchestra consisting mainly of children and comprised 11 strings and five woodwind. There were six singers—all children.

The bare necessities of life, though not more, were thus assured and he and Signorina Carbognani set themselves up in lodgings in via Francesco d'Assisi. They obtained a bank loan of 500 lire. Within two months of his appointment a son, Domenico, was born, but four months later, on 2nd October, 1887, the child died.

Mascagni worked hard. He organized the Philharmonia and gave a few private lessons in Cerignola itself, as well as in some outlying places, travelling in a shaky cart dragged along by broken-down horses. Within a year of his appointment, a requiem mass, *Tuba mirum,* was written, and performed by the Philharmonia. The Cerignola journalist Michele Sinischalchi, who was also the music critic of the *Avanguardia* of nearby Lucera, described the work as "really strong and original, full of beauty" and predicted a brilliant future for Mascagni. The Philharmonia came in for particular praise.

All this was undoubtedly an improvement on his previous impecunious wanderings, during which his "piece of bread" was frequently missing, but it did not make him happy for long. It become increasingly obvious to him that Cerignola was not the solution, that his appointment was a blind alley, and that he must attempt to escape. He had to be very careful: he could not afford to offend those Cerignola worthies who had been so helpful, and were now so pleased with him. He had to play a double game, keeping his eyes open for any chance of escape, while avoiding any offence to those he still needed.

Mascagni used to buy the *Corriere della sera* at Marinelli's, the Cerignola newsagents. One day in July 1888, the *Corriere* had not arrived, and Marinelli offered him the other Milan daily, the *Secolo*. This paper carried an advertisement for the Concorso Sonzogno, promoted by the *Teatro illustrato*. He immediately decided to compete, and his first impulse was to use the finished act of his *Ratcliff* as a one-act opera. On second thoughts this did not seem feasible. He asked Sinischalchi, who by now was his friend, for help in obtaining a suitable libretto, and the secretary of the Naples Conservatoire, Rocco Pagliara, was recommended as librettist and commissioned. Pagliara was prepared to start at once. Mascagni, however, changed his mind, and after some argument, this project was dropped. Sinischalchi made various other suggestions, but none of them suited Mascagni. Finally, he wrote to his Livorno friend "Nanni" (Giovanni) Targioni-Tozzetti, who suggested using the play *Cavalleria rusticana*, which both had seen. Mascagni replied with the urgent request that he should convert this play at once into a suitable libretto.

Mascagni's miserable and unhappy circumstances during his work on *Cavalleria* may well bear special significance. After this first work, Mascagni composed a further 15 operas. Yet only his first, *Cavalleria*, remains in permanent repertoire; the second, *L'amico Fritz*, is occasionally performed; the rest are more or less forgotten.

Commenting on this fact, the writer Giorgio Vigolo said that it was indeed a "cruel miracle which gave Mascagni his masterpiece at the beginning of his career, followed by a slowly progressive, fatal enfeeblement". Musicians and music critics have been intrigued by it and have put forward various reasons to explain why Mascagni should have begun with his masterpiece, and been unable to match it later. None of their explanations is convincing.

All fields of artistic achievement can reveal the paradoxical fact that the best is sometimes produced under the most adverse conditions. If this applied to Mascagni, the "cruel miracle" is explained: the great initial success which brought at once lifelong financial security may have proved a hindrance rather than a spur for later efforts.

Mascagni's first letter to Targioni-Tozzetti was sent in October 1888. Work on the libretto began soon afterwards. Sketches and corrections on postcards went to and fro between Cerignola and

Livorno. The competition's closing date was 30th May, 1889, so that about eight months were in hand after the choice of subject had been made. From January 1889, Guido Menasci, a Livorno journalist, helped Targioni-Tozzetti to complete the libretto, on Salvestri's recommendation.

Meanwhile, Argenide Carbognani was pregnant again. In a special ceremony intended for those who are unable to appear in public, she was married to Mascagni at their home (illus. 32) on 3rd February, 1889. Eight days later their second son was born.

Operatic composing requires a piano; in the whole of Cerignola there were hardly 20 such instruments, mostly the property of "elect and special citizens". Eventually he had to hire one from a firm in Bari for 12 lire a month. Work progressed rapidly, with an almost daily exchange of postcards containing suggestions and amendments.

Meanwhile, Mascagni requested information from Puccini regarding the Sonzogno competition. This advice was important as Puccini had entered his opera *Le Villi* for the same competition four years earlier (see p. 61). Puccini was strongly against it, and proposed to submit the *Cavalleria* manuscript to his own publisher, Ricordi. This was done, but Ricordi rejected the work with the words *"Non ci tengo"* ("I don't care for it"), an error of judgment for which he never forgave himself. This refusal settled the issue, and Puccini duly entered Mascagni's opera for the competition, just before the end of the prescribed period, and without the prelude with its "Siciliana", which had not yet been composed.*

The manuscript's rejection by Ricordi was a further blow for Mascagni. His restlessness and irritability increased and he felt that he must get away from Cerignola at all costs. He wrote again to Puccini, and asked for help. Many years later, when the two composers were no longer friends, Puccini, with his tongue in his cheek, arranged for this letter to appear in a newspaper. It contained the following passage: "Please find me a few private lessons in Milan, find me a place in the orchestra of the Dal Verme, anything at all just so that I can get away from here". The publication of this letter displeased the people of Cerignola; it belied the love story of "Mascagni and his Cerignola" which had provided such good publicity, and was so acceptable to the Cerignolesi. But Puccini had underrated Mascagni's resourcefulness. Mascagni replied in the press that Puccini had quoted the passage outside its proper context; he

*As Mascagni had entered his opera without the prelude (see p. 150), it had to be presented to the commission before the audition began.

had only made this request in order to save his beloved Cerignola expense. 1888 had been a year of bad harvest, and his post became a luxury which the citizens could ill afford: for the sake of economy they even had to dismiss their midwife and close the grammar school.

Mascagni's letters to his librettist show his intense anxiety after the closing date of the competition. On 27th June, 1889, he writes that he can find neither peace nor sleep in expectation of the verdict which "may well be fatal for me." The whole issue is "a matter of life and death". It became known that 73 operas had been entered.

For eight months he lived in stress and tension, without hearing a word. Not even an acknowledgment of the entry had been received. "Nothing but apprehension and fears" is how Signora Mascagni later spoke of this period. They had practically given up hope when, in the early hours of 22nd February, 1890, a telegram from the secretary of the Royal Academy of S. Cecilia in Rome invited Mascagni to come to Rome to play his opera before the members of the appointed commission.

In the five years following the first award, the Sonzogno competition—partly as a result of the incidents connected with Puccini's first opera—had acquired an equivocal reputation. In order to improve its image, people of considerable distinction and reputation for independence and integrity had now been invited to adjudicate. The jury of five members were to be assisted by Alessandro Parisotti, the Secretary of the Academy of S. Cecilia. Leopoldo Mugnone, later chief conductor of the Scala, had been retained as conductor for the performance of the prizewinning entries of the second *Premio*.

The audition took place on 26th February, 1890. On the following day, the 27th, Mascagni wrote a most interesting letter about it to his Cerignola friend, Luigi Manzari, the Mayor's son-in-law. The letter has a curious history. Manzari kept it in his safe until 1927, when Daniele Cellamare, a Mascagni admirer from Cerignola, obtained it with the intention of publishing it. Mascagni initially objected to its publication, but eventually (it is said at Mussolini's personal request) gave the editor of Mussolini's paper *Popolo d'Italia*, the necessary permission and confirmed its authenticity. He did insist on omissions in four places. It is almost certain that three of the omissions contained derogatory remarks about Sonzogno, whom Mascagni had not yet met at the time of writing the letter. One of the omissions relates probably to a hostile remark about Umberto Giordano, with whom Mascagni later became friendly. This is the text of the letter:

"Dear Luigi,

"I am keeping my promise to write to you and to our friends about what is happening in Rome with this competition; it is a rather serious matter. I shall try to be as clear and brief as possible, because I have a lot to say.

"To start at the beginning, I arrived in Rome on Monday at 3 p.m., went to the *Albergo del Sole,* and later to the Royal Academy of S. Cecilia, but there was no one there. When I presented myself again on Tuesday at eleven, as the telegram requested, I was courteously received by Marchetti, and by Parisotti, the Secretary. Now the surprises started.

"After a little while, more people turned up, and I began to wonder how many of us there would be. They say twelve! Poor me! I can give you a few facts, which come from one of the judges. The first four, selected in that order, were; first, Ferroni; second, Mascagni; third, Pizzi; fourth, Bossi. Three of the four certainly do not represent the "youth" for which this competition was intended. Bossi is professor at the Naples Conservatoire and Pizzi won a competition in Bologna with an opera in four acts.* Ferroni is professor of composition at the Milan Conservatoire, successor to Ponchielli.

"That leaves little *me* to fight it out with the giants, but as Ferroni has to be *hors concours,* I take first place. However, this first place is only a technicality, as we are all meant to let them hear our music on equal terms. So back to the 12 apostles—or 11 on account of Ferroni's exit, or rather ten, as one of them wishes to remain anonymous and does not disclose his name. Who could it be? From the others I have nothing to fear, unless they have special influence. You have no idea how they try to influence the jury! There is, for instance, Baravalle,** one of the 12, or rather 10, who has such recommendations to . . .

"Seppilli*** is supported by nobody less than Sonzogno himself: I feel sure that I am the only one who is 'untouched' by any influence. As a matter of fact even the good, the important ones matter little . . .

"Fourteen days before I arrived, Pizzi already knew the results! Bossi had been here for three weeks, but I feel I can measure up to them, in spite of their backing. The real struggle is only beginning now, a fight man to man, but it is going to be neither fair nor equal. Only the first one was really equal, because the name cards were still sealed—and I came first. Now it's unequal, now the names are public, and I shall be worst off. When I got to hear of all these goings on, my first feeling

*Emilio Pizzi (1861-1940) lived for many years in London where he composed the oratorio *Death and Resurrection,* and the opera *The Bric-Brac Will.* The opera which won in Bologna was his *Guglielmo Ratcliff.*
**Vittorio Baravalle's (1855-1942) entry was the opera *Amore d'artista.*
***Armando Seppilli (1860-1931) was later artistic advisor to Messrs. Sonzogno, became Melba's accompanist, and conducted at Covent Garden.

was one of profound discouragement. But I pulled myself together. To hell! Wasn't I sure of my own stuff, of my own music?

"It was nice to see Bossi, Pizzi and Seppilli, old (so to say) friends from the Conservatoire. We are together a lot, and it is enjoyable to be with them, pleasant and interesting chaps as they are. I do most of the talking. They find me changed, particularly in morale—they say I am no longer the Mascagni I was. Little do they know what this competition means to me. To them it doesn't matter much. Bossi is teaching at the S. Pietro a Majella Conservatoire [Naples]. Last month Pizzi sold an opera to Ricordi for 20,000 lire. Seppilli eats, drinks and sleeps with Sonzogno (*mangia, beve e dorme con Sonzogno!*) . . . They are quite right; I have changed. I was never lucky. When the auditions started, I had to give up first place (mine by rights!) to Bossi, who is older, and to Giordano because . . .

"My turn came last night (Wednesday) at 9. No need to tell you the state I was in—the whole day I couldn't eat a thing. I arrived in good time and was pleasantly welcomed, particularly by Galli and Sgambati.

"The prelude was quickly accepted [see p. 147] and my audition started at 9.30.

"In the room was a grand piano with the vocal score. By my side were Marchetti* and Parisotti, who turned the pages for me. Platania** sat on the settee; on a big table stood a conductor's lectern with the orchestral score, and in front of the lectern was Sgambati*** with D'Arcais**** on his left and Galli,***** libretto in hand, on his right.

*The five judges are named in this paragraph.

Filippo Marchetti (1831-1902) was the composer of the opera *Ruy Blas,* based on Victor Hugo's book. This opera enjoyed some popularity in England, and Bernard Shaw mentions that his sister sang the rôle of the Queen of Spain in a London performance. He was president of the Academy of S. Cecilia in Rome from 1881-86.

**Pietro Platania (1828-1907) was Director of the Conservatoires of Palermo and of Naples and a composer of sacred music. He was much respected as a master of counterpoint.

***Giovanni Sgambati (1841-1914), whose mother was English, had been a pupil of Liszt's. At 26 he was nominated professor at the Academy of S. Cecilia. At the time of the competition he was Master of Music to the Italian Royal family.

****The Marquess Francesco D'Arcais (1830-90), a composer and well known journalist and music critic, died a short time after the award was announced.

*****Amintore Galli (1845-1919), composer and music critic of Sonzogno's *Secolo* who, together with Boito took part in the Garibaldi expedition of 1866, was head of Messrs. Sonzogno's music department, editor of the Sonzogno periodical *Teatro illustrato* and of Sonzogno's Opera anthologies.

"Now came the supreme moment. My main fear was that I would be unable to break through the indifference of the judges. I started confidently but trembled inside. For the 'Siciliana' I did my best with that croaky voice of mine, sang with my whole heart and did not look at anyone. I just kept my head high, looked at the wall and sang and sang.

"Great surprise: the moment I finished and was about to play the orchestra's re-entry, I heard them shouting: 'Bravo, bravo, Maestro', and they all got up and asked why I had not sent the prelude and this and that which, to be frank, I did not really understand at all. I felt confused, and very moved. I too got up, and heard Sgambati say: 'I should never have thought that I would have a new musical experience at this stage, but I must say the finale of that Siciliana surprised me. Never have I heard those two chords [illus. 35] used so beautifully.'

"And afterwards I heard him ask quietly: 'I say—they have two harps at the Costanzi, haven't they?'

"I realized that the ice was broken. They wanted me to repeat the Siciliana, and so the prelude ended with real success.

"O Lord, I really did not have the feeling of playing in front of those professors, the best professors that there are today in Italy. I had the feeling of being in our Ofanto Club playing the Juanita and the Befana for Don Peppino Cannone and Don Carlo Tozzi, who always cheered me so generously.

"I continued, much encouraged.

"They all enjoyed the first chorus. They thought the Carettiere's song theatrically strong, and with popular appeal. The prayer pleased them more than any other piece; Marchetti was enthusiastic and Platania approved of the real parts and said that I had learned my lessons well. All the rest went well, too. Marchetti quite frequently patted me on the back, said softly, 'Bravo,' and, 'Very good,' and pointed with his finger on the page to passages he particularly liked. There was another burst of enthusiasm after Lola's 'Stornello'. Marchetti seemed quite moved. They all had pieces of paper and made frequent notes. The Drinking Song pleased them very much and Sgambati said, 'There is no doubt that this is the sort of music the public likes'. I immediately seized on this remark and said that I thought I had to write music for the public, theatrical music, which the terms of the competition required. I said that, because most of the other subjects in this competition are mythological, ideological or oratorio-like.

"In the end we came to the finale, that great question mark. I would never have expected it, but that too made a very good impression. I said at the end that I was fully prepared to write a new finale if the judges thought that desirable. But they said no, and accepted it completely as it stands.

"Afterwards Sgambati asked me a thousand questions, all very friendly, and I said I would like to revise the whole work. Sgambatı added, 'I am sure you'll have enough time for that before it is performed at the Costanzi' but he realized immediately that he had gone too far and retracted, by saying with a smile, 'if it is going to be performed!' I understood, and smiled with him. D'Arcais asked me about Verga's proprietary rights. I pushed it all on to Salvestri.* D'Arcais finally said: 'Anyway, we will have to see to it'.

"I took my leave. Everyone shook me by the hand and praised me. The coolest was D'Arcais, the warmest were Marchetti and Sgambati. Galli was a little reserved, but I know that he favours me. Sgambati said to me when I left: 'Bravo—you can be proud of this opera. You have let us hear beautiful and good music.'

"They did not ask a single question about theory, instrumentation and the distribution of parts, and not a single critical comment did the judges make. I am really proud of that. They liked the subject, and the libretto was regarded as first class.

"But now comes the unpleasantness, now come the doubts. Are the judges going to be overruled? . . .

"If all goes as it should, I am bound to be first. In Rome they're already talking about *Cavalleria* and everyone knows the good impression it has made on the judges. Don Peppino Manfredi heard indirectly that my opera had pleased them much more than the others. But there are some other good works, too, particularly those by Bossi and Pizzi.

"I should not really leave Rome before I know the result. The secretary, Parisotti, does not wish me to leave either. He said that all the judges favour me, and that: 'the music of all the other operas produces divided opinions among the judges, but your music is not being discussed at all; they all like it, and so they should.' And he started to sing the Carettiere's song. A friend!

"I myself have a great desire to wait for the result, which will be known by Monday or Tuesday morning, but because of my finances it is difficult for me to stay.

"My mind is quite at ease and my success with the judges compensates me for my hard work. So, with my money gone, I will return to Cerignola on Saturday and await the final result in peace and faith.

"Forgive the bad writing and the awful style of this letter; I wrote it in great haste, without re-reading it!

"Greetings to all, all, all, all from

"Pietro Mascagni."

*Mascagni had known his fellow Livornese Salvestri (born 1841) in his home town. Salvestri (see pp. 126 and 139) had given advice with the libretto as well as making the first approach to Verga. He died shortly after this letter was written, in October 1890, in Livorno.

30 As used on the operatic stage
(Covent Garden version)

29 According to Verga's design

31   On 24th February, 1884, the *Illustrazione Italiana* carried a full page of *Cavalleria* pictures drawn by Ettore Ximenes (1855-1926) who later became the well-known sculptor

Three days later (2nd March) he wrote to his wife:
"My dear Lina,

"You can't imagine how much your telegram and letter annoyed me. When I don't write or send telegrams, it is a sign that I am very busy with my own affairs. You have no idea what goes on here in Rome.

"My presence was of supreme importance. What a battle! What hatred! They are all against me, but I don't mind that and I'm not afraid of any of them. They all know the impression my *Cavalleria* has made and they are all frightened of me. And if, as I hope, the judges won't allow themselves to be influenced against me now, victory is mine, I am certain of that."

Victory was his, and on 9th March, Mascagni eventually approached Verga for the first time. He wrote:

" Forgive me if I take the liberty of asking you a favour which I feel certain your kindness will not refuse. I believe that Signor Giovanni Salvestri has already written to tell you that I entered in the Sonzogno competition an opera, *Cavalleria rusticana*, which is completely taken from your so very well known work. I had asked Signor Salvestri to obtain your permission regarding copyright, but Salvestri told me then that there was no hurry, because the competition was to be judged with the names of the entrants remaining undisclosed, and that for this reason one could wait until the prizewinners were announced."

Continuing with evident emotion, Mascagni mentioned the possibilities which had now for the first time opened up for him, feeling certain that Verga would not wish to interrupt his "golden dream" and would not deny him the authorization for the performance. He fully admitted Verga's right, when granting authorization, to impose "such conditions as you regard as useful or necessary."*

Verga replied to the letter by giving provisional permission on the lines Mascagni had suggested, but added that he felt he should have been informed somewhat earlier and that he would have been quite prepared himself to help with the work. Within a few days he would send a draft agreement for signature, and set out the terms which he proposed.

To this Mascagni replied on 27th March:

"You can hardly imagine how anxiously I awaited your letter and how your courtesy and kindness delight me. I take the liberty of thanking you from the bottom of my heart and I beg to assure you of my ever-lasting gratitude and devotion.

"I am absolutely mortified to learn that you yourself would have been ready to help, and to link your famous name to my humble one. O Lord,

*The final paragraph of this letter is reproduced in illus. 33.

if I could only have guessed that! What an honour that would have been for me, how proud I would have felt. But believe me, if one lives in misfortune and in misery, one does not even dare think on such lines!

"In order to submit my music to the Sonzogno competition I approached several poets—personal friends of mine among them. All of them replied in the same way; they wanted money. And being unable to afford even the smallest sum, I had to bow my head in resignation and give up the idea of competing. At that moment, a dear friend of mine, Professor Targioni, well aware of my financial position and intending to do me a good turn, offered to write your *Cavalleria* up for me. You can imagine how I jumped at his suggestion. The competition required an opera in one act, and, in my opinion, no subject lent itself better than your *Cavalleria,* which in one single act embraces all true and human passions.

"I have worked with ardour, with all my soul and with faith. I entered my work and, as you are aware, it won. For some time I had been thinking of obtaining your consent and my friend Salvestri had assured me that he had seen to it. Instead, and to my greatest regret, I learn from your letter that you knew little, or rather nothing, of the matter. How much better it would have been if only I had written myself to you right at the beginning!

"Anyway, I acknowledge your reply with gratitude. I have shown your letter to Targioni who, I think, has written to you himself. I can assure you that his libretto reproduces your *Cavalleria* almost word for word, and therefore completely preserves that colouring and atmosphere which have made your work immortal. Even the members of the jury had words of praise for the libretto, and this, of course, not for its invention, but entirely for the fidelity of its transcription.

"I myself would like to tell you this: among the 73 presented works, there must have been not only good ones, but better ones than mine. If the judges decided to place my work first, it is due to the theatricality and the strong and dramatic colouring of my music which your very true, human and passionate subject inspired in me. I sincerely hope that I will meet you in Rome for the performance, which is to be given in the second half of April. We can then see what we ought to do, and please do rest absolutely assured that I myself as well as Targioni will be only too pleased to accept not only your advice but (and I hope you really did mean it) your collaboration as well.

"As far as your financial interests are concerned, please be so kind as to show once more your gentle consideration. Today, to be frank, I cannot even take the smallest step. But I have every hope of selling the opera after its first performance, and then we can come to the understanding which you suggest in your letter.

"For four years I have been living here at Cerignola, forgotten and forsaken by all. A life of drudgery, of want and of misery. Today at last I can see a future, thanks to my efforts, to my work, and most of all to your *Cavalleria,* which has inspired in me such passionate and theatrical music. Can you imagine that I could ever forget your name, a name which, as the result of your attitude to me, will remain forever linked with unselfish kindness and graciousness!

"I beg you to excuse my disjointed and ungrammatical letter, written in a state of—I trust forgivable—excitement.

"I repeat the expression of my devotion and sign myself

"Your humble servant,

Pietro Mascagni."

A few days beforehand, on 21st March, Targioni-Tozzetti had written to Verga to give his side of the story.

"Maestro Mascagni has today shown me a letter you sent him to Cerignola and, as I do not want to delay introducing myself, I hasten to write.

"To start with, please let me explain and try to justify the Maestro and myself for not having approached you directly.

"Over a year ago Mascagni, compelled to stay in Cerignola as conductor of the peasant orchestra there, wrote to me proposing that I should write a libretto for him. He had already knocked on many doors, but the poets had all replied as the blind beggar boys do in Bologna: without money they won't sing.

"However, with the impression of your *Cavalleria* still fresh in my mind, I suggested that I should versify your Sicilian drama for him. I told him, too, that this adaptation required permission from the author.

"The Maestro liked my idea, and a little while later he wrote to me stating that you had given verbal permission for the adaptation to Giovanni Salvestri, who had asked for it on our behalf. Thereupon, and in order to help my very gifted and artistic friend, I set about the task with great love, helped by Guido Menasci, and in two months of making, unmaking and remaking, the adaptation was completed.

"I certainly ought to have approached you, but the closing date of the competition drew near and Mascagni could not wait—indeed I sent him the final postcards with the lyrics in answer to his urgent telegrams.

"My collaborator and I have kept strictly to the original work, and if our adaptation has one merit, it is its fidelity, almost to the letter, of that admirable play which you have given to the Italian theatre . . . we have always tried to be translators (*traduttori*) and not betrayers (*traditori*) of your *Cavalleria.*

"For the competition, the libretto must now stand as it is, though for the subsequent performances both Menasci and I are quite ready to make all amendments you may consider necessary.

"I hope, sir, that this letter will persuade you to forgive his silence, to your devoted,

G. T. T."

It does not seem likely that under normal circumstances Verga would have asked for a formal agreement, but the contradictory and somewhat underhand tactics of Salvestri and Mascagni had put him on his guard. A suitable draft-contract, based upon suggestions from the Society of Authors, was drawn up by Verga's solicitor and friend, Salvatore Paola. Brother Mario, whose handwriting was very clear, copied the text on to a piece of official stamped paper (illus. 36).

The essential feature of the agreement was that Mascagni was given permission to versify (or have versified) and to adapt for music Verga's work *Cavalleria rusticana* and to have it performed, under the obligation to account to Verga for "that part of the profits which the law of copyright stipulates".

Verga signed the agreement on 7th April. Mascagni signed on 9th April, and returned the document with renewed expression of gratitude and devotion, as well as thanking Verga for his good wishes for the work's success. Everything seemed clearly, properly and fairly settled. Mascagni was undoubtedly convinced that he had been treated very generously and he was probably quite sincere about the devotion and humility which he expressed in his letters to Verga.

However, neither the devotion nor the humility were to last long; the change began soon after Mascagni met Sonzogno. The relationship between Mascagni and Sonzogno, particularly at its beginning, is not well documented. It is known that Mascagni regarded Sonzogno as "the boss", in whose presence he was on his best behaviour. He was even careful in what he dared to say about Sonzogno behind his back, in case such remarks should find their way back to him. He treated him with that type of deferential respect which is so often accorded to the influential and the wealthy. He did not accept Sonzogno's artistic judgment as of any real value, but as "important" in a material sense. He regarded, for instance, Sonzogno's suggestion of a ballet in *Cavalleria* as quite ludicrous and expressed this view in a letter to his wife, but he did not dare to contradict Sonzogno directly.

We should know even less about that relationship were it not for a chance remark at their first meeting on 1st March, 1890. Sonzogno asked Mascagni where he lived. Upon the reply "in Cerignola". Sonzogno smilingly admitted that he had never heard of the place, and asked where it was. Years later, Mascagni related this remark to his biographer Daniele Cellamare, who was as devoted in his admiration of Mascagni as he was in his attachment to Cerignola (his own birthplace). Sonzogno's ignorance of Cerignola aroused in him such antipathy against the friend and "benefactor" of his idol Mascagni that, 75 years after Sonzogno had made this remark, he wrote: *

"Sonzogno must have known as little about history as about agriculture, not to have heard of this beautiful town in Apulia: not only was it very near to the scene of an historic battle between the French and Spanish in 1503 [see p. 99], but it is the granary of Italy as well."

To this antagonism to Sonzogno we owe the knowledge of some of Mascagni's critical remarks, though in spite of later friction (which made Mascagni sell his opera *Iris* to Sonzogno's competitor, Ricordi), Mascagni remained in his public utterances always loyal to Sonzogno. This applies particularly to all questions connected with *Cavalleria rusticana*, where the two regarded themselves as in the same boat, and took great care to remain and appear united.

In April, Mascagni travelled to Milan to check the copying of the score's parts. He met Puccini again, and also Maresca who did not wish to forgive him. He travelled on to Livorno and made peace with his father.

On 2nd May he was back in Rome, this time in style, as Sonzogno's guest. The rehearsals had started and he was in a state of exultation when he wrote to his wife on 3rd May, 1890:

"My dear Lina,

"I don't know any longer whether what I am doing here is reality, or whether it is a fantastic dream.

"All my previous successes fade compared to what is happening now. I see the important people, I see celebrities turning towards me, full of enthusiasm about me and my music.

"Yesterday I went to the Costanzi and when I entered the rehearsal-room I heard Stagno sing the Finale: *'Vi saprò in cuore il ferro mio piantar'!* I went in; there were Sonzogno, Mugnone, Stagno and the Bellincioni. They repeated the whole opera for me! My dear Lina, what an effect! It did not seem to me to be my opera any more! They sing it with extraordinary passion. They are enthusiastic about it. They praised me and fussed over me so much that I became too confused to say a single word!

"Bellincioni said she felt as if she were singing Verdi—and you should hear how she sings! Sung like that, the two romances really are beautiful, and I listened to them with my mouth wide open.

"There is no need to tell you much about Stagno: the word 'sublime' is enough. In the finale he is immensely touching. One must just hear how he sings it! It is an absolute creation! But where both of them reach the highest peak is in the duet. When I heard that, I felt sure that the public could not possibly hiss or whistle! No, they can't, I'm sure they can't. Absolutely not.

"Now that Stagno sings it, the Siciliana has taken on a completely different aspect. He has already changed practically all the words of it because they just weren't Sicilian. Now he sings in his own manner, really as the Sicilians do, and he makes a stupendous effect in the finale.

"After the rehearsal, Sonzogno called me and suggested that dances should be added, and that the opera should be divided into two acts—though not now, only after the performance in Rome. I don't need to add anything to that because I am sure you understand what it means : that Sonzogno is buying the opera !

"When we left, Mugnone and I saw Sonzogno home, and then Mugnone came with me and told me several things which impressed me very much. He told me that Sonzogno was buying *Cavalleria*; that *Cavalleria* was going to be performed at the Scala next year; that Sonzogno was going to give me a commission for another opera—in fact he told me so many things that I no longer understand anything and wonder whether I am going crazy.

". . . Be patient and pleased : the results will by far exceed the expectations.

"Greetings to all, etc.,

Pietro."

His prediction proved correct; the results did exceed all conceivable expectations and the night of 17th May proved one of the most successful first nights in operatic history.

Sgambati, the Master of the Queen's Music, had succeeded in persuading Queen Margherita to attend. So obvious was her enjoyment of the performance that the public's enthusiasm was the greater.

The rather shy, still boyish-looking 26-year-old composer, poorly dressed in a suit which was far too big for him, took the audience by storm. Gemma Bellincioni (one of the best known sopranos of the time), her husband, the tenor Stagno, the other principals and the conductor Mugnone had innumerable curtain calls, but there was no doubt that Mascagni was the hero.

The librettist, Targioni-Tozzetti, was not present. After the performance, Mascagni sent him a telegram: "*Cavalleria* splendid result. Verga was there, congratulating about music and libretto. Much regret your absence. Mascagni."

The remark that Verga enjoyed the music rings quite true. Not only is *Cavalleria*'s music good and effective, it was at that time progressive music as well, music of a type which Verga felt should be written. That Verga should have praised the libretto seems far less likely, and may well have been Mascagni's embellishment.*

The libretto writers' task had been comparatively easy. To a considerable extent they had simply to let Mascagni set Verga's words to music. What was really new in the libretto were only three choruses and one song** and a few bits and pieces. As author of story and play, Verga no doubt looked with a critical eye at the libretto, and some of the things he found were not likely to make him care for it very much.

For instance, when the curtain rises and brilliant sunshine unveils the morning mist in the Piazzetta S. Teresa, it also unveils that a line of the first chorus is lifted from a poem by Severino Ferrari, a poet of the Carducci school. And if Verga saw the Siciliana in its original form, which according to Mascagni forced Stagno to change practically every word because "they just were not Sicilian", his reaction to it can well be imagined.

Many of the operatic libretti of the 19th century have little in common with their literary sources, and are based on the ballad and romance writing of Berchet and Carrer. In the libretto of *Cavalleria rusticana*, these old influences vie with the new. According to Cattaneo some of its vocabulary stems from old melodrama phraseology, e.g. *"quell'invida", "eterna fe'", "Ei fulgente ha dischiuso l'avel"*. Other expressions are based on contemporary idiom. This leads to inconsistency and to muddled phrases (*accozzi*) such as Alfio's *"Io me ne vado, ite voi altre in chiesa"*, which gives a similar impression to that produced by "You good ladies proceed to church —myself, I'm buzzing off".

From a literary point of view, the *Cavalleria* libretto was certainly not impressive and the critics were not slow to condemn it.

*The famous argument which this opera started, as to whether Mascagni or Puccini would inherit "Verdi's sceptre", was senseless and fatuous, as neither Mascagni's nor Puccini's music is a development of Verdi's classical style. Mascagni's and Puccini's music is that of realism and, remarkably enough, just as Italian literary *verismo* had its roots in France, so, too, had the music of *verismo*: what Emile Zola and the other French writers had done for Italy's literature, Bizet did for Italian music. *Cavalleria* and all subsequent *verismo* operas are fundamentally developments of *Carmen*, and to a lesser extent of *The Pearlfishers,* and not developments of Verdi's operas.

**This assessment was accepted as correct by the Milan Court of Appeal. Antonino Gandolfo, *La Cavalleria rusticana in tribunale*, Studio editoriale, Catania, 1936.

This upset the two librettists; influenced—or misled—by Mascagni's telegram which reported Verga's congratulations, they wrote to Verga on 20th May, 1890:

"We have heard from several friends, as well as from Maestro Mascagni, that you were not displeased with the libretto which we adapted from your famous play. Your opinion upholds us against the biased judgments of those journalists who denigrate our modest work. We would feel safe against their malice if your opinion could be made known to the public.

"Recommending ourselves to your courteous frankness,
                                                              "We are, etc."

Verga, who shared the misgivings of the critics, did not feel inclined to oblige.

The relationship of the two librettists with Mascagni did not remain undisturbed or uninterrupted, and the libretti of three of Mascagni's "middle period" works, *Iris, Le Maschere* and *Isabeau,* were written by Illica.* However, the relationship proved on the whole durable, and Targioni-Tozzeti and Menasci wrote the libretti for eight of Mascagni's 16 operatic works.**

The literary imperfections of *Cavalleria rusticana's* libretto did not prevent the opera from becoming one of the most successful operas ever given. Its fame spread rapidly and the catalogue of its productions has remained unequalled.

Within its first year, *Cavalleria* was performed in three productions each at Rome and Florence, in two productions each at Livorno, Turin, and Palermo, and in single productions at Milan, Naples, Bologna, Venice, Genoa, Trieste, Perugia, Ancona, Verona, Pisa, Messina, Catania, Brescia, Cerignola, Bari, Barletta, Trani, Chieti and Lecce. By the end of the 12 months practically all European capitals had heard the new opera and further productions in nine Italian and 40 non-Italian towns were in preparation. In Belgrade the audience cheered so exuberantly that the whole opera had to be repeated.***

---

*Giacosa's co-librettist for several Puccini operas. He was so unorthodox and individual in his versifying that his lines were referred to as "Illicasyllables".

**They are also known as the authors of the Italian translation of the French libretto of *Werther,* Massenet's opera based on Goethe's novel.

***According to Cellamare, this had only occurred once in previous operatic history, when Cimarosa's *Secret Marriage* was so enthusiastically received at the court of Vienna in 1792 that it had to be performed all over again.

32　Via Mascagni, Cerignola. The arrow points to the *Cavalleria* room

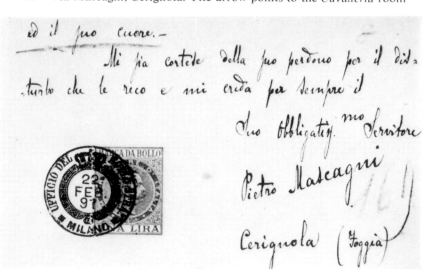

33　The last paragraph of Mascagni's letter to Verga of 9 March, 1890. The letter was an exhibit in the court case which explains the stamps on the left

34　Mascagni . . . "now he was elegant and jaunty" (p. 161)

35　Sgambati said: "Never have I heard these two chords
used so beautifully" (p. 151)

Sonzogno handled Mascagni's publicity very expertly. The 1890 Christmas number of Sonzogno's *Secolo illustrato* offered its readers a free photogravure of the *Pifferata di Natale* (a small Christmas piece for piano) specially composed by Mascagni; so many readers sent this to Mascagni with the request to autograph it that Cerignola's post office had to engage additional staff.

Sonzogno succeeded in obtaining the management of the Scala for the 1890-91 season. Shortly after Christmas, the opera was performed there. It proved enormously successful. The composer was again and again called before the footlights. He already seemed changed. Writes Gatti, the chronicler of the Scala:

"No longer was he the shy young man he had been in Rome, in ill-fitting clothes, and bewildered by the triumphant reception; now he was elegant and jaunty [see illus. 134], self-assured as well as sure of his public, whom he thanked with a sincere smile."

Financially all went brilliantly; already in January 1891, he could write to his friend Pericle, "*Cavalleria* has made me rich, for now and forever". Another son was born and christened Edoardo after Sonzogno, who became the child's godfather and attended the christening.

Plans for a second opera matured quickly and arrangements were made for the first night of *L'amico Fritz* in Rome in October, 1891. The opera was dedicated to Sonzogno.

CHAPTER VIII

CAVALLERIA LITIGATA

Colla presente privata scrittura da valere
nel miglior modo che di ragione
Il sig. Giovanni Verga, domiciliato a Catania,
è attualmente dimorante in Vizzini, ed il
sig. Maestro Pietro Mascagni dimorante a Cerignola (Foggia) per sé ed eredi, sono addive-
nuti al seguente contratto:
Il sig. Verga dà facoltà al sig. Maestro Mascagni di versificare (o far versificare) ridurre
per musica, e far rappresentare il suo lavoro
drammatico intitolato Cavalleria Rusticana
Il sig. Maestro Pietro Mascagni, per sé e suoi,
si obbliga di corrispondere al sig. Verga o a chi
per lui, quella parte d'utili che la legge attri-
buisce al sig. Verga sugl'introiti, per diritti
d'autore.
Fatto il presente contratto di comune accordo,
e in piena buona fede, rimossa qualunque ec-
cezione.
Firmato a Vizzini il sette aprile 1800novanta
    Giovanni Verga
Firmato a Cerignola il nove aprile 1800 novanta
    Pietro Mascagni

Registrato a Milano addì
al N. Vol. Fog.   Reg. Atti Privati
sate lire
N.   IL RICEVITORE
    IL CONTROLLORE

36   The Contract (p. 156)

37   Salvatore Paola
December, 1887

38   Verga and Federico De Roberto,
1881

39   Verga, December 1887

40   Verga and Capuana, December 1887

37, 39 and 40 are photographs by Verga

CAVALLERIA LITIGATA

D URING the summer of 1890 Verga was in Sicily, and spent
most of his time with his brothers in Vizzini. The newspapers
carried notices of the great success of *Cavalleria*, but neither
Mascagni nor Sonzogno had communicated with him again. He was
surprised, and began to feel annoyed. Eventually he wrote and asked
for his share of the proceeds.

The Italian law of copyright had been introduced in 1882, eight
years before the first performance of *Cavalleria*. The relevant provisions were contained in its Articles 5 and 6; they had not as yet
been put to the test.

> Article 5 read as follows: "When the rights to publish or
> perform an opera belong jointly to two or more persons, it
> is, without evidence to the contrary, presumed that all are
> entitled in equal shares. Each one may exercise the right to
> publish or perform, save that they must account to the
> other joint owners for their share of any royalty or com-
> pensation due to them."

> Article 6: "The author of a libretto or other written item which
> has been put to music cannot dispose of the right to
> reproduce the music. The composer of the music is entitled
> to reproduce or have reproduced both the music and the
> words, but in that case he must account to the author of
> the words as laid down in Article 5."

In response to his request, Verga received a note from Sonzogno
with a cashier's order for 500 lire. This, so Verga's advisers estimated,
represented less than a two-hundredth of the sum he was according
to the law entitled to expect from the known performances of the
opera.

Verga refused to accept the money, although his financial
position at the time was precarious. He even had to write to Dr
Saluzzo (see p. 46) that, to his "deepest displeasure" and "consternation", he did not for the moment possess adequate funds for certain

loan-repayments which were due. A letter to his friend Salvatore Paola gives proof of his financial distress.

"Don't be surprised that this note arrives a few minutes after we have just seen one another; when asking the sort of favour I am now asking you, one has to spare even so great a friend as you are the unpleasantness of having to say 'no' verbally.

" 'What a preamble!' you will say. To put it into a nutshell: in order to settle my affairs, I need to discount a bill of 5,000 lire at the Bank of Sicily, and for that I need your guarantee.

"If you could do me this favour, I should be very grateful. But more than anything else, I want to avoid using your friendship as a means of forcing you. If for any reason you think that you should not sign it (although your guarantee should not cause you any difficulty on this occasion) tell me so, frankly and without fear of upsetting me. You have given me so many tokens of your friendship that I do not need this new one for proof. I want to feel sure that you don't say to yourself 'what a nuisance', and yet say 'yes' to me, in order not to say 'no'. As a solicitor, you may well have many reasons for not wanting to see your signature going the rounds—it is not only a question of trust.

Yours, G. Verga.

"P.S. In case you do want to, please sign horizontally, near the stamp in the place marked with a cross."

Sonzogno was undoubtedly fully aware of Verga's financial plight. In a letter to Verga he expressed surprise at his attitude, offered 1,000 lire, and elaborated the offer by stating that he considered this "more than adequate compensation" inasmuch as he had paid the librettists only 500 lire. Nothing was said about Verga's claim, nor of his contract with Mascagni.

Again, Verga refused to accept. He explained that he had not been brought up "to accept tips" and pointed out that in the agreement which both Mascagni and he himself had signed, the conditions had been clearly defined: in case of any doubt, it might be useful to refer the matter to the Italian Society of Authors for their opinion. This drew an offer of 1,500 lire, as well as Sonzogno's approval of Verga submitting the dispute to the Society of Authors. Verga replied that in submitting the case he was fully prepared to accept the Society's decision, and that he assumed Sonzogno and Mascagni would do the same.

In a letter to Salvatore Paola, which he sent from Vizzini on 11th September, 1890, Verga made his attitude clear:

"My dear Salvatore,

"Forgive me for bothering you, but the matter I am writing to you about could, as you will see, be of great importance, and I do not want to do anything without your advice.

"Sonzogno offers me 1,500 lire *à forfait* [in a lump sum] for my copyright in *Cavalleria rusticana*. I want to insist on that percentage, on my royalty, which the law provides and which my agreement with Mascagni, which reads as follows, stipulates [illus. 36]:

" 'Signor Giovanni Verga, domiciled at Catania, at present living at Vizzini, and Maestro Pietro Mascagni, of Cerignola (Foggia), have for themselves and for their heirs and assignees entered into the following agreement.

" 'Signor Verga grants Maestro Mascagni the right to adapt his play *Cavalleria rusticana* into verse (or to have it set into verse) and to set it to music and to have it performed.

" 'Maestro Mascagni, for his part, undertakes to remit to Signor Verga, or to whomsoever should act for him, that part of the proceeds to which, according to the law of copyright, he is entitled.

" 'This present contract is made by mutual agreement in good faith and with the exclusion of any exception whatsoever.

" 'Signed at Vizzini, 7th April, 1890. Pietro Mascagni.'

"Sonzogno, the publisher of the opera and Mascagni's assignee, wishes to come to an agreement with me (realising that he ought to!). He started off by offering me 500 lire, which offer he has now raised to 1,500. However, he tries to evade any discussion of my share of the royalty upon which I insist and which, according to our agreement, is due to me. Both of us belong to the Society of Authors, and as the result of the intervention of some friends we have agreed to submit the dispute to their jurisdiction.

"The chairman of the Society's legal committee has written to say that, for the verdict to have binding effect, the dispute has to be submitted to one or more arbitrators, in equal numbers. He has named those of the Milan members who serve on the legal committee, 11 in all, including himself. I want to nominate them *all* as arbitrators, not only to avoid any sign of preference, but also to give their verdict more authority. In the present state of our literary law the judgment is bound to create a precedent, and the resulting moral responsibility will force them to consider their verdict very carefully.

"I beg you to draft the points of claim which I have to submit to the arbitrators; the salient item is to find the formula which will make them admit that I am entitled to whatever share of the proceeds they will allot to me, according to the terms of my agreement with Mascagni, and not to let them award me a compensation for my copyright or the payment of a lump sum *à forfait*: however much this would be, it would always be less than what should be mine. Sonzogno is well aware of it, and for that reason he insists on a 'once and for all payment' and tries at all costs to avoid having to implement our agreement.

"If it seems to you that my case is clear and incontestable, I shall not yield, and shall only agree to terms if I receive the share due to me.

"I know very well that if Sonzogno does not want to compromise, I may eventually be forced to take him to court and accept the result. Our law is not as clear as the French law in this respect: French law attributes to the author of the libretto the same rights as to the author of the music, i.e. 50 per cent of the royalty. I believe that in our case the French law would still be of importance if an Italian court is called upon to decide an analogous case.

"Do me the favour, my dear friend, of sending me your advice as soon as possible, and also the draft; time presses.

Yours, G. Verga."

Memorandum for Paola (appended to the letter):
"I do not know for certain whether Sonzogno has bought the opera from Mascagni, or whether he is only the publisher. All negotiations so far have been with him. Has Mascagni got to be a party to the agreement? Or is it enough to sign with Sonzogno as the assignee publisher who has a contract with Mascagni?

"N.B. I would really prefer to deal with Sonzogno—who, although he is a thief, is at least a solvent thief—rather than with Mascagni, who is an insolvent swindler."

The financial disparity between the two opponents was enormous. Sonzogno's publishing firm had been prosperous for a long time. His music-publishing venture enjoyed considerable success. Furthermore, Sonzogno had good hopes of retaining control of the Scala, enabling him to arrange that, almost exclusively, operas in which he had a financial interest were produced there (see p. 57).

All these interests were, however, sidelines, as Sonzogno was in financial and editorial control of the *Secolo,* a lucrative Milanese daily paper. He had founded a prosperous musical periodical as well, the *Teatro illustrato.* He was also about to buy an old theatre whose subsidy the municipality had withdrawn, the *Teatro della Cannobiana,* and intended to open it as *Teatro lirico* in 1894. This he could use to tighten his hold on the Scala even more, and so obtain absolute control of the Scala's management for several seasons. Financially as well as in influence within his sphere, he belonged to the most powerful people not only of Milan, but of all Italy.

Sonzogno was a forceful, energetic and dynamic personality. He was not completely unscrupulous, but was accustomed to use money and influence without much restraint when it became expedient to harm an opponent or competitor, and he was surrounded by yes-men. *Cavalleria rusticana* was proving as successful a work as any music publisher could possibly wish for, but Verga had dared to antagonize him, and had annoyed him by what he regarded as the presumptuous tone of his letters.

Few sources of information are accessible which would enable one accurately to reconstruct Sonzogno's line of thought. It may well have been as follows:

First of all, Verga's demands may have seemed quite unreasonable to him. Verga himself had not done a stroke of work in connection with this opera. He had, in fact, admitted that he did not even know that the work was being done; to make financial demands, and to refuse to accept 1,000 lire as compensation for nothing more than supplying a story, seemed rapacious. The accepted rate for a libretto was 100 lire per act. On that scale, he had compensated the librettists handsomely, and Verga handsomely twice over. Whatever the new law meant, what he was offering was surely all that could be justifiably expected. To request more (for work one had not carried out) seemed outrageous. Who was this fellow Verga anyway? He was as immoral as they made them. It was said that he had had a mistress in Florence, whom he afterwards took to Catania with him, to marry her off to his best friend. This was typical Sicilian behaviour. As if this were not enough, he continued to sleep with her, until the deceived friend quite rightly threw her out. The whole affair caused a lot of scandal, as one might expect.

Then, when he had arrived in Milan, Verga continued to behave scandalously. He was an unmitigated philanderer! Carducci, the greatest living Italian poet, detested him. One late afternoon the poet had unexpectedly arrived from Bologna (where he lived) to visit his friend "Lidia"* in her Milan flat. He found Verga there, who eventually left but not without caressing her hand in front of Carducci, and making remarks about the softness of her skin. It was obvious to Carducci that the two had been to bed together. In the flat, he found Verga's visiting-card with a baronet's crown! This Sicilian outcast and *parvenu* calling himself "Cavaliere" without being entitled to it! A hack writer, who had written a clumsy and silly convent love

*"Lidia" was Lina Piva-Cristofori. Carducci liked to change the names of his lady friends to similar names taken from Horace.

story, in letter form on top of it! In Carducci's opinion this *Capinera* was sheer nonsense, without any merit at all.

Then there was D'Annunzio, another person who really counted in literature—he did not like Verga either. In typical arrogance, Verga habitually derided D'Annunzio; jealousy, no doubt, because his own stuff had flopped. The *Malavoglia* novel, that shipwreck story, had, as Scarfoglio had noted, become a shipwreck itself. *Mastro-Don Gesualdo,* too, had failed. The *Cavalleria* play was Verga's only success, or modicum of success, but how could its success be compared to the real success of the opera? Within six weeks the opera had made more money than the play had made in six years, and the fun was only beginning. Money would pour in from every country in the world; in South and North America alone, an opera could now make a hundred times more money than in Italy. Speculating on its success, and envying those who could do things better than he could himself, Verga was now making extortionate demands.

What may have annoyed Sonzogno most was that Verga, with his odd background and his frequent failures, was socially accepted everywhere, and was regarded as irresistible to women. Milan society had opened its doors to him. All the more reason to teach Verga a lesson and to resist his demands! He did not think that Verga would go to court: litigation was an expensive business. Verga himself had nothing, and his friends would certainly not lend him money for that purpose; anyway, only fools go to court. If Verga should dare to sue, he would show him who was the stronger! As a taste of things to come, Sonzogno caused critical and derogatory comments about Verga to appear in the *Secolo.* The gist of these was that Verga obviously failed to practise what he preached. He had repeatedly claimed that "the hand of the writer must disappear", that a "work of art must be able to stand on its own feet". Such views were all well and good, but after the genius of Mascagni and his librettists had transformed Verga's play into a work of art, all Verga wanted to do now was to "hang on" to it, to exploit Mascagni, and to claim money for work he had not done. How did that match the professed lofty principles? As a deterrent to those who might want to try the same tricks, and claim royalties which were morally not justifiable, such attempts had to be resisted.

What was Mascagni's position in this dispute? From his letters it is quite clear that he sincerely appreciated Verga's generous action in authorizing the performance of the opera without demanding any payment. There was no reason why he should feel antagonistic to Verga; he must have felt proud to let Verga share in that bonanza which he had brought about, and must also have known that Verga was being wronged. However, the maintenance of a good relationship with Sonzogno, the one person through whom all these riches were coming to him, remained more important than anything else. Mascagni gradually became very arrogant towards most people, but he remained servile in his attitude to Sonzogno. If Sonzogno thought that Verga's demand should *not* be met, it was in Mascagni's interest to support him unconditionally—at least in public—whatever his private thoughts might have been about the rights and wrongs of the matter.

The references in the *Secolo* irritated Verga considerably. On 19th September, 1890, he again wrote to Paola, and thanked him for his reassurance in considering his case "indisputable and unassailable".

In a later letter to Paola he wrote:

"Campi* is not a Salvatore Paola, my dear friend . . . even if, in compensation, he is an M.P. However, as the elections are approaching, he does not really want to quarrel with Sonzogno! I do know my chickens, my dear friend, I do know them!

"And if things go wrong, and I have to have recourse to court action, where do I start? At Catania (as my domicile), at Foggia (for Cerignola) where Mascagni lived when he signed the contract, at Livorno, his present residence, or at Milan, Sonzogno's domicile?

"For your speedy and splendid reply to my last letter, I thank you with all my heart, and all the more so since I am told that you were suffering from toothache at the time!"

Towards the middle of October 1890, Verga returned to Milan. On 18th November he wrote to Dr Saluzzo that the judgment of the Society of Authors had now come to hand; the committee had expressed the view that Verga was fully entitled to the proportion of the profits which the law stipulated.

As soon as he heard of this decision, Verga arranged for Sonzogno to be contacted again. He pointed out that they had both agreed to abide by the Society's verdict, and that an agreement on the lines the Society had suggested should now be arrived at forthwith. The only reaction to this request were further notices in the

*In order to conduct negotiations on Verga's behalf, a Milan solicitor had to be chosen, and Emilio Campi was selected.

Secolo, suggesting that Verga continued to make unjustified demands. In spite of all this, Verga was still reluctant to go to court, not only in view of the expense, but also of the waste of time litigation would entail. However, the chairman of the legal committee of the Society of Authors explained that no other way existed which would make the "platonic" opinion of the Society legally effective. Encouraged by Salvatore Paola, he eventually brought an action against Mascagni and Sonzogno, submitting his case through Messrs Campi. He requested from the court the implementation of Articles 5 and 6 of the Law of Copyright of 1882, No. 1012.

On 3rd January, 1891, he wrote to Salvatore Paola:

"Dear Salvatore,

"Regarding the case against Mascagni and Sonzogno which is due to be heard on 20th February, I need opinion and advice which only you are able to give me convincingly.

"In his reply to the Society of Authors, Sonzogno found no better argument in Mascagni's defence than to submit that I myself had repudiated my contract with Mascagni by granting other people, *after this contract* had been signed, the right to use my *Cavalleria* as a subject for an operatic libretto. I certainly have never given anyone any such a right subsequent to my contract with Mascagni.

"Long before the contract, to be exact on 3rd June, 1888 (the contract with Mascagni is dated 7th April, 1890), I had, out of sheer kindness and without asking for payment or contract, the weakness to write a letter to a certain Bartocci Fontana—who had used my *Cavalleria* for a botch of a three-act libretto for the opera *Mala Pasqua* by Gastaldon. [For the text of this letter see p. 138.]

"Please read it carefully and let me know whether this can possibly invalidate my contract with Mascagni as Sonzogno claims. Campi is of the opinion that my letter does not prejudice the contract in the slightest. He also contends that the contract contains a clause binding on both parties—apart from the fact that the contract was signed two years after my letter to Bartocci Fontana was written! Incidentally, Bartocci Fontana had made his work very different from mine, not only in its title but also in the treatment of the subject."

On 13th January, 1891, Verga again wrote to Paola:

"Sonzogno is at present trying to keep Mascagni out of the way (imagine, he did not even let him come here for the first performance of *Cavalleria* at the Scala)* so that the writ could not be served on him

*Verga seems to have been misinformed on this point.

either in Cerignola (where we were told he had left) or at at Livorno, where he was meant to be.

"In order to comply with the legal requirements for serving the writ, the solicitor had to write to the Mayor of Cerignola by registered letter with advice of receipt to ascertain the facts of Mascagni's residence there. As you can imagine, I am pretty desperate about this loss of time and money—though, on the other hand, if they resort to such expedients it shows that they realize how weak their own case is. There is a rumour that Sonzogno is buying the *Cavalleria* opera for 150,000 lire. Is that good from my point of view, or bad? Am I entitled and does it seem to you justifiable, to demand an interim payment in view of the notoriously fat profits *Cavalleria* provides for publisher and composer?"

On 9th March, 1891, he writes again:

"I confess to you that I am very worried about the outcome of my case on account of the obstinacy of my solicitor here. Campi says I must let him do as he thinks fit and that the responsibility for taking the appropriate steps of the procedure is his.

"But if the case is adjourned on account of defects of procedure, or worse still, if a judgment, obtained in default, is set aside for this reason, much time and money will have been lost. What can I do? I have already had to swallow so much bitter unpleasantness! If I only had you here, I would not be in this painful uncertainty."

Judgment was given on 12th March, and Verga was awarded half of the net profits already earned, as well as half of all net profits to be earned in future. Jubilantly he reported to his friend on 15th March, 1891:

"I am sure my brother has already informed you of the telegram with which I announced complete victory, as I asked him to do. I feel I owe it to a large extent to you—to your wise counsel and the brotherly affection with which, in spite of all your heavy professional commitments, you have studied my case.

"As you will see from the judgment, the victory could not be more complete. The whole of Milan is delighted and talks of nothing else— my case even had the sympathy of those who don't know me, but who have been to the Scala and have given me credit for half of the success.

"My solicitors feel safe about the outcome of a possible appeal, but should a compromise proposal be afoot I shall only accept it with your approval."

Mascagni and Sonzogno lodged their appeal. In order to refute one of its arguments, i.e. that the judgment was "out of keeping with precedent in other parts of the world", Verga's solicitors had requested an opinion from a French society which was held in great respect in Italy, the *Société des Auteurs, Compositeurs et Editeurs de Musique*. On 20th April, 1891, the following report was received by Messrs Campi. It was from M. Victor Souchon, the *Agent Général* of the Society, with offices at 17 rue du Faubourg Montmartre:

"Your letter of 8th April (I was out of Paris when it arrived) requests an opinion on questions relevant to the case you are conducting on behalf of M. Verga.

"The usual practice in France, supported by numerous court decisions, is that the original author who, through a novel or a play, has provided an idea for a new work, becomes automatically the new work's co-author and shares its copyright. There is no doubt about this and no difficulty whatsoever: it is standard practice.

"You ask for examples. There are almost too many! In order to give you just a few of the best known, I mention Verdi's *Rigoletto*; the copyright is shared with Victor Hugo whose *Le Roi s'amuse* had provided the subject; Salvayre's *Dame de Montsoreau* is shared with the novelists Maquet and Dumas; *Ascanio* by Saint-Saëns is shared with the novelist Alexandre Dumas; *Patrie* by Paladilhe is shared with the playwright Sardou; Verdi's *La Traviata* is shared with Alexandre Dumas fils, the author of *La Dame aux camélias*, etc., etc.

"In all these cases neither Sardou nor Dumas nor Maquet nor Hugo assisted materially with the new work; they simply permitted their work to become the subject of a new work, and authorized its adaptation.

"Whoever says 'authorized' refers to copyright, and raises the question as to who has the right to grant such an authorization. This is the salient point, and the examples which I have quoted quite clearly support your own case.

"Who is Verga? He is the author, just like Maquet, Dumas, Sardou or Hugo. What had those who took his work, in order to adapt it for an opera, to do? They had to ask for his permission. What conditions was M. Verga entitled to impose? Incontestably, those of sharing the proceeds resulting from his adaptation. This is so obvious in France that such details are here arranged almost before the adaptors even put their pen to paper.

"What is the accepted share of the proceeds which are to be attributed to the author? This varies considerably, and depends entirely on the demands of the original author. It depends on what he thinks of the project as far as his own name is concerned, and whether the adaptation might enhance his reputation.

"For example, Sardou reserved for himself in *Patrie* two-thirds of the share due to the authors of the libretto—so that if this opera pays 12 per cent of the gross receipts to its authors, Salvayre would have six per cent (the authors as a general rule share with the composer half and half), Sardou four per cent, and the adaptor two per cent.

"A composer may voluntarily forgo part of his share in favour of the adaptor; everything depends upon the arrangements between those who are entitled to the copyright. The arrangements themselves are flexible.

"*Rigoletto,* for example, gives its original author a bigger share, because Victor Hugo has reserved for himself four-tenths of the total.

"In the *Dame de Montsoreau* we see that half the rights go to Maquet alone, who benefits to this extent either because Dumas agreed to forgo his own rights in favour of his original collaborator, or because Salvayre gave up part of his rights. In *Ascanio,* Alexandre Dumas has one quarter of the total. Can you see my point? What I mean is that four works by four different authors show four different methods of distribution, though the share assigned to the composer remains nearly always half of the *total.* In France, the publisher is not entitled to the copyright of theatrical works—this is shared only between the authors and the composer.

"A summary of what is the correct reply to your question is therefore the following: it is, in principle, and quite firmly established here, that the original author of a play or of any other such work transformed into an opera or a comic opera participates in the rights of the authors of the new libretto. The share itself must be agreed between the original author and his new collaborators. Exactly the same applies to works taken from novels. The share of the original author is, in every respect, an undeniable right!

"It is very much in the interest of all Italian authors that these questions of collaboration should be ruled exactly as they are in France. The Italian courts have, in my opinion, every reason to allot to M. Verga his due share.

"By its laws and conventions, Italy has given too many tokens of her concern for authors to permit such a grave assault on literary property to succeed. The verdict ought to be a pledge of security for the rights of the Italian authors of the future.

"To add a few recent examples:

"Reyer's opera *Salammbô* pays a quarter of the rights to the heirs of Flaubert, who was the author of the novel, one quarter to Du Locle, the libretto writer, and one half to Reyer.

"In *Carmen,* the heirs of Mérimée (on whose novel the work is based) have voluntarily ceded their rights in favour of Meilhac and Halévy. These last two therefore receive a half share, and Bizet has the other half.

"As a general rule one can say that one quarter goes to the original author, one quarter goes to the libretto's adaptor, and one half to the composer.

"I am, sir, at your disposition for any further explanations you may find necessary for the clarification of the facts mentioned, and am, etc."

Verga was pleased to see this opinion. It appealed to his sense of fairness, and he thought that it expressed exactly what he himself felt to be just. He took the unusual step of informing his solicitor that he regarded the proposition referred to in the last paragraph as just, and that, in spite of having been awarded a bigger share in court, this was the division he desired.

Pending the appeal, the necessary discussions with his own solicitors were at times exasperating. On 27th May, 1891, he wrote:

"O Paola, O my Turiddu Paola, where are you? Where were you yesterday while these Deputies and ex-Ministers managed to ramble on for hours without saying a thing! Where is the clear and forceful logic of your conclusions, instead of those useless reams of theirs which no one reads or needs to read?"

The appeal was heard on 16th June, 1891. On 17th June Verga wrote to Paola:

"Pietro [Verga's brother] will have told you about my telegram in which I reported the victory. I say victory, because, in spite of the reduction which the court has made, the sums which Mascagni and Sonzogno owe me so far, plus those to come, free me from any financial embarrassment. Victory, because I think an award in those terms must be safe even in the event of an appeal to the Supreme Court; that it will be considered as just by public opinion (with the exception of the *Secolo*, of course), and also because I myself consider it fair and just.

"I have sent you the *Lombardia*, and its exact report of the judgment will explain everything to you better than I can.

"Of course, the *Secolo*—the worthy journal of that 'Maecenas' Sonzogno—will continue its lament in furious articles. The lesson which has been taught to this man's overweening pride—which he regarded as unassailable—is a severe one. His cash box, too, will take a sound beating, as he has to account to me for his profits of more than 400,000 lire. This, according to the last verdict, makes my share come to at least 100,000 lire so far, and this within two months!

"Twenty-five per cent of all net income is due to me, not only from the performances but also from every publication of the music together with the words, therefore also from the sale of the libretto, the vocal score, etc. The difference between gross and net—so Boito and others assure me—should not be more than ten per cent! Boito authorizes me to call him as witness that this is the expected average ratio, and so does Ricordi."

Sonzogno and Mascagni again appealed, this time to the Supreme Court of Appeal in Turin, the Italian equivalent of the House of Lords. About this appeal Verga wrote to Paola on 14th July, 1891:

"I am plainly satisfied with what the last verdict gives me, and I myself will not appeal and demand the previous fifty per cent. I am, however, in a great hurry to see a practical result as you, who know the grave state of all my financial affairs, can well imagine."

This grave state of affairs was well known to Sonzogno as well, and he intensified his delaying tactics.

On 4th September, 1891, Verga wrote again to Paola:

"You know that the state of my affairs just does not permit me to wait at all. An adjournment for me would be tantamount to losing the case. I am quite satisfied with the twenty-five per cent awarded to me. I wish for no more than that the Supreme Court of Appeal confirms this, and rejects their appeal.

"The enormous fortune this opera is bringing! Reliable information says that they have taken 847,000 lire up to 11th August!

"Sonzogno has now offered me, through Peppino Giuffredi, 20,000 lire 'once and for all'. He knows perfectly well that he only stands to gain by playing for time, and tries to wear me down.

"To accept 20,000 lire seems to me to be suicidal. Campi, who knows of my straits, can do no better than to advise me to accept if Sonzogno should offer 50,000 lire!"

On 16th September he wrote:

"Valdati [Campi's junior partner] suggests that as soon as Sonzogno presents his accounts (whatever they are) I should ask the court that I be paid, provisionally, twenty-five per cent of the sums due to me. Then, without prejudice, I shall within five days of it have 7,000 lire plus costs paid to me.

"The accounts Sonzogno presented to Campi in order to comply with the judgment show only 117,000 lire as receipts. Of this he deducts 82,000 lire as expenditure, thus reducing his net profit to 35,000 lire!

"Only imagine it! The expenses include 10,000 lire for Sonzogno's travelling, 6,000 for telegrams, etc., and yet, instead of the 8,700 due to me according to *that* reckoning, they offer me 25,000 lire! So much for the morals of their accounting!"

Three months later, on 28th December, 1891, Verga wrote in better spirits:

"For some time now my affairs have begun to take a turn for the better, and, with God's help, I shall soon be over all these troubles which beset me and my family."

On 1st February, 1892, he wrote:

"Campi now advises all my friends to persuade me to accept an offer of 40,000 lire! . . . I think I had better insert your name among my solicitors connected with this appeal. If you can come to Turin in the late spring it would be splendid, but even if you can't it cannot do any harm to have your name included.

"I enclose Sonzogno's accounts, a real monument of impudence in which the theatres abroad do not appear at all! He says that we can go to court in each foreign country if we want to.

"Many of the places in Italy are omitted; the figures which he declares are ridiculous. No account is taken of the sales of the vocal score which, according to Ricordi, should have brought in 20,000 lire or so, and not even all the performances in those theatres where Sonzogno's *Secolo* has reported attendance-figures are included!

"Finally, Sonzogno debits all his fantastic overheads exclusively to the share of the authors and even makes me liable for the 47,000 lire he gave to Mascagni, which therefore appears twice! Altogether a most ill-advised statement which really will show him up in a bad light, with the judges as well as with public opinion."

The appeal was to be heard on 15th February, 1892. A few days before, Verga wrote:

"Yesterday we were at last able to submit our case in reply. I should have liked to go to Turin myself but could not afford it.

"I have decided to go for Sonzogno as hard as I can, because he is only aiming at wearing me out with all his delays. He has even obtained an adjournment of the investigation into the accounts until the twenty-seventh of this month by means of a medical certificate of illness which his solicitors submitted."

On 9th August, 1892, Verga finally emerged victorious.

The verdict settled the matter, but Sonzogno was still not finished. He continued his delaying tactics, and used every possible trick to try and force Verga to accept a once-and-for-all settlement. On 29th December, Verga again wrote to Paola:

"I enclose my signed bill of exchange, renewable for only fourteen days. Everything makes me feel sure that the transaction with Sonzogno will be settled now—it could have been signed before the thirty-first, were it not for the usual solicitors' delays.

P.S. The money necessary for this renewal is to come from the tenancies."

Verga was under severe and increasing pressure on account of his daily rising debts. He felt that he had only halfhearted support from Campi, who played a double game by attempting, if not to please Sonzogno, at least not to antagonize him too much. To make a powerful and certainly not very scrupulous tycoon disclose proper accounts presented almost insurmountable difficulties. Verga was only *fully* supported by Salvatore Paola, who was 600 miles away! All this forced him into his own crucial mistake. His representatives eventually persuaded him to agree to accept the sum of 143,000 lire as a fair "final compensation" within the terms of the law. The agreement was signed on 2nd January, 1893, and the figure it contained was at that time regarded as high. However, it proved to be a serious mistake.

The expert in "tragic errors", the master chronicler of the Malavoglia family's fatal mistake, the writer who had so movingly portrayed Gesualdo Motta's false step, the man who had given the world the concept of those *vinti* who seal their doom by a forgivable error, now, half knowingly perhaps, committed his own fatal error.

He knew from the beginning that he should not have done so, but felt forced by circumstances to sign the agreement. It proved, in the long run, as grave an error as any of those made by the characters he invented. What mattered most was not so much the riches he had missed—though this was bad enough—but that he had helplessly to stand aside and see the work which he had so substantially helped to create, become the work of others. He had to watch the children of his own fantasy change their parents, and become the children of his enemies. In a sense he even had to pretend, when he met them, that he did not know them any more!

As for *Cavalleria rusticana,* its triumphant progress continued. In London it had its first performance in 1891, at the Shaftesbury Theatre. In July 1893, the opera came to London again, with Mascagni attending a performance at Covent Garden. Queen Victoria —not really an ardent opera-lover—was present herself and commanded that Mascagni be introduced to her. What Her Majesty actually said to Mascagni we do not know, but from a letter to his wife in Cerignola dated London, 15th July, 1893, we have Mascagni's version of it:

"The Queen approached me and said in French, 'I am absolutely delighted to meet you. For a long time I have wished to meet the composer of *Cavalleria,* as I feel moved to tears whenever I hear it. You must always write music like that, and when you compose a new opera, you must think of *Cavalleria*.' Her Majesty then asked what opera I was working on *now*, and when I replied that I was working on three, she replied smilingly, 'What? On three operas at the same time? I understand, I understand— you are *so* young!"

41   Tiepidi, a view from the farmhouse

42   Tiepidi, a pair of mules ploughing

43   The giant cone of Etna often forms the backcloth of Verga's stories

44   Donkey, mule and horse still provide transport and motive power on the land

CHAPTER IX

THE WITHDRAWAL

THE WITHDRAWAL

IN 1893, at the time of the conclusion of his agreement with Sonzogno, Verga was 53 years old. His venture to the mainland of Italy, he sadly had to admit, had resulted in failure. He had had successes, no doubt, but, on the whole, he had not been able to achieve what he had set out to do.

Disappointed with his experiences, he decided to return to Catania. He still travelled frequently, in particular to Milan, but no longer kept rooms there, and stayed, generally for short periods only, in hotels.

He had paid off his debts, and the money from his court case also enabled him to realize an old ambition; to occupy his parents' home in Catania's Via S. Anna, and to decorate and furnish the place as his own.* The house contained four separate flats; his own was quite spacious and he usually employed a cook-housemaid and a waiter-manservant; he generally lived alone and, apart from his brother Mario, had only on rare occasions anyone staying with him. He enjoyed solitude.

His relationship with Giselda had entered a phase of decline soon after his visit to Florence on the occasion of the first performance of *Cavalleria* there. Giselda remained in Florence and earned her living as an assistant inspector of teaching at girls' colleges, and by private lessons. She also studied for a degree, and in 1891 obtained a teaching appointment at a technical high school at Bari, and (in 1892) at Perugia. In 1893 she became inspector of studies for girls' colleges and lived for ten years in Venice. Still later she moved to Milan. Her financial position (she had to support her mother, who lived with her up to her death at the age of 84 in 1914) was precarious until she received, upon her husband's death in 1912, the widow's pension to which Rapisardi's professorship entitled her.

A novel, *Maria,* had appeared while she was still living with

---

*It also enabled him to satisfy the Church's demands regarding the piece of land he owned near Mineo, thus freeing it from its obligations and converting it into an ordinary freehold (see also p. 47 and p. 233)

Rapisardi. In 1886 she published a book of short stories under the title of *Cose che succedono* (*Things Which Happen*), which was reprinted in 1914 under the title *In Toscana e in Sicilia* (*In Tuscany and in Sicily*). The first of these short stories, *Amor campagnuolo* (*Country Love*), was the "jewel" referred to in Verga's ill-fated letter (see p. 117). Those of her stories which are set in the neighbourhood of Catania clearly show Verga's stylistic influence:

Le avrebbe sputato sul viso le avrebbe

(He would have spat right into her face, he really would).*

When, many years later, Verga was asked by his nephew how his affair with Giselda had ended, he answered, "the less said about it the better". Giselda died at Lodi, on 3rd February, 1946, at the age of 95, outliving Verga by twenty-four years; all her life she retained her sincere affection for him.

Evelyn, who had become a close friend of Giselda's in Florence (see p. 125), also passed through a difficult time after her separation. On her return to Florence she became interested in journalism and worked for a while on the *Fieramosca* (see p. 99). She published verse, novels, and children's books under the pseudonym of "Contessa Lara", and the choice of this pen name, which is taken from her idol Byron's poem *Lara, A Tale* (the sequel to *The Corsair*) is revealing. Lara is the assumed name under which the pirate chief Conrad, his outlaw's life over, attempts to return to society. He hopes to remain unrecognized, a somewhat mysterious person, but his past follows him. He is recognized, involved in a feud, and killed. Lara, so it is generally accepted, contains features of Byron himself.

Under the name of Contessa Lara, Evelyn established for herself a firm place in Italy's literary history—though she could not have known how well the pen name would come to fit her. Several of her books of poetry were outstandingly successful. She become famous as well as prosperous and, contrary to the obligation in her separation agreement, she moved to Rome. No objection was raised, and she lived there in style and elegance, if always with some sadness.

At the age of 47, she was brutally murdered by a young painter who had been her lover and whom she had supported. Tiring of his demands and his threats of violence, she had made up her mind to dissociate herself from him, and had for her own protection bought a revolver. He shot her with this weapon on 30th November, 1896, in her own house, 27 Via Sistina.

*(See also pp. 77-78).

Later during the same night, her murderer returned with a doctor who neither informed the police, nor arranged for her transfer to hospital. She was left alone all night. She died miserably, on 1st December, 1896. Her last words: "I die just as poor Bennati died for me," were true in every respect. Prompt and correct medical attention could have saved them both; the operation of laparotomy, which of course should have been performed at once (the bullet had entered her abdominal cavity just above the umbilicus), was well within the surgical competence of the time.

Among the very few people who came to her house and brought flowers after her death were Capuana and Pirandello. Some newspapers made unkind references to her, and, although a few correspondents pointed out that her behaviour would have been seen in a very different light had she been a man, she was on the whole condemned by public opinion. The writer Matilde Serao was one of the few who publicly came to her defence.

The series of misfortunes which beset her did not end with her death. A public auction of her books, furniture, and jewels in March 1897, raised 42,000 lire, but a notary fraudulently converted the money, took refuge in the Vatican and was not prosecuted.

The court case against the murderer, who cynically threw mud at his victim's memory, lasted from 3rd November, 1897, to 10th November. He was sentenced to eleven years and eight months' imprisonment.

Her body, provisionally interred in a municipal grave, should have been transferred to a proper grave. As the result of the fraudulent disappearance of the auction money, as well as of the 70,000 lire which had resulted from the sale of her house in Florence, no money was available. A literary journal opened a subscription to pay for a place in a churchyard; an adequate sum of money was collected but this, too, ended in the wrong hands.

Eventually the time limit which the regulations permitted for the transfer of the body from the *Deposito municipale* at Verano to a private grave expired; what remained of the body of one of the most beautiful girls of her time was thrown into a large ditch which served as the communal grave for the destitute. She was soon forgotten. Years later, Benedetto Croce devoted part of a chapter in his *La letteratura della Nuova Italia* to her work, and Maria Borgese published a biography, *La Contessa Lara,* in which she courageously corrected many wrong assumptions. Some of her poetry is of lasting interest.

Verga's wish to return to Sicily was intensified by the "longing for home and the native countryside" which, as expressed in a letter to Luigi Capuana, he felt the more strongly the older he got. However, the main reason was the wounded feeling of the artist who had hoped for recognition and failed to win it because the time was not ripe. His disenchantment had one very sad result: Verga no longer felt his once so powerful urge to write. All his great work was done within a relatively short period. On his return to Catania in the prime of his life, in good health, and with 30 years still ahead of him he did not press on with his main ambition, the writing of *The Cycle of the Doomed*. This series of novels which was meant to embrace all strata of human life, a work which he had begun with unparalleled if unrecognized mastery, remained unfinished.

After *I Malavoglia* and *Mastro-Don Gesualdo* had appeared, the *Duchessa di Leyra* was the next novel to be written. All the preliminary work for this book had been done, and the plot was ready in Verga's head. The leading characters were descendants of people he had invented earlier on, the Duchess herself being Mastro-Don Gesualdo's daughter. The literary task involved was thus comparatively simple, but, in spite of all this thorough preparation, Verga never succeeded in accomplishing it. When later the public recognition for which Verga had so long and fervently hoped came his way, this became one of the great literary puzzles of the time.

The curious fact that a man who had been so devoted to writing, should quite suddenly lose all desire for it, led to a good deal of speculation. Some people thought that Verga did not write any more because he preferred to fight law cases. After the Sonzogno affair, they claimed, he had become obsessed with court actions and actually enjoyed litigation; others said that personal, as well as family problems, mostly financial, had forced him to neglect his literary work; again others thought that he preferred sitting in his club to writing, and that he had become immersed in local and national politics. Finally, it was believed that he had lost self-confidence, in particular the confidence in his capacity successfully to solve the difficult linguistic and literary problems which the presentation of the *vinti* in the social setting of the *Duchessa* presented (see pp. 79-80). This loss of confidence must undoubtedly have occurred but may well have been an effect rather than a cause.

After the failure of *I Malavoglia,* his latent streak of sadness and pessimism gradually increased. The *Cavalleria* dispute accelerated this process, and his disappointment was intensified by the

bitter awareness that someone who deserved success much less
than he did was succeeding where he had failed. Eventually, his
sadness reached at times the intensity of a depressive phase.

Verga had no false notions about his own work, and was capable
of surprisingly accurate self-criticism. He knew that *I Malavoglia*
was a masterpiece, and in the very letter to Capuana in which he
admitted the book's fiasco, he spoke, "putting aside all stupid and
hypocritical modesty", of that *"griffe de lion"* which "in Italy at
present only you and I possess".

However, without this *"griffe de lion"* Gabriele D'Annunzio
had left the other two far behind in public recognition, and at the age
of 20 secured for himself what the 23 years older Verga had only
dreamed about.

Verga disliked D'Annunzio for a number of reasons, some of
which were personal. In his early verse, D'Annunzio leant heavily on
Carducci. In his prose, he was, if he did not directly imitate Verga,
at least seriously influenced by him (see p. 78). Verga conceded
D'Annunzio ingenuity, but felt he used it to deceive the public. In a
letter to Felice Cameroni (3rd November, 1888) he lists D'Annunzio's
failings as conventionality, fraudulent cunning, affectation and in-
sincerity. If this was an accurate assessment, these traits had not
prevented D'Annunzio's enormous success, a success which soon left
its mark on his personality.

"The timid and somehow unspoilt child," wrote his friend Scarfoglio,*
"became calculating. Gabriele , who had left Rome candid, modest, and
gentle, returned from his holiday in the Abruzzi, during which his success
became evident, a cunning, conceited and pretentious man."

D'Annunzio's success was facilitated by the resourceful new
approach to literature which the publisher Angelo Sommaruga, a man
of considerable influence on Italian literature, had initiated. According to Scarfoglio, Sommaruga

"was the product of the fusion, or rather of the collision, of two opposed
and apparently irreconcilable elements: of scholarly culture and of bluff.
A quarter of a century ahead of the rest of the world, he had invented that
impudent and insolent publicity which first perturbs and almost frightens
the public, then mesmerizes it, and eventually imposes its will on it. For
Sommaruga, the publisher was not the manager of a literary trend but a
producer of merchandise, whose task it was to get rid of the biggest
possible quantity."

*Edoardo Scarfoglio, *Il libro di Don Chisciotte*, Quattrini, Florence, 1911.

With a totally new technique for the period, he created the popular success of two writers both of whom Verga disliked: Carducci and D'Annunzio.

Carducci, for many years Professor of Literature at Bologna University, was a very gifted poet who held within his lifetime unparalleled power in Italian literature. He was rather pompous and very righteous, and his influence was increased by the widely held, and probably accurate belief, that he was the Queen's lover. He disliked, and was disliked by, Rapisardi, a rebel and excommunicated unbeliever. Rapisardi published in 1877 a poetical work, *Lucifero,* in which he made Dante refer to a man "sick with rabies and drunk with bile and wine", who believes that "his place is at my [Dante's] side", and who "has set himself up as the people's tribune, sends out poisoned darts and is quite unable to find any honest man—apart from himself".

To contemporaries it was quite clear that these strong but not altogether unjustified remarks were meant for Carducci. The remarks unleashed the most violent literary polemic in a country where polemic has a far more recognized place in literature than in Anglo-Saxon countries. Carducci's pupils and followers joined in the battle and heaped insult and ridicule on Rapisardi. For a while Rapisardi tried to give as good as he got, and in the course of the polemic even announced another philosophical-critical poem, his *Giobbe (Job).*

At this news, some Carducci sympathizers canvassed a number of Catania shopkeepers by means of a printed circular, purporting to come from Rapisardi, which invited them to advertise their wares in his poem for the price of one lira a verse. A number of merchants, particularly of groceries and delicatessen, sent Rapisardi money and a description of the goods which they wanted praised. Furthermore, a parody of the new book, lampooning Rapisardi, written by the Carducci followers Guerrini and Ricci, was published in 1882, before the appearance of Rapisardi's own poem.*

The whole of literary Italy seemed to be up in arms against Rapisardi. In Sicily itself he maintained a core of admiring followers, who defended in him the fellow-Sicilian who was being vilified by envious mainland detractors; this enabled them to use the polemic as a welcome vent for their antipathies to the mainland. However, the general consensus was that Rapisardi had the worst of the encounter.

---

*It was printed (by Treves in 1882) as the "serene conception" of one Marco Balossardi, a jocular variation of Rapisardi's name, which makes it sound childish and silly.

"The duty of the poet," Rapisardi said later in answer to a journalist's question, "does not consist in the founding of new schools, nor in aligning himself to old ones. The poet's duty is to express himself, to express reality as he sees it and to express it with sincerity."* This, in spite of private and public persecutions, is what Rapisardi actually did; and if he did not always do it with great poetry, he did it with considerable courage.

Verga had taken no part in this polemic.** In spite of the bitter animosity dating from the Giselda affair, in spite of his sarcasms about Rapisardi's "meannesses, jealousies and stupidity", his feelings were on the side of the friend he had wronged, and he disapproved of Carducci's methods.

Verga always viewed the popularity of those writers he did not think too much of with mixed feelings. This may partly have been due to envy but this is not the whole picture: their success shook his faith in the "justice" of literature.

For a time he was comforted for his own lack of success by his firm belief that "Time is, or is going to be, a gentleman". Gradually his belief in his own phrase waned. The resulting feeling of injustice intensified the bitterness and deepened his gloom, and eventually led to a dignified retreat, and to obstinate and proud silence.

Only one bright ray penetrated his preponderantly gloomy emotions after his return to Catania; a friendship which was as important for the last decades in his life as it was important for posterity—the friendship with Federico De Roberto. This young writer, Verga's junior by 21 years, attached himself to him, combining the feelings of filial admiration with devoted friendship. In due course, he assumed a position in Verga's life which can be compared to that of Boswell in Johnson's.

De Roberto was born in Naples in 1861. His father, an officer of the Bourbon army of occupation, had married and settled in Catania. He first met Verga in 1881 when, as editor of the literary journal *Don Chisciotte,* he approached him for a contribution: a special edition of his journal was to be sold in aid of the earthquake

*Mario Rapisardi, *Antologia* (ed. Ermanno Scuderi), Giannotta, Catania, 1968.

**Verga was rather reverently referred to in the *Giobbe* parody:

E reverenti salutiam la vera	Salute to Verga's work, we can profess
la viva gloria di Catania, il Verga,	That it Catania's glory does reflect,
in cui l'ingegno più virile alberga	In him more real genius we detect
di tutta questa Italia romanziera.	Than all the other novelists possess.

victims of Casamicciola. In 1890, De Roberto went to Milan as literary critic of the *Corriere*. He returned to Catania after a year, in order to continue with his main work, the novel *I Vicerè* (*The Viceroys*) which he published in 1894, and which became the most important historical novel of Sicily. Verga, who was personally very fond of De Roberto, was often unduly critical of his writing, and regarded the *Vicerè* as "too long as well as too long-winded".

After Verga's death, De Roberto published a series of newspaper articles which became the basic source of information for every Verga biography. De Roberto would have been well capable of writing a full Verga biography, and he had every intention of fusing and extending his articles into such a work. However, a protracted illness made him lose interest before the work was properly under way and his articles remained sketches. They clearly reveal his fondness for and his attachment to a friend whom he regarded as the person nearest to him.

The reasons, other than Verga's loss of confidence, put forward to explain his failure to continue with his writing (see p. 186) also need to be examined separately.

COURT CASES

How further legal actions came about, after the settlement made everything appear cut and dried, makes a somewhat involved story.

Sonzogno and Mascagni and the success of Mascagni's *Cavalleria* had contributed to Verga's bitterness, though to some extent the outcome of his legal battle had pleased him.

His author's rights had been recognized and Sonzogno humilated, but he was never fully reconciled to the agreement itself. He had been forced to accept it; at heart, he felt cheated.

The opera's continued success became a constant reminder that he should never have agreed to give up his percentage of the proceeds. To his further irritation, he remained the target for biased and unfavourable notices in Sonzogno's *Secolo* as well as the victim of other pin-pricks. The necessary reference to his name in the score of *Cavalleria rusticana*, for example, was made in ridiculously small lettering, and, before long, was reduced to a mere footnote in the smallest print (illus. 45). Later on, his name was removed altogether from all the scores. He had won his case, but was losing his *Cavalleria*. The success of the opera also caused a decline in the fortunes of the play, which was henceforward only presented by second-rate companies. In the truculent production of Giovanni Grasso, success was achieved by distortions and vulgar effects, by bloodstained knives, and so on, all this rather objectionable to Verga.

It is impossible to assess accurately the extent to which Verga's work had contributed to the success of Mascagni's opera. Contemporaries accepted the view that the dramatic power of Verga's story was a significant influence, a view shared by the music publisher Giulio Ricordi, whom Verga knew well. Verga had been in touch with Ricordi when he attempted to persuade him to publish Perrotta's opera *Bianca di Lara*.

Giulio Ricordi had missed the opportunity to buy Mascagni's *Cavalleria* (see p. 147), and this disappointment continued to irk him. He now felt that an opera based on another of Verga's dramatic short stories might be equally successful, and suggested to Puccini that he set the story of *La Lupa* to music. This story, from the book *Vita dei campi*, the same book which had contained the *Cavalleria* story, is based on an incident of which Capuana had told Verga, and which had occurred in Mineo, his home town (see p. 87).

A mature woman, the mother of a grown-up daughter, falls in love with a young man who works together with her in the field. She confesses to the young man that she loves him. He retorts by disclosing that he is in love with her daughter, who does not want him. The mother forces her daughter to marry the young man, and succeeds in making her son-in-law her incestuous lover. By this time the daughter has fallen in love with her husband. The husband realizes the disgrace of his situation, but again and again yields to his mother-in-law's temptation. To rid himself of his incestuous desire he eventually decides to kill her, while she, aware of his axe though unafraid, walks to their secret meeting place.

Probably upon recommendation by Eleonora Duse, Verga had converted this short story into a play, which was to be performed before long. Verga was in Catania when he heard from Ricordi about Puccini's interest. He was very pleased and the thought that this might annoy Sonzogno and Mascagni was perhaps what pleased him most. Puccini, too, was delighted with the new idea, and began to compose with inspiration. At that time (1894) he had already achieved fame with *Manon Lescaut*—after having failed with *Edgar*.

It was agreed that Puccini should come to Catania to meet Verga and to gather local impressions. On Verga's suggestion, Ricordi commissioned Federico De Roberto for a fee of a thousand lire to write a libretto.

Giulio Ricordi was a shrewd businessman,* who liked to affect the rôle of the fatherly friend. In his letters he was in the habit of addressing Puccini as "Doge", a nickname Puccini had acquired on account of his tastes in wearing apparel.

At the beginning of the summer of 1894 Puccini was in Catania. A good deal of work had to be done; adjustments to the libretto were to be made—there was too much dialogue, the rôle of Mara (the daughter) was insufficiently developed, most of the characters were rather unattractive and not one "luminous" figure emerged. However, the collaboration progressed well and Puccini was working with pleasure on the score.

A visit to Malta is a popular excursion from Catania. Puccini, too, made and enjoyed this trip, and being an enthusiastic photographer at that time, he took pictures of unfamiliar scenes, the farmsteads, general views, "Maltese types", and of the island's imposing naval fortifications. To photograph fortifications was, of course, strictly forbidden, and Puccini was warned off by a police officer—but as soon as the officer had turned his back, Puccini resumed the use of his camera. This led to his arrest as a suspected spy. He was taken to a police station and searched, and a note on the following lines was found.

"Dear Doge,

"You have now been travelling for a considerable time, and, needless to say, have used up a good deal of money. I certainly don't grudge this to you, but I do find it disappointing that you have not sent us a single act yet!

"I really think you should set to work with more determination, and I do hope to receive something from you soon.

"Remember, please, that it is imperative that you keep your mouth shut, and that you do not talk to anyone about your plans!

"Yours, Ricordi."

A British policeman in Malta was in 1894 most unlikely to have heard the name Puccini. The letter was obviously incriminating, and

*The strong position, as well as the harsh business acumen, of the music-publisher tycoons of the period is illustrated by a cartoon from the Milan *Momento* of 1889 which shows an elderly man, with the features of Ricordi, slapping a whistling boy's face, and saying "No-one is permitted to whistle in the street if he has not previously arranged terms with the firm which controls all composers and holds the exclusive rights to every musical note". The cartoon is entitled: Musical Monopolies. From *Storia di Milano*, XVI, p. 701.

the odd names aroused even more suspicion; it took a few hours before Puccini was released.

Detention at a police station was for Puccini not altogether a new experience,* and although in his view detention at a British police station compared favourably with Italy, the experience itself was unpleasant, and changed his mood: on returning to Catania he found that his enthusiasm for *La Lupa* had gone, and he wished to leave at once.

During the return journey to Livorno he made up his mind to abandon the project altogether and to resume work on a libretto which he had put aside in favour of *La Lupa*. He used the music he had composed for *La Lupa* for this new project, *La Bohème*—an opera which might not have been written were it not for an unknown British policeman's conscientious attention to duty.

The theatrical version of *La Lupa* was, with mediocre success, first performed in January 1896, in Turin and subsequently in Milan, Florence and Rome. In Turin, the first act was successful, but the reception of the second was lukewarm. Verga did not attend the performance, and in a letter to De Roberto explained that his own behaviour had been held responsible for the failure of the play: his refusal to show himself on the stage after the well received first act had "chilled and vexed the public. But this sort of thing I neither desire, nor know how to do, and I am not going to change my attitude." The libretto which De Roberto had adapted from *La Lupa* was later used by the Sicilian composer Pierantonio Tasca, whose opera *La Lupa* was performed for the first time at Tasca's birthplace, Noto, in 1933.

For Verga the whole affair had turned into another disappointment. No one mentioned *I Malavoglia* any more; *Mastro-Don Gesualdo* was forgotten; "the only one of my works which still lives is *Cavalleria,* and this on account of Maestro Mascagni and not of me", he wrote bitterly.

In 1902 a new plan emerged, out of the blue, which offered another opportunity to annoy Messrs Sonzogno and Mascagni. Verga scrutinized it with welcome anticipation. Domenico Monleone, a composer of "pleasantly melodic vein", approached Verga for permission to write a new opera based on *Cavalleria*. Domenico's brother Giovanni was to write the libretto.

Anxious to be correct, Verga again asked the legal committee

*He had been arrested for disorderly behaviour, and poaching wild fowl during the close season. Later, a firearms offence had led to trouble.

of the Italian Society of Authors for their opinion, and put his own case as follows:

The first person to obtain his permission to set *Cavalleria* to music had been Stanislao Gastaldon. Later, the Mascagni version was produced, leading to disputes and litigation which were eventually settled. Now, a third operatic version was suggested. Verga considered himself entitled to give permission for this new work, just as he had given permission first to Gastaldon and later to Mascagni. Did the Society accept this view?

The Society agreed but suggested that Verga should obtain an indemnity agreement, and make it a condition of his permission that Monleone should bear the whole responsibility for any costs which might arise from possible legal action should Mascagni and Sonzogno choose to challenge this permission in court.

In due course the opera was composed. In order to take the bull by the horns, it was entered for the Sonzogno competition of 1905. It did not win a prize, but it was published by the music publisher A. Puccio. In view of the delicate legal situation, it was decided to perform the opera to begin with abroad, and in 1907 the work was given in Amsterdam, with encouraging success. It was even performed there as a *Cavalleria* double bill with Mascagni's *Cavalleria*, Maria Tensini Ternetti singing both Santuzzas. Performances in Budapest followed and tours of Germany and Austria were contemplated. In view of its success, it was decided to risk a performance in Italy, and in July 1907 Verga received a telegram from the Monleone brothers stating that, in spite of "mistrust", the new *Cavalleria* had scored a great success in Turin. This proved the signal for Mascagni and Sonzogno to go to court, alleging (i) unlawful imitation of the Targioni-Tozzetti and Menasci libretto by Giovanni Monleone, (ii) illegal and unfair competition by Domenico Monleone (the composer) and Puccio (the publisher), and (iii) illicit authorization by Verga.

Verga's case was that by the compromise of 1893 he had not divested himself of his author's rights. He felt, therefore, entitled to give his consent to Monleone in the same way as he had previously given it to Gastaldon, and later to Mascagni.

Sonzogno and Mascagni claimed that this was not so, and that the judgment of the original case had established Verga's co-authorship of the Mascagni opera. In support of their case of unfair competition, certain figures were submitted to show the great financial success the Mascagni opera had enjoyed from its very beginning.

The court's verdict was in favour of Mascagni and Sonzogno, and the Court of Appeal upheld the judgment.

However, the figures which had now been presented to the court in order to prove the immediate success of Mascagni's opera were quite different to the figures for the same period which Mascagni and Sonzogno had presented at the time of the original court case, and which had been the basis for the agreement of 1893.

The wilful distortions of the *Cavalleria* receipts at the time of the original court case had rankled with Verga ever since. Verga's lawyers, certain as they were of Sonzogno's dishonesty, maintained that it would be too difficult to prove the fraudulence in court. This difficulty had of course contributed to Verga's decision to accept a "once and for all compensation", the decision which he had had every reason to regret. Sonzogno had now "bitten the devil's tail"* and delivered the proof of his own crookedness into Verga's hands. Verga's solicitors felt that this could be used to prove that the agreement of 1893 had been obtained by fraud. A case against Sonzogno and Mascagni alleging fraud was accordingly prepared and submitted.

Meanwhile another disappointment arose. The payments due to Verga from the successful performances in Budapest were not forthcoming. The Monleone brothers attempted to evade their commitments, and claimed to be without funds. This attitude changed Verga's view of the whole affair and he now regretted that he had ever consented to a plan which had only added to his own troubles.

The unfavourable court judgment meant that the new opera could only be performed in countries which had no copyright agreement with Italy, and the Monleones arranged for performances in Constantinople. Verga did not approve of this and was anxious to dissociate himself completely from all further performances. He favoured the idea that Monleone's music should be used for a new opera altogether, to be based on Verga's short story, *Mistero*.**

Meanwhile the fraud case came before the court and led to a prolonged argument as to whether this was the type of fraud which should have been brought to the notice of the court within five years of being committed (if this were the case, the period of prescription had elapsed) or if it was the type of case which could be acted upon

*To bite the devil's tail is a popular Sicilian expression for giving away information potentially damaging to oneself.

**One of the stories from the *Novelle rusticane*. Monleone composed his opera "Il Mistero" in 1921. He died, 67 years old, in 1942.

within five years of the discovery of the fraud, in which case the outcome appeared more hopeful.

In the first judgment it was held that the period of prescription had expired, but an appeal against this decision offered hope for a reversal of the verdict. The appeal was to be heard in Rome, but for various reasons the hearing was adjourned again and again.

In spite of successful performances of Monleone's work in not less than 12 opera houses outside Italy, the payments still did not arrive. This led to further court actions, as the Monleones, while putting the profits into their own pockets, left Verga to pay the expenses of the case brought by Mascagni and Sonzogno, contrary to the indemnifying agreement. Verga now claimed his share of the profits, as well as a repayment of the costs which he had incurred as the result of Sonzogno's action. His case was successful, or partly successful, and in the autumn of 1911 he was awarded 5,900 lire, a disappointing sum which reimbursed him for only half of the costs already incurred. A further disadvantage of this judgment was that the court had found only Monleone liable, and had excluded the publisher Puccio from the responsibility for repaying Verga's expenses. Monleone had no means. Suddenly it dawned on Verga why this arrangement with Monleone had gone wrong, and indeed *had* to go wrong: Monleone was a *jettatore*, a man possessed of the evil eye. As a logical consequence of his discovery, Verga tried from now on to avoid writing Monleone's name in his correspondence, and referred to him as the *così detto*, the "so-called". When writing his name could not be avoided, it was followed by the sign of the "horned hand". The hand with the first and fourth fingers outstretched is a symbol generally used in Sicily to avert the power of the evil eye.* (see illus. 46 and 47).

New hope for a settlement came in sight when Monleone's situation was improved by his marrying a lady of means, but he was a *jettatore* and no good came of it: Signora Monleone managed to avoid any responsibility for the financial obligations of her husband.

The fraud case against Mascagni and Sonzogno and the litigation in conection with the Monleone opera dragged on for many years. Other court cases arose as well; Verga had to take proceedings against a film company which violated his copyright by producing a film version of *Cavalleria rusticana* for Sonzogno and Mascagni without his permission. Some court actions were still pending when Italy's

*Verga's drawings are faulty as they make the hand to appear to have six fingers.

ATTO UNICO [1]

La scena rappresenta una piazza in un paese della Sicilia. — Nel fondo, a destra, Chiesa con porta praticabile. — A sinistra l'osteria e la casa di Mamma Lucia. — È il giorno di Pasqua.

(A sipario calato.)

TURIDDU.

O Lola c'hai di latti la cammisa
si bianca e russa comu la cirasa,
quannu t'affacci fai la vucca a risa,
biatu pi lu primu cu ti vasa!
Ntra la puorta tua lu sangu è spasu,
ma nun me mpuorta si ce muoru accisu...
e si ce muoru e vaju 'n paradisu
si nun ce truovo a ttia, mancu ce trasu.

(Traduzione.)

O Lola, bianca come fior di spino,
quando t'affacci tu, s'affaccia il sole;
chi t'ha baciato il labbro porporino
grazia più bella a Dio chieder non vòle.
C'è scritto sangue sopra la tua porta,
ma di restarci a me non me n'importa;
se per te mojo e vado in paradiso,
non c'entro se non vedo il tuo bel viso.

SCENA PRIMA.

Coro.

DONNE *(di dentro).*

Gli aranci olezzano	tempo è si mormori
sui verdi margini,	da ognuno il tenero
cantan le allodole	canto che i palpiti
tra i mirti in fior;	raddoppia al cor.

UOMINI *(di dentro).*

In mezzo al campo tra le spiche d'oro
giunge il rumore delle vostre spole;
noi stanchi riposando dal lavoro
a voi pensiamo, o belle occhi-di-sole.
O belle occhi-di-sole, a voi corriamo,
come vola l'augello al suo richiamo.
(Il coro entra in iscena.)

DONNE.

Cessin le rustiche	tempo è si mormori
opre: la Vergine	da ognuno il tenero
serena allietasi	canto che i palpiti
del Salvator;	raddoppia al cor.

UOMINI.

In mezzo al campo tra le spiche d'oro
giunge il rumore, ecc., ecc.
(Il coro traversa la scena ed esce.)

SCENA II.

Santuzza *e* **Lucia**.

SANTUZZA *(entrando).*

Dite, mamma Lucia..

LUCIA *(sorpresa).*

Sei tu?... che vuoi?

SANTUZZA.

Turiddu ov'è?

LUCIA.

Fin qui vieni a cercare
il figlio mio?

SANTUZZA.

Voglio saper soltanto,
perdonatemi voi, dove trovarlo.

LUCIA.

Non lo so, non lo so, non voglio brighe!

[1] Il presente melodramma è tolto dalle Scene Popolari omonime di G. Verga.

45   Raference to Verga's name in the score was made in rediculously small lettering and reduced to a mere footnote (p. 190)

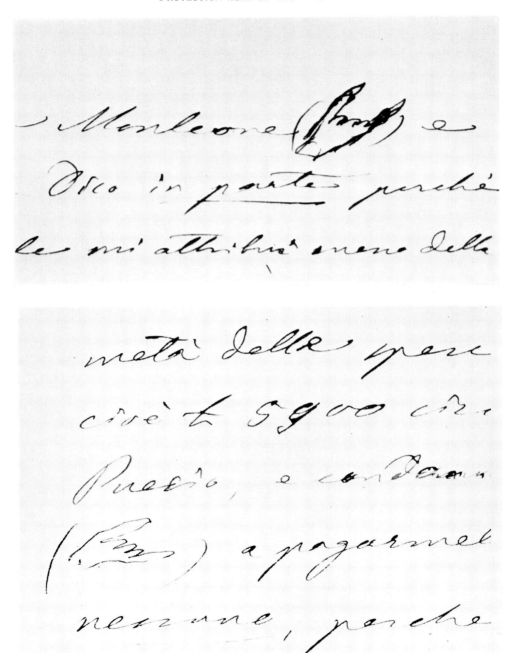

46 and 47   Monleone's name (in a letter to Dina) followed by the sign of the horned hand (p. 196)
Faultily drawn, it suggests six fingers

entry in the 1914 war caused a great slowing down of all litigation. When the war ended, Verga was 76, and felt too old and tired to fight on. He preferred, or felt forced, to let things "go to the devil". The last reference to the *Cavalleria* litigation is contained in a letter of 19th September, 1919, from Catania, when the 79-year-old Verga wrote to his brother Mario: "The *Giornale dell'Isola*'s announcement of my victory in the case against Mascagni and Sonzogno regarding the film version of *Cavalleria* only means an increase in my death duties, I'm afraid."

Twenty-eight years had elapsed since the first court actions in 1891! It is not surprising that it was believed by some who were not familiar with the full facts that Verga had degenerated into a quarrelsome old man who engaged in court cases for his enjoyment and pursued them fanatically to the exclusion of more important activities.

This line of thought is unfair. If the court cases are viewed in perspective, there can be no doubt that the first action against Sonzogno and Mascagni was necessary. Verga had been treated very badly; not only would it have been a grave mistake on his part, it would have been contrary to the interest of all Italian writers not to have brought this action.

However, the agreement he was forced into in 1893 carried within it the seeds of future troubles and the case regarding the Monleone opera sprang from this agreement. Verga's grudge against Mascagni and Sonzogno was so bitter and deep-seated that he probably gave Monleone his permission against his own better judgment, merely as a means to annoy the two men he despised and hated. That Verga consulted the Society of Authors beforehand shows that he wished to avoid, and not to precipitate, court action. The fact that the opinion of the Society of Authors proved wrong was for Verga as unpleasant as unexpected. The Society's expertise gave him a false sense of security, and he could not foresee that the indemnity agreement would prove useless. That Monleone, in spite of a limited financial success of his opera, would be unable or unwilling to pay, was also unexpected: it is almost tempting to accept Monleone's evil eye, Verga's own explanation for all these calamities, as the correct one!

This leaves the fraud case against Sonzogno to be considered. The prescribed time limit for such actions must have appeared as a formidable obstacle. However, a difference of opinion as to whether the limit of prescription was to begin with the commission or with the discovery of the fraud, was quite legitimate. Furthermore, the prospect of seeing Sonzogno and Mascagni convicted of fraud, even if only morally, was a temptation which Verga, in spite of the 14 years which had passed since the agreement, simply could not resist.

The court case regarding the film rights (which Verga won) was straightforward. The actions he had to bring in connection with the family property, too, were not engendered by pathological lust for lawsuits. These actions certainly wasted time; much thought, planning and travelling became necessary in connection with them, but Verga's personal involvement in them was very limited.

To sum up, the explanation that Verga ceased to write because of the pressure of incessant court actions is not acceptable, particularly as, in fact, he did not entirely cease to write. He still wrote short stories and plays, he adapted his works for the theatre, and helped friends with translations from the French. But his main artistic ambition, the five part cycle of the doomed: that he did not pursue.

ADMINISTRATIVE DIFFICULTIES

An alleged preoccupation with financial matters affecting family interests is another reason frequently given to explain Verga's withdrawal from major literary work. The preservation of the estate and the upbringing of his brother's children, had become his duty as the result of special circumstances. His sister Rosa had died, unmarried, in 1878, the year before the death of their mother.* His brother Pietro, widowed in 1896, died in the spring of 1903. Verga was appointed legal guardian of Pietro's three children and took his duties connected with their education and their property very seriously. As his brother Pietro had been "easily influenced and had put too much trust in some people who did not deserve it", these duties brought some unpleasantness and legal actions in their wake. With the help of Salvatore Paolo, Verga recovered certain sums for his nephews.

The need to collect the rentals for land which was let to tenants was irksome, but with occasional help from his brother Mario, and later with the help of his nephew Giovannino, he managed to keep things going. The main administrative problem was the *agrumeto* (orange and lemon orchard) at Novalucello. The merchants and

---

*His other sister, Teresa, had caused a good deal of worry. After the death of their mother she married, against the wishes of the family, Enrico Felice, a Maltese port interpreter. The couple's financial circumstances, particularly after the birth of a daughter, were precarious, and Verga was repeatedly called upon to help.

exporters he had to deal with he regarded as a "punishment of God".
In 1908 he wrote:

"I have carried Novalucello on my back for six years and it was not an
easy thing to put it in order. But now I think we have got there—or at
least I hope so, for the sake of us all. The greatest sacrifice was my novel
[*The Duchess of Leyra*], on which I could only work by fits and starts.
Literature? I know all about that, worse luck. And I think it is more
honest to live the hand-to-mouth existence of a market gardener . . . "

Again, the affairs of farm and estate were bound to waste time,
but cannot explain the aversion to writing.

FINANCIAL PROBLEMS

Money troubles had beset Verga all his life, and had not prevented him from writing his masterpieces. They had interrupted his
work and necessitated journeys, but never prevented him resuming
work as soon as the emergency had passed. While writing *Mastro-Don
Gesualdo,* for example, Verga had, together with his brother Mario,
to visit London.

The visit was necessitated by an inheritance. Don Salvatore
Verga (see p. 30), a knowledgeable coin collector, had died at the
end of 1880, and left a collection of 800 greco-siculic silver and gold
coins to his son-in-law and nephew Mario. The director of the
museum at Syracuse, Targia, was asked for advice. He held that some
of the coins were valuable, and should be taken to London.

A family friend, Tommaso Catalina, was serving as a Secretary
at the Italian Embassy, and photographs of the coins were sent to
him. He submitted them to Messrs Sotheby,* who wrote on 15th
November, 1881:

"We have examined the photographs of coins you were good enough
to submit to us. We should say the coins must be good, but it is impossible
to form any judgment as to value from mere photographs.

"We would recommend the owner of the collection to let us have it
to catalogue in a proper manner and in due time to bring forward for
sale. It would be sure to reach its full value.

"Yours very truly,

"Sotheby, Wilkinson & Hodge."

Meanwhile, the photographs were sent to experts at the British
Museum. Good offers were made for some of the coins but Verga
and his brother thought it best to sell the collection as a whole. Mr.

*Then Sotheby, Wilkinson and Hodge of 13 Wellington Street, Strand.

Reginald Poole* offered £819 for the pieces of interest to the British Museum, but thought that the collection might bring £1,550 if sold "piece by piece".

It seemed clearly necessary to take all the coins to London. Armed with one of the latest guidebooks, the *Londres en poche et ses environs (Guide Conty)* of 1881—still to be found in Verga's library —and with a room reserved at the Hotel Dieudonné in Ryder Street, the two brothers arrived. Their guidebook had warned them against arrival on Sundays:

"Sunday is a woeful day for the strangers whom one can see wandering from park to park and from church to church. On Sundays everything is suspended in that *grande machine britannique.*

"England's physiognomy, generally cold, seems even more chilling on that day. One feels as if under a very dark cloud. But true disaster overtakes you if you arrive on Sunday by the Thames: without pity, and without any respect for hospitality, the customs officer will impound your luggage till the next day."

The visit to London did not prove very enjoyable. Verga annoyed a London policeman, an experience which cast a shadow over his stay. He wrote to Capuana that no doubt there was "real greatness" in London, but it was difficult to find it in the "immensity" of the city.

"I have seen all I could, I have almost broken my legs and my back in the process—and tomorrow I leave with a sigh of relief . . . If I had to document my impressions, I would have to write a whole book; mere impressions are difficult to justify. You must, for instance, know that here one must *not* pass one's water, or at least it is severely forbidden to unbutton one's trousers and to perform any act or movement that would betray that one had yielded to a small but pressing need. All well and good if public morality were really as strong as all that!

"But . . . at night under the very eyes of the police you can see girls of ten to twelve years offering themselves . . . (Ah, if you were here, you bald old sinner!), and then there are religious societies of men and women (mixed!) who carry blue banners, sing psalms in the parks, and preach one after the other in public!"

Cattaneo feels that this letter shows the narrow-mindedness of an Italian traveller, "indifferent to the fascination of Victorian London and incapable of perceiving the greatness of an empire which Disraeli and Gladstone had then brought to its greatest splendour".

*Keeper of the Department of coins and medals 1870-93.

He maintains that Verga's moralizing assumes a comic Sicilian colouring, and is in reality not in the least based on religious motives, but only on the difficulties of finding a "lonely corner" out of sight of policemen.

However, the purpose of the journey was achieved: London had lived up to its reputation as the world's art market, and Mario Verga and his brother sold the collection for £1,200 at the Holborn Town Hall in Gray's Inn Road—to a virtual neighbour!*

Within a very short time Verga was back at work. As on this occasion, the need to cope with financial problems never seriously interfered with his work while he was still keen to write.

VERGA AND POLITICS

This leaves the assumption that his participation in political issues, his active membership of his club, and a gradual envelopment by the sleepy life of a provincial town had led to his literary sterility.

The Circolo Unione in the Via Stesicoro-Etna, where Verga and De Roberto generally played cards in the evening, was harmless enough. Verga had indulged in the habit of the evening card game even at the period of his greatest productivity as a writer, except that his evenings were then spent at the Caffè Cova in Milan, instead of the Unione Club at Catania. The social life of the provincial town had never been a temptation to him. Increasingly aloof and reserved, social pursuits never occupied his time, even if he occasionally saw a few friends besides De Roberto and Salvatore Paola.

His interest in public affairs and politics was spasmodic and never led persistently to time-consuming political interest. Several examples, which at the same time demonstrate his exaggerated fears for Italian unity, can be given.

On 1st March, 1896, the Prime Minister, Crispi's, Abyssinian venture had ended with the calamity of Adowa and the loss of many lives, among them the brother of a beloved friend (see p. 212). Crispi was forced to resign, and the people of Milan demonstrated against the war. Verga, together with many others, believed that the catastrophe was at least in part caused by the bad quality and insufficient quantity of the materials of war, and that the soldiers had been let down by the profiteers. The demonstrations in Milan continued for five days. Verga wrongly saw them as a danger to the new

---

*The Italian dealer Alessandro Castellani. The best pieces of the collection eventually found their way into a Brussels museum.

national unity, and this caused him to show a lack of sympathy for the attitude of the Milanese, which to him appeared cowardly. Although Rome was the capital, the people of Milan thought of their own town as the *capitale morale*. In a letter to a publisher, Verga referred to Milan as the *"capitale morale del Canton Ticino"* (see p. 56). This showed neither tact, nor respect for Swiss principles, but it does not, as alleged, show Verga as a pre-fascist national interventionist.

1897, the following year, was a year of more disasters. The bad harvest led to price increases, and to unrest which in 1898 became even more violent. In Milan—on the whole little affected by the economic circumstances—it was demonstrations against the murder of the son of a radical member of Parliament that led in May 1898 to bloody clashes with the military. The repression of those demonstrations by the army under General Bava Beccaris was unpardonably severe. Verga was critical of the government's actions, but refused to sign a protest against the excesses of the repression which Cesare Lombroso* was keen to organize, because he saw in every social agitation a potential danger to Italy's national unity.

The earthquake which destroyed Messina and Reggio di Calabria in December 1908 was one of the worst disasters the world had as yet known. A flotilla of British destroyers brought the first outside help to Sicily. Aid from the Italian mainland was much delayed, and severe mismanagement tragically complicated all assistance. An unnecessary declaration of martial law precluded unauthorized help, and caused the Greek steamer *Sfakteria,* which carried medicines and provisions, to be denied a safe conduct. The antagonism of the various authorities resulted in their working against one another. Thousands of wounded, who were buried under the débris, were left to their fate, while available manpower was used to recover money and jewellery from the strong-room of the Bank of Italy. Homeless people were mistaken for looters and shot. The so-called "detailed plan of action" existed on paper only; in reality, there was a complete breakdown of services, and telegrams took five days to deliver. The Prime Minister failed to visit the disaster area and, weeks later, the homeless were still without shelter.

Almost all newspapers condemned the government. Many Sicilians expressed personal criticism of the government's conduct.

---

*Cesare Lombroso (1836-1909) was the man who established the function of psychiatry in legal proceedings.

Two of Verga's closest friends, Luigi Capuana and Federico De Roberto, both joined in the public criticism, but Verga's ever-present fear that Italy could fall apart again prevented him from adding his name.

Verga's feeling is perhaps easier to understand if one bears in mind that Italian unity had only been achieved when Verga was already grown-up, and that the danger of a secession of Sicily, possibly followed by a disruption of Italy, seemed always to be latent. It made some of Verga's utterances appear more reactionary than they were meant to be, and this was exploited by the biographers of the Fascist era.

One of the remarks of Verga's which made the Fascists claim him as a spiritual precursor was his wish that the Italian fleet "should bombard the coast of the United States". This nonsense, an exaggerated reaction to an injustice, and an outlet for acute grief, was interpreted as the expression of his staunch "nationalism". What had led Verga to make this odd remark was the New Orleans lynching which followed the murder of David Hennessy.

David Hennessy, the Irish-born chief of police of New Orleans, was engaged in energetic crime eradication when he was murdered in October 1890. A criminal organisation which included people of Italian descent, the so-called *Stoppaghera,* had caused trouble: about a dozen people, mostly of Italian origin, were arrested and charged as accomplices to the murder. Six of these had been found innocent and the jury ordered their discharge. Dissatisfied with this decision, a crowd led by "well-known New Orleans citizens" broke into the jail and murdered 11 Italians.

This had understandable repercussions in Italy : not only had the connection of the murdered Italians with Hennessy's death not been proved, but several of the lynched were held on different charges altogether. In Italy the lynching was seen as a manifestation of the American belief that the last immigrant is always wrong, and the last immigrant at that time was Italian. The Italian fleet was quenching a rebellion in Crete; according to Verga, bombarding the American coast would have been better than shooting a few poor rebels. Verga's pathetic and anguished notion was more than 50 years later used by the Fascists as a proof of his warlike spirit, to extenuate their own obvious hubris in declaring war against the United States.

None of these events could have preoccupied Verga to any great extent. In fact, it seems incontestable that his reluctance to write is not explained by his court cases, nor by his family and estate interests, nor by his occasional involvement in political issues.

Only one theory can explain it and this is that Verga suffered from clinical depression. His permanent "state of grief", of which there is ample evidence, cannot possibly be regarded as psychiatrically normal. It was brought about by the failure of his books and was aggravated by the unfortunate *Cavalleria* experience, the hapless Monleone episode, and perhaps also by his permanent financial difficulties, family misfortunes and other disappointments. This state of grief did not admit of the mood and effort which is required for sustained creative writing. It caused a definite mental affection, diagnosable—if only in retrospect—as a "reactive depression", which is caused by severe disappointment in anyone predisposed to melancholic reactions. It was not an anxiety state.

"Anxious thoughts occur in depression, and depressive thoughts in anxiety, but the two disturbances are fundamentally different from each other. The depressed patient is like a prisoner who has accepted his doom. He knows or assumes that there is no escape; unconsciously he even longs for the end. He fears it, but his muscles do not quiver, his heart does not beat fast and his throat does not choke. He feels empty and dead inside."*

The above description tallies with the clinical picture which, by all accounts, Verga presented. Fifty years after his death this suggestion, which has not previously been made, is not easy to prove. However, proof for it can be attempted as the result of the recent publication of what is in effect a most interesting psychological case history, and altogether a remarkable and extraordinary document: the *Letters to Dina*.**

Sufficient relevant information about Verga's depression was of course accessible prior to this publication, but, surprisingly, the obvious conclusions were never drawn. A report by the journalist Ugo Ojetti,*** for example, dating from 1894, gives a characteristic

---

*L. Alexander, *Treatment of mental disorder*. W. B. Saunders and Co., Philadelphia and London, 1953.

**Giovanni Verga, *Lettere a Dina* (ed. by Gino Raya), Ciranna, Rome, 1962.

***Ugo Ojetti, *Cose viste*, as quoted in Nino Cappellani, *Vita di Giovanni Verga*, *Le Monnier*, Florence, 1940.

description of such symptoms. Ojetti wrote thus about a "discussion" which took place in a Milan coffee house:

"It was almost impossible to make him talk. Pozza said, 'For years I have tried and have asked him whether he likes Mascagni's *Cavalleria,* but he does not reply.' Rovetta said, 'Is it possible that the author of *Cavalleria rusticana* has never heard Mascagni's *Cavalleria*?' Verga looked at him, smiled a little, licked his moustache, took a little sip as if to avoid words—and was silent."

Gradually, though inexorably, his depression deepened, and his attitude of withdrawal changed to one of complete and almost impenetrable retrenchment.

CHAPTER X

LOVE, AND RETRENCHMENT

LOVE, AND RETRENCHMENT

W HEN Verga visited Rome he always stayed at the Hotel
Milan because it was a "first-class place with prices consider-
ably lower than the luxury group". There, in 1881, he met
Brucco, Count of Sordevolo, and his wife, Francesca Giovanna
Annunziata née Castelazzi. The Count was an ageing man; the
Countess was twenty-one,* and twenty years younger than Verga.

One must assume that the relationship between Verga and
"Dina", as the Countess was called, became adulterous almost at once,
though, for obvious reasons, no letters survive from that period of
their relationship during which the Count was alive. Neither her
age nor her marriage proved a hindrance, nor was Verga disturbed by
the fact that those were the years of his professed love for Giselda
Fojanesi-Rapisardi and of his adulterous relationship with Paolina,
Countess Greppi—as well as of other affairs.

Verga's personality was attractive to women, and he had many
a chance to get married had he wished to do so. Possibly under the
influence of his frequent wish to be alone, he must have decided
early on in life that a sexual relationship with a married woman
provided the ideal companionship. His attitude to marriage is already
on record in a letter to Edouard Rod,** who had married his Mlle
Gonin in 1882, and visited Italy on his honeymoon. Rod thanked
Verga for having been graciously entertained, and assured him that
the married state was thoroughly to be recommended. Verga replied:

"I shall never get married, my dear Rod, but if anything could make
me doubt the wisdom of this determination it is the evidence of your
domestic happiness, which I sincerely hope for you will continue
forever."

It is characteristic that when Countess Dina, after their relationship had gone on for more than ten years, became a widow in 1891,
she received a letter from Verga which showed "so little affection

*Born on 25th March, 1860.

**The date of the letter is 31.12.1882. Giovanni Verga, *Lettere al suo
traduttore* (ed. Fredi Chiappelli), Le Monnier, Florence, 1954.

for her" that she, hurt and offended, returned the letter to him and refused to see him for two years.

Their correspondence was resumed in February 1893—within a few days of the agreement in the *Cavalleria* case. The Countess wrote and complained that she had seen him and that he had failed to greet her. He replied immediately:

"I did not recognize you for the simple reason that I did not see you, but I am so glad that *you did* see me, after, alas, so long a time! I do know that with those eyes of yours you can do all sorts of things! Of course, I shall be delighted to meet you and, if possible, even before the ball [the *veglione,* a masked ball in the Scala building], where you are bound to be so in demand that one will have a job to get anywhere near you! However, I doubt whether my letter will reach you! Surely 15 Via Brera is the front gate of the Military Command? Are you commanding the Division now? And why do you write to me at Via di Barnaba, where I have never lived? I am at the Hotel Continental, and am always yours,

Verga."

This is the first of a series of letters which forms a unique documentation of an unusual relationship. Both parties were now free to marry, and this is no doubt what the Countess fervently desired. However, at first Verga was too disinclined to give up his accustomed freedom—he was at the time of the first letter fifty-three years old—and later too depressed, and too anxious for solitude, to contemplate living with anyone, in particular with Dina; fond as he undoubtedly was of her, he found her at times trying and even exasperating. Dina tried her best to make him understand her point of view; at one stage she came perilously close to confronting him with the choice of marriage or a complete break. However, to the credit of her good sense, she did not persist with this demand, once she realized his unalterable determination to remain alone. Wisely, she regarded the continuation of her friendship with Verga, even if she saw him later only very occasionally, as preferable to complete loneliness.

Such were the circumstances that produced this remarkable chronicle of 30 years of the life of a great writer. In the full intimacy of expression which springs from a well established and happy sexual relationship, Verga wrote to Dina 687 letters within 29 years, an average of a letter every fortnight. The letters give an uncommon insight into his life and thoughts. So prolonged and frank an exchange of views and news as this would normally only occur with a married couple, but in that case conversation would replace some, if not most, of the correspondence. Verga and the Countess, however, always lived apart and only spent occasional holidays together. His home was in Catania and the Countess' home was first in Milan, and later in Rome.

For many years Verga had supported Dina financially; after his death the Countess' circumstances deteriorated critically. In September 1938, 16 years after Verga's death, when she was 78 years old, she entered the House of the Daughters of San Camillo in Rome. She paid—at least at the beginning—20 lire a month. Outliving Verga by 23 years, she died there at the age of 85 on 7th May, 1945.

In March 1940, the 80-year-old Countess had written to Italy's Minister of Education:

"I find myself in such dire straits that I have to resort to the only way out of my difficulties which I can possibly think of, and that is to sell the 687 letters addressed to me by our poor, great, and lamented Giovanni Verga. It was a correspondence which continued for 30 years, and lasted up to the time of his death."

This transaction was concluded three years later—for 5,000 lire.* Before parting with them, the Countess cut off the postage stamps, added a few explanations, and destroyed several pages, probably of erotic content.

The letters she had written herself were destroyed by Verga upon their receipt. His nephew, Giovanni, recalls that one day, while assisting his uncle with some correspondence, a letter from the Countess had found its way in among the business letters, and he began to read it. As soon as Verga became aware of this, he got hold of the letter with every sign of annoyance, and immediately destroyed it.

Only two of the Countess' letters survive. One of them, written in anxiety upon hearing the news of an earthquake near Catania (see p. 229), shows a highly strung and rather exaggerated reaction. As if in compensation, the second of the two surviving letters is beautifully written, and reveals a deeply moving but restrained disappointment: it is the letter of a remarkable woman, a gracious reply to the cruel friend who, in his mood of despair and his longing for solitude, finally refused her offer to visit him after she had not seen him for ten years!

Most of the letters were first published in 1962 by Gino Raya.

*The receipt is dated 11th February, 1943. Three years later, on 8th June, 1946, the letters were removed to their permanent home, the library of Catania University.

who had edited them* with care and annotated them with painstaking scholarship. They are important not only as a day-to-day account of his life, but because they change posterity's picture of Verga, and enable us to understand and judge his personality much better than before. They also provide the answer to the vexed problem of his protracted silence, and are in their own right a relevant medical history of a case of reactive, progressive depression. Regrettably, the publication of the letters raised legal problems and in fact caused litigation.

A resumption of the intimate contact between Verga and Dina was safely re-established within a month of her first letter. They met regularly. A short note suggests that at the hour which she had indicated (3 p.m.) she is to walk past his hotel, where he will wait for her (if the weather is not too bad!). He wishes her all the best for her "coming battle."

The "battle" was one of the Countess's piano and song recitals. Dina, apart from being a gifted painter of miniatures, was also a talented singer and musician, and attempted a concert career. In June 1896, she gave a recital in London and the envelope of Verga's letter gives her address as "Chez Mme Theodorus, 45 Colville Gardens, Bayswater, W.1." He wrote to her:

"Yours is a bold venture for which I wish you all success, but to make a place for oneself in London amid such a crowd of competitors is a difficult job . . . How did the concert go? What do they suggest to you? London is so big, and so far away from us in all respects!"

In the same letter he reports that Ersilia, his sister-in-law (his brother Pietro's wife), was seriously ill:

"My house has become an inferno—with three small children—the youngest hardly two years old. Can you imagine me, surrounded by a worrying family? Me, who have always kept clear of it until now!"

Depressive utterances recur frequently. "I don't work, I can't do anything, I am finished" (August 1896). In order to "flee from the black clouds" and to "escape", he declares that he has resumed work on the *Duchess of Leyra,* and finds that the words *"ars consolatrix"* are true.

Dina's only brother, a young officer, lost his life in the Adowa

*521 letters (*Lettere a Dina*). The remaining 166 letters had been mislaid and were not available at the time. A complete edition has since been published by Gino Raya under the title Giovanni Verga. *Lettere d'Amore,* Tindalo, Rome, 1970.

48　Dina, Countess Sordevolo (a photograph probably taken by Verga)

49 Mario Verga and his wife leaving the farmhouse at Tiepidi (taken by Verga)

50 Mario and Lidda Verga with Verga's orphaned nephew, Giovannino (p.213), (taken by Verga)

Turiddu: Did you do that on purpose?

Santuzza: Yes, I did it on purpose.

Turiddu: By the blood of Judas!

Santuzza: Well, go on; kill me!

Turiddu: You did it on purpose! You did it on purpose!

Santuzza: Go on, kill me—I don't mind.

Turiddu: I don't even want to kill you now!

He turns to go.

Santuzza: You are leaving me?

Turiddu: Yes, that's what you deserve.

The elevation bell sounds from the church.

Santuzza: Don't leave me, Turiddu! Can't you hear that bell ringing?

Turiddu: I don't want to be led by the nose. Do you understand?

Santuzza: Do what you like with me, beat me, kick me. I'll take anything from you. But not from her.

Turiddu: Let's finish. I'm having no more of these scenes. I'm going.

Santuzza: Where are you going?

Turiddu: Where I want to—to Mass.

Santuzza: No, you just go to church to show Lola that you have left me for her sake. To show her that I don't matter to you.

Turiddu: You are mad.

Santuzza: You must not go, Turiddu. You must not go to church to-day in order to commit a sin. Don't insult me like that in front of that woman.

Turiddu: It's you who do the insulting. You want to show everybody that I mustn't go anywhere without you—that you keep me tied to your apron strings like a little boy.

Santuzza: What does it matter to you, what she says? Do you really want me to die in despair?

Turiddu: You are mad.

Santuzza: Yes—it's true—I am mad. But don't leave me alone with this madness in my head.

Turiddu: (*tearing himself away from her*) Let's finish it all. To hell with it.

Santuzza: Turiddu—for the sake of our Lord—who now descends into the consecrated host—you must not leave me for her.

Turiddu goes.

Ah! Curse your Easter!

CAVALLERIA MUSICATA

CAVALLERIA MUSICATA

ALTHOUGH there was always a piano in his *salotto,* music did not play an important role in Verga's home life nor did he play a musical instrument. The first musical influence of any importance reached him through the composer Giuseppe Perrotta, whose parents owned a villa at Sant'Agata li Battiati, and had become friends of the family (see p. 51).

Verga's novels contain many references to music. The heroine of the *Peccatrice,* for example, is an accomplished pianist who at night plays the "Kiss" waltz by Arditi "deliriously". In the drawing-rooms of Florence, Verga's musical education progressed appreciably. He attended musical soirées in the houses of friends, where Mozart, Beethoven and Chopin, as well as the romantic music of Germany could be heard: when he wrote *Eros* in 1874 his piano-playing heroines no longer played Arditi's *Il Bacio,* but Schubert and Liszt.

In Milan, he could often be seen at La Scala, immaculately attired in his *marsina,* the morning coat, and in the company of his elegant friends. His musical understanding had by that time progressed so far that he became a convinced Wagnerian. He attended Milan's disastrous *Lohengrin* première, and the bon mot is attributed to him that *Lohengrin* "in disclosing where he came from, also told the musicians of Italy where to go to". By the time, therefore, that he expressed his wishes for music for *Cavalleria rusticana* he must at least have been a very interested and well-educated listener.

Verga expressed these wishes in a letter to his friend Perrotta two months after its first performance. His ideas were surprisingly predictive. He asked for:

"a piece for small orchestra to introduce the play, a sort of short overture and musical recapitulation of its contents, to be played before the curtain rises. It should be simple, clear and effective, well attuned to the subject without being too intricate or difficult, and should breathe the true spirit of Sicily and of rural life.

"The sound of a love song in the night, the longing of Turiddu singing under Lola's window, and the lament of Santuzza who waits in vain for him. Life in the village coming awake, the church bells which summon to the mass. A note of jealousy, and of that love which returns and persists and forms the basis of it all. Finally the frantic outburst of jealous fury, the scream for help, and the outcry of the mother and the beloved."

Perrotta composed the overture as requested and Verga liked it. However, it was considered too difficult for the public to understand, and for the available orchestra to play, and so was not used. This rejection hurt the over-sensitive composer, to whom Capuana had once felt compelled to write:

"You really ought to learn a lesson from Giovanni [i.e. Verga] and me: if the two of us had been discouraged by every difficulty in our way, we would by now have forgotten how to read and write! The future belongs to those who persevere!"

The advice had had no effect, and, to Verga's regret, Perrotta remained so discouraged that he abandoned the idea of writing any further pieces of operatic music for *Cavalleria*.*

A different possibility soon presented itself. The composer Stanislao Gastaldon approached Verga for permission to use *Cavalleria* for an opera with a libretto to be written by Bartocci Fontana. Before giving his permission. Verga asked to see the libretto. It was not to his liking but nevertheless on 3rd June, 1888, he wrote to Bartocci Fontana as follows:

"I welcome your desire to use my *Cavalleria rusticana* as basis for an operatic libretto. I must, however, tell you—in absolute frankness—that in the way you have used it, this subject does not seem to me to lend itself to musical drama. However, I do not want to make my own view a reason for a refusal, and I am quite willing to let you use my play, and shall be pleased if you find within it what you hope to achieve. Yours sincerely, G.V."

The opera was published by Ricordi and performed in 1888 under the title *Mala Pasqua (A Bad Easter)*. It was not a success, but the opera's failure** in no way affected the fortunes of Verga's play, which was continuously performed for several years, and given in practically every town in Italy. Generally it was very successful, though it failed in (Austrian) Trieste. It significantly influenced Italian

*Perrotta's *Cavalleria* overture was first performed in Catania in 1906. In 1910 he committed suicide during a phase of deep depression (see p. 225).

**Its only surviving piece is a serenade, later revived by the tenor Benjamino Gigli under the title of *Musica proibita (Forbidden Music)*.

theatrical writing and acting, and its title became a household word.

On 19th February, 1890, Verga received a letter:

"Milan, 15th February

"Three or four years ago—I cannot really remember—I approached you with the request to grant permission to a composer, a friend of mine, to set your wonderful *Cavalleria rusticana* to music, and with great courtesy you granted this request.

"However, the composer—I do not know why, but rather believe for reasons of health—gave up the idea. Now another friend of mine, a young man of great promise, who is competing for the current Sonzogno prize, has asked me for the same favour.

"I replied that I felt as if I already had your permission, as I was sure that you would grant it to me again.

"Afterwards, plagued by various vicissitudes, among them a long and grave illness, I forgot about writing to you until my friend a few days ago wrote that he was in fact competing with an opera on the subject of *Cavalleria* and that your formal permission was therefore urgently required. I now appeal to you on his behalf to be kind enough to grant him this great desire—a desire in which I sincerely join him.

"The name of my friend is Pietro Mascagni and he is conducting in Cerignola. If you—to save time—could write to him direct, I would be very grateful.

"With the expression of sincere gratitude and respect,

I am yours, etc.,

Gni. Salvestri."

Quite justifiably Verga regarded this letter as an impertinence. Verga had known Salvestri, rather vaguely, in Turin in 1884 (see p. 126). He had spoken to him once or twice, but had no recollection whatsoever of ever having seriously discussed with him, not to mention consented to, a musical adaptation of *Cavalleria rusticana.* His annoyance increased greatly when, three days later, on 22nd February, he learned from the newspapers that an opera entitled *Cavalleria rusticana,* shortlisted from 73 entries, was to be played (see p. 148) within the framework of the Sonzogno competition in Rome, on 25th February. Apart from Salvestri's letter, Verga knew nothing about this work. He had heard neither from the composer, nor from the man who had adapted the words.

How could such an extraordinary situation have arisen?

Pietro Mascagni, born in Livorno on 7th December, 1863, was Verga's junior by 23 years. His father, Domenico, was a baker.*

---

*He came from S. Miniato al Tedesco, 25 miles from Livorno on the road to Florence. The mother, Emilia, née Rebua, was Livornese.

Pietro's great musical gifts became obvious early on, while he was a choir-boy at the church of S. Luigi Gonzaga.

His story follows a familiar pattern: father's unwillingness to let young Pietro take up music; intercession by a local nobleman, Count Florestan de Larderel (to whom the composer later dedicated *Cavalleria*); the interest of a generous uncle, Stefano Mascagni, who made himself responsible for the costs of his nephew's musical education.

The first compositions of the 15-year-old Mascagni were pieces of church music. A symphony for piano and orchestra followed a year later. At 18, he wrote *In Filanda* (*In the Spinning Mill*) for chorus and orchestra, and submitted the work to the musical competition connected with the 1881 Exhibition in Milan. Wisely as well as characteristically, he dedicated the work to the composer Amilcare Ponchielli, head of the Milan Conservatoire, where he hoped to study. The work won an honourable mention, first class. A later composition also deserves mention. His cantata *Alla Gioia* (1882) resulted from a performance of Beethoven's Ninth Symphony (the choral) which he attended in Livorno. Exhilarated by the great work, he sat down when he returned home and composed his own version of Schiller's *Ode an die Freude*.

Later in the same year (12th October, 1882) he successfully passed the difficult entrance examination to the Conservatoire of Milan. This was the examination Verdi had failed, and by doing so has made the "Conservatorio Giuseppe Verdi" the only scholastic institution in the world which is named after a would-be pupil who failed to gain admission.*

The course at the Conservatoire was exacting: it lasted four years, and was interspersed with stiff examinations. The successful graduate won the right to use the title *Maestro*.

At the Conservatoire, Mascagni met Puccini, who was his senior by five years. They soon struck up a friendship and even shared a room for a while. Mascagni was a competent double-bass player, an accomplishment he had acquired in record time, and which he put to use by playing in the orchestra of the *Teatro dal Verme* for three lire a night. It is said that Puccini's and Mascagni's style of

*Carlo Gatti (see p. 62) claims that Verdi was a pupil of the Conservatoire after all, and bases this claim on the following extraordinary reasoning: as he was not accepted, Verdi was forced to take private lessons. Among his teachers was one Vincenzo Lavigna, who also taught at the Conservatoire, and *"La questione delle mura non ha importanza sostanziale"*: "the question of the walls has no real importance".

living and their resourcefulness in dealing with creditors is echoed in the first act of *La Bohème*.*

Between the two friends there was, however, one fundamental difference. Puccini was a first-class pupil, and in every respect a serious student who, during his final year, was not only the star pupil of Ponchielli's composition class (see p. 61), but of the whole institution. Mascagni too possessed without any doubt whatsoever the musical gifts necessary to stay the course, but lacked the application to do so. He attended the Conservatoire for little more than the academic year of 1882/3. Early in his second year, in February 1884, he suddenly left, apparently of his own accord, and joined a touring company which was performing operetta in Cremona.

Several years later, in December 1892, after his great success with *Cavalleria*, he was questioned about this defection in an inter-view. His answer was defensive:**

"In what little experience I have of life it seems to me that the tale of other people's troubles must be much more amusing than that of their pleasures. I do not think this is due to malice—if you understand what I mean—but rather because happiness, fame, and perhaps good fortune as well, always carry something within them which causes dislike, and makes other people turn their noses up.

"Searching my notes and my memory for the years of my wanderings brings my most difficult years back to me. I was a nobody, and the vainglorious dreams of the 22-year-old had to yield to the demands of my appetite—a formidable appetite which gave me as much to think of as lack of appetite or indigestion can possibly give a millionaire.

"I studied at the Milan Conservatoire from 1882 to 1884. I cannot complain of my teachers, who with gentle persuasion encouraged me to work, nor of my fellow students, who almost all liked me. I was there for about a year, when I happened to read a translation of Heine's *Guglielmo Ratcliff*.*** I found Maffei's verses beautiful and, based on my

---

*The need to deal with creditors was a favourite conceit of the *"Scapiglia-tura"* (Milan's 'Chelsea set' of the period). The founder of the movement, Giuseppe Rovani, left a coffee-house without paying for what he had consumed and wrote on the white marble table-top four lines which later became famous.

Non è credibile	It's quite incredible
Com' è terribile	How it's so terrible
La vista orribile	To see a horrible
d'un creditor.	Creditor's face.

**Daniele Cellamare, *Pietro Mascagni*, Flli Palombi, Rome, 1965.

***William Ratcliff, a tragedy by Heinrich Heine, published in 1823, when he was 26 years old.

school knowledge, I judged them most harmonious. I could not rest until I had written three pieces of what should have been my first opera. I sketched part of the duet in Livorno during the summer holidays of 1882, and completed it in Milan the following year.

"All this did not prevent me from being very lazy and from feeling at the same time a yearning for independence and for freedom to roam the world.

"Living so close to the art which I had only caught a glimpse of, made me concoct all sorts of plans, each one sillier than the other—and seeing so many nobodies above me—and how conceited those people were!—induced me to leave the Conservatoire and to accept an engagement as deputy conductor of an operetta company which was giving a short series of performances in Cremona."

This marked the beginning of Mascagni's wanderings. He started with the Forlì company, but soon changed to the company of the actor-manager Luigi Maresca. The reason for the change was the attractive soubrette of the new company, Argenide Carbognani. For nearly three years they toured together, mostly performing in the smaller places. Rewards fluctuated between scanty and very poor; and in order to buy his "mouthful of bread" he had to sell small possessions. The termination of his studies had at first irritated, and later alienated his father, who did not wish to have anything to do with a son living "a vagabond's life", and who refused to help financially. During his journeys Mascagni continued to work rather spasmodically on his *Ratcliff*, and in a letter to a friend in Livorno he requested information about London (which he required for the first act) and about Douglas' journey.

He became increasingly unhappy and irritable. By August 1886, if not sooner, he had realized that he had made a mistake, and he began to speak of his "disgrace". The financial difficulties of the company, and Mascagni's state of nerves led to friction with Maresca. After several altercations they even came to blows during a performance in Foggia. On the morning of his departure from Foggia, on 28th December, 1886, Mascagni fell down a staircase after some further fisticuffs, and injured his right foot. More trouble was ahead: Miss Carbognani was four months pregnant.

The next town to be visited was Cerignola, about 20 miles from Foggia on the road to Barletta, near the Ofanto River. Many small southern Italian towns contain unexpected delights. Not so Cerignola which the 1887 Baedeker dismisses in three words: 26,000 inhabitants, uninteresting. The company was booked to present operettas for six weeks at its *Teatro Mercadante*, Mascagni playing the piano accompaniments. By the time he arrived there, he had made up his mind that he could continue his itinerant life no longer.

His plans for escape ripened. The most important requirement seemed local help and sympathy. Aided by his youthful good looks, and a personality which enabled him to charm at will, he set out to look for them.

The long winter evenings posed at that time a considerable problem for the inhabitants of a town like Cerignola. Without radio or cinema, with a single theatre which gave only occasional performances, time must have hung heavily on their hands: any entertainment offered was more than welcome.

The town's social club, the *Circolo Ofanto,* possessed a piano, and the musically interested Mayor, Giuseppe Cannone, together with his family, encouraged and supported musical evenings. This club seemed to offer Mascagni the chance to make himself popular.

Mascagni was, of course, a first-rate musician and an excellent pianist. Three years of touring with an operetta company had made him familiar with all the current and past popular tunes. To the members of the *Circolo Ofanto* he could offer heaven-sent entertainment; soon he had made himself indispensable there.

A number of difficulties remained. Mascagni was under contract to Maresca, who was not prepared to release him. His immediate need was money. Towards the end of the company's stay in Cerignola he asked Maresca for what was due to him. This started a row which continued after the beginning of the last performance on the night of 17th February, 1887. The two came to blows, and the audience could see Maresca slapping Mascagni's face. They liked the good-looking Mascagni and sympathized with him.

While the performance was going on, Mascagni's few belongings, including his *Ratcliff* sketches, were packed into a large suitcase by some friends and whisked away from the lodgings which he shared with Argenide Carbognani. Immediately after the performance, Mascagni and Signorina Carbognani left the theatre, unrecognizable and heavily cloaked, and walked in the cold night across the town towards the road to Foggia. A vehicle was waiting to take them to an isolated farmhouse at Stornarella, four miles along this road. Two Albanians who lived nearby helped to make a fire and produced something to eat. It had turned three o'clock in the morning, and the fugitives had to sleep on sacks of seeds. The next day they ventured into Stornarella. The few inhabitants of the village were friendly; they took them for an eloping couple, one of those frequent abduction stories. Anxiously the couple waited for news from Cerignola.

Maresca had obtained the help of the police in his search for Mascagni as some box-office takings were missing. The police forced the door to Mascagni's old room but could find no clue to his whereabouts. Questions put to neighbours produced no result either. Maresca's company was due to perform in Sicily and had to leave. Maresca stayed behind for three days but, as the searches proved fruitless, he, too, left to rejoin his company. The news of his departure was relayed to Stornarella and Mascagni returned to Cerignola.

The first part of the plan was thus successfully accomplished. The second was to secure a living at Cerignola. The day before his escape, on 16th February, Mascagni had written to his father in Livorno:

"My dear Father,

"I have not written to you for a long time, because I wanted to wait until I could give you some good news. I have finally decided to quit my life of a nomad and mountebank, and to settle as a teacher of music here in Cerignola.

"At a meeting which will take place tomorrow, I hope to be appointed municipal conductor here. For the moment, I shall teach singing and piano, but soon I shall conduct my opera at the municipal theatre here and enlarge the music school. I am very satisfied—and besides, it is better to earn five lire this way than twenty with a touring company.

"Furthermore, I shall have ten or so private pupils. Cerignola is a somewhat backward place, but they do like me here, and it should not be too difficult to borrow sufficient money to set myself up decently.

"Could you possibly write to Messrs V. . . . and tell them that I will send them all I owe them soon. Please try to recover my big case from them because of some papers I need, as I must give the mayor here certain documents. It is also essential that you do as follows: please ask Maestro Soffredini to give me a certificate stating that I have studied at his Institute, that I am capable of giving lessons of every type, etc.; make him say as much as possible! The more documents there are, the better for me; and could you, perhaps, through Soffredini,* also get a certificate from Maestro Menichetti of Pisa, and one from Cav. Magroni, the inspector of the Institute? Maestro Luigi Pratesi, too, could be asked to give me a testimonial stating that I am competent to teach music, piano, etc. Also do please ask all these people to write their titles,

---

*Alfredo Soffredini (1854-1923), a Livornese composer who later became a music critic in Milan.

appointments, Civil Orders, etc., below their signatures. That sort of thing makes it more impressive, and is very effective!

"I am very pleased with developments. Meanwhile, I am working seriously at my opera, which will soon be finished. You will see that I will make good after all. I beg you to do all the things I ask for as quickly as possible: my life may well depend on it."

Some of the facts of this letter were anticipatory, some not strictly accurate. However, on 25th March, 1887, 21 members of the town council of Cerignola met under the chairmanship of the Mayor. On the agenda was the proposed appointment of a teacher of singing and music, and the Mayor supported Mascagni's application. Counsellor Chiomento spoke in opposition to the appointment, which he regarded as an unnecessary luxury. The result of the vote was seven against and 14 in favour of Mascagni, who was therefore duly appointed, with a stipend of 100 lire per month and the obligation to be available for the establishment of the "Philharmonia" and of the school of singing, and for the instruction of individual pupils, without further payment. The Philharmonia became an orchestra consisting mainly of children and comprised 11 strings and five woodwind. There were six singers—all children.

The bare necessities of life, though not more, were thus assured and he and Signorina Carbognani set themselves up in lodgings in via Francesco d'Assisi. They obtained a bank loan of 500 lire. Within two months of his appointment a son, Domenico, was born, but four months later, on 2nd October, 1887, the child died.

Mascagni worked hard. He organized the Philharmonia and gave a few private lessons in Cerignola itself, as well as in some outlying places, travelling in a shaky cart dragged along by broken-down horses. Within a year of his appointment, a requiem mass, *Tuba mirum,* was written, and performed by the Philharmonia. The Cerignola journalist Michele Sinischalchi, who was also the music critic of the *Avanguardia* of nearby Lucera, described the work as "really strong and original, full of beauty" and predicted a brilliant future for Mascagni. The Philharmonia came in for particular praise.

All this was undoubtedly an improvement on his previous impecunious wanderings, during which his "piece of bread" was frequently missing, but it did not make him happy for long. It become increasingly obvious to him that Cerignola was not the solution, that his appointment was a blind alley, and that he must attempt to escape. He had to be very careful: he could not afford to offend those Cerignola worthies who had been so helpful, and were now so pleased with him. He had to play a double game, keeping his eyes open for any chance of escape, while avoiding any offence to those he still needed.

Mascagni used to buy the *Corriere della sera* at Marinelli's, the Cerignola newsagents. One day in July 1888, the *Corriere* had not arrived, and Marinelli offered him the other Milan daily, the *Secolo*. This paper carried an advertisement for the Concorso Sonzogno, promoted by the *Teatro illustrato*. He immediately decided to compete, and his first impulse was to use the finished act of his *Ratcliff* as a one-act opera. On second thoughts this did not seem feasible. He asked Sinischalchi, who by now was his friend, for help in obtaining a suitable libretto, and the secretary of the Naples Conservatoire, Rocco Pagliara, was recommended as librettist and commissioned. Pagliara was prepared to start at once. Mascagni, however, changed his mind, and after some argument, this project was dropped. Sinischalchi made various other suggestions, but none of them suited Mascagni. Finally, he wrote to his Livorno friend "Nanni" (Giovanni) Targioni-Tozzetti, who suggested using the play *Cavalleria rusticana*, which both had seen. Mascagni replied with the urgent request that he should convert this play at once into a suitable libretto.

Mascagni's miserable and unhappy circumstances during his work on *Cavalleria* may well bear special significance. After this first work, Mascagni composed a further 15 operas. Yet only his first, *Cavalleria*, remains in permanent repertoire; the second, *L'amico Fritz*, is occasionally performed; the rest are more or less forgotten.

Commenting on this fact, the writer Giorgio Vigolo said that it was indeed a "cruel miracle which gave Mascagni his masterpiece at the beginning of his career, followed by a slowly progressive, fatal enfeeblement". Musicians and music critics have been intrigued by it and have put forward various reasons to explain why Mascagni should have begun with his masterpiece, and been unable to match it later. None of their explanations is convincing.

All fields of artistic achievement can reveal the paradoxical fact that the best is sometimes produced under the most adverse conditions. If this applied to Mascagni, the "cruel miracle" is explained: the great initial success which brought at once lifelong financial security may have proved a hindrance rather than a spur for later efforts.

Mascagni's first letter to Targioni-Tozzetti was sent in October 1888. Work on the libretto began soon afterwards. Sketches and corrections on postcards went to and fro between Cerignola and

Livorno. The competition's closing date was 30th May, 1889, so that about eight months were in hand after the choice of subject had been made. From January 1889, Guido Menasci, a Livorno journalist, helped Targioni-Tozzetti to complete the libretto, on Salvestri's recommendation.

Meanwhile, Argenide Carbognani was pregnant again. In a special ceremony intended for those who are unable to appear in public, she was married to Mascagni at their home (illus. 32) on 3rd February, 1889. Eight days later their second son was born.

Operatic composing requires a piano; in the whole of Cerignola there were hardly 20 such instruments, mostly the property of "elect and special citizens". Eventually he had to hire one from a firm in Bari for 12 lire a month. Work progressed rapidly, with an almost daily exchange of postcards containing suggestions and amendments.

Meanwhile, Mascagni requested information from Puccini regarding the Sonzogno competition. This advice was important as Puccini had entered his opera *Le Villi* for the same competition four years earlier (see p. 61). Puccini was strongly against it, and proposed to submit the *Cavalleria* manuscript to his own publisher, Ricordi. This was done, but Ricordi rejected the work with the words *" Non ci tengo"* ("I don't care for it"), an error of judgment for which he never forgave himself. This refusal settled the issue, and Puccini duly entered Mascagni's opera for the competition, just before the end of the prescribed period, and without the prelude with its "Siciliana", which had not yet been composed.*

The manuscript's rejection by Ricordi was a further blow for Mascagni. His restlessness and irritability increased and he felt that he must get away from Cerignola at all costs. He wrote again to Puccini, and asked for help. Many years later, when the two composers were no longer friends, Puccini, with his tongue in his cheek, arranged for this letter to appear in a newspaper. It contained the following passage: "Please find me a few private lessons in Milan, find me a place in the orchestra of the Dal Verme, anything at all just so that I can get away from here". The publication of this letter displeased the people of Cerignola; it belied the love story of "Mascagni and his Cerignola" which had provided such good publicity, and was so acceptable to the Cerignolesi. But Puccini had underrated Mascagni's resourcefulness. Mascagni replied in the press that Puccini had quoted the passage outside its proper context; he

*As Mascagni had entered his opera without the prelude (see p. 150), it had to be presented to the commission before the audition began.

had only made this request in order to save his beloved Cerignola expense. 1888 had been a year of bad harvest, and his post became a luxury which the citizens could ill afford: for the sake of economy they even had to dismiss their midwife and close the grammar school.

Mascagni's letters to his librettist show his intense anxiety after the closing date of the competition. On 27th June, 1889, he writes that he can find neither peace nor sleep in expectation of the verdict which "may well be fatal for me." The whole issue is "a matter of life and death". It became known that 73 operas had been entered.

For eight months he lived in stress and tension, without hearing a word. Not even an acknowledgment of the entry had been received. "Nothing but apprehension and fears" is how Signora Mascagni later spoke of this period. They had practically given up hope when, in the early hours of 22nd February, 1890, a telegram from the secretary of the Royal Academy of S. Cecilia in Rome invited Mascagni to come to Rome to play his opera before the members of the appointed commission.

In the five years following the first award, the Sonzogno competition—partly as a result of the incidents connected with Puccini's first opera—had acquired an equivocal reputation. In order to improve its image, people of considerable distinction and reputation for independence and integrity had now been invited to adjudicate. The jury of five members were to be assisted by Alessandro Parisotti, the Secretary of the Academy of S. Cecilia. Leopoldo Mugnone, later chief conductor of the Scala, had been retained as conductor for the performance of the prizewinning entries of the second *Premio*.

The audition took place on 26th February, 1890. On the following day, the 27th, Mascagni wrote a most interesting letter about it to his Cerignola friend, Luigi Manzari, the Mayor's son-in-law. The letter has a curious history. Manzari kept it in his safe until 1927, when Daniele Cellamare, a Mascagni admirer from Cerignola, obtained it with the intention of publishing it. Mascagni initially objected to its publication, but eventually (it is said at Mussolini's personal request) gave the editor of Mussolini's paper *Popolo d'Italia*, the necessary permission and confirmed its authenticity. He did insist on omissions in four places. It is almost certain that three of the omissions contained derogatory remarks about Sonzogno, whom Mascagni had not yet met at the time of writing the letter. One of the omissions relates probably to a hostile remark about Umberto Giordano, with whom Mascagni later became friendly. This is the text of the letter:

help and advice he so willingly gave, his letter of 15th May, 1913, makes it obvious that he still felt ashamed of his collaboration in "this counterfeit art, the only good of which is the profits". He requested Dina to keep his help a strict secret, and yet at the same time tried to "see his own stories in a series of silent pictures", and to acquire a "cinematographic mentality". This he wanted so as to be of more help to Dina, who was adapting five of his other short stories for filming.

Regarding *The Foxhunt,* he wrote on 28th June, 1913, that "the first part, the gallop across the Roman countryside of those elegant hunting people, is fine up to the point of the faked fall of the young man, who uses this trick to be alone with the girl. But the difficulty is to show, without words, the scene in the hut which follows."

On 6th July, 1913, he expressed his annoyance about the film censorship of the *Capinera,* that "innocent and rather childish story." On 10th December, 1913, he claimed that he had never enjoyed a film, and recalled that he had found the "tedious length of *Cleopatra, Quo Vadis* and *The Last Days of Pompeii* enormously boring."

At the beginning of May 1914, an earthquake at Acireale provoked an alarmed letter from Dina. She implored him to leave Catania, and called Sicily the "island which nurtures deceit, ambush and treachery in its entrails". Verga was worried about his nephew Giovannino, who had been operated on a few days previously for acute appendicitis. Post-operative complications had set in, and Verga slept in the nursing home in order to be nearby: he had no intention whatsoever of leaving Sicily. He did not want to be disturbed in any way, he only yearned for solitude. When the Countess wrote that she would come to Catania in June 1914, her suggestion was not acceptable to her seventy-four-year-old friend, who wrote to her on 1st July, 1914:

"No, no, no, you mustn't do such mad things, or you will make me commit an even bigger folly myself! I would rather take the train and go to the devil! If you knew into what a state your letter has put me! Don't you understand or don't you want to understand that I just cannot, cannot do anything further? That I stand with my back to the wall? As you can see, I do what little I can do quite willingly, and I give with all my heart. But more, no! I cannot! For God's sake don't aggravate the difficulties I'm struggling with!"

The operation on Giovannino and the ensuing anxieties had made him even more depressed. On 24th June, 1914, he wrote:

"Do you know the story of that so-called 'savage' Indian tribe who carry their old to the top of the mountains, so that the birds can eat those who are of no more use to themselves, or to the others? That's how it is with me, and don't you laugh about your old Indian!"

Reluctantly, Dina had to give up her plans for the meeting. She spent the summer of 1914 in Cutigliano Pistoiese, while Verga remained in Catania. The war had begun and initially Verga was anxious that the Italians "should get back on to the right track in this political muddle which threatens to carry the whole world away, and which would only double all our troubles—of which we already have enough!"

"And if war comes," he wrote on 12th December, 1914, "that would be a fine thing, here as much as anywhere else! Already one can't get hold of the money one is owed any more, and our famous lemons are only good for our bile, and for nothing else!"

Even on 1st February, 1915, Verga still expressed the hope that "this blizzard which rages over Europe, and brings so many troubles even to those who are far away from bloodshed and destruction, would pass quickly, without causing Italy more harm."

The economic situation was steadily deteriorating. To make matters worse, it became evident that the water supply which was essential for the irrigation of the citrus orchard at Novalucello had suffered as the result of the earthquake of May 1914. "We're finished," he wrote in despair on 1st March, 1915, but continued to send Dina her hundred lire per month. The payments would, however, now sometimes be delayed, and then arrive with apologies for being late, due, as he emphasized, to his reduced circumstances.

The demand for stories which could be adapted for films was continuing, and even increasing. He authorized Dina to adapt for films any of his works which she thought suitable, with the exception of *La lupa*: this story he was reserving for De Roberto, who had written the libretto for the opera.

Gradually Verga accepted the need for Italy's entry into the war. His nephew Giovanni, as well as Antonino Catalano, the husband of his niece Caterina, were called up. This was another blow, as he felt that without his nephew's help he was now no longer able to look after the orchards, where "everything is going to the dogs, and there is the additional trouble of the terrible lack of water caused by that last earthquake."

His oldest and greatest friend, the seventy-six-year-old Luigi

Capuana, died in November 1915. A few years previously, and to Verga's sincere regret, a slight cooling-off in their friendship had taken place. Verga's comment about Capuana in his letter of 2nd March, 1909 (see p. 224) shows a somewhat critical attitude and, as if in reply, a letter from Capuana to a mutual friend (Francesco De Felice) peevishly refers to Verga as "this very dear friend of mine, who for the last twenty years has had the good fortune of not having to work, whereas I, at seventy-four, am still forced to write and to teach."

The reason for the slight estrangement was the curious story of Capuana's marriage. In 1895, five years after he had parted from his Beppa, Capuana happened to read in Rome the newspaper report of a young woman who had attempted suicide on account of an unhappy love affair. She had been saved, and was recovering in hospital. Capuana, always greatly interested in female psychology, felt an irresistible urge to visit the young woman in hospital and to find out more about this intriguing story.

The name of the young lady was Adelaide Bernardini, and a comparatively short time after Capuana's visit to the hospital she and Capuana were living together. His financial resources were very limited, and Ada did her best to make the poorly furnished rooms homely, and to run their household on economical lines. After seven years spent happily together, Capuana was in 1902 appointed Professor of Lexicography and Stylistics at Catania University, and he took Ada with him. The salary of the new post was adequate, but Capuana was heavily in debt;* since he was now in possession of a regular income, he was expected to commence repayments, and he fulfilled this expectation as best he could. He was, however, quite unable to put anything aside.

He was due to retire in 1914 at the age of 75, but as this meant only twelve completed years of university service, he was not entitled to a pension. Special steps were taken to secure him an *ex gratia* pension and, although eventually nothing came of it, the prospects for it seemed at one stage quite favourable. His pension would—if he was legally married—provide a widow's pension as well. For this reason Capuana married Ada, in some secrecy, in Catania in April 1908. Verga was one of the witnesses at the ceremony and was amused by the coyness with which both bride and bridegroom gave their ages. Luigi Pirandello, too, was a guest at

*For one thing he owed his brother Francesco alone 23,000 lire.

the wedding. He was their junior by more than twenty-five years and his literary beginnings had been much influenced by Capuana and Verga. Both had befriended him, and Pirandello on his side held them in fond esteem.

At first, Capuana used to speak freely about the story of his original encounter with Ada. However, Ada became increasingly sensitive about it, and eventually strongly objected to the episode ever being mentioned, even to close friends.

Shortly after the wedding, she heard to her consternation that Luigi Pirandello had decided to use her own story for the plot of a new play. She suspected that her husband had told Pirandello the details, but Capuana pleaded innocence, though probably only in order to avoid trouble with Ada. She eventually believed him, and became convinced that it must have been Verga who had told Pirandello of her past. Verga never cared much for Ada, and on Capuana's request and in order to help his old friend, he admitted to having done so. As a result Ada became hostile and eventually even succeeded in inducing her husband to adopt a critical attitude towards him.

Verga's feelings for Capuana were not affected by all this, and his friend's death grieved him deeply. He acted as a pallbearer at the funeral, and at the request of a journalist he recited from memory a few lines of poetry which his friend had written in his youth, after a sentimental crisis.

In his will Capuana left the *I Malavoglia* manuscript (see p. 86) to Ada, who intended to sell it. When Giovannino, Verga's nephew, heard of this, he bought it from her—only to lose it again in the manner mentioned before (see p. 38). Pirandello's play, which contained Ada Capuana's story, *Vestire gli ignudi (To Clothe the Naked)* was produced in 1922. It had world-wide success and was performed in 15 countries.

During the war, the correspondence with Dina continued. It dealt mostly with his difficulties and his financial troubles, with interspersed patriotic interjections. Novalucello was all but ruined; no one was prepared to pay his debts; the collecting of outstanding moneys was a nightmare; the film projects were going wrong, and so was everything else.

For the film rights of *Tigre reale,* produced by Giovanni Pastrone with a team of well-known early cinema artists (Pina Menichelli, Febo Mari and Alberto Nepoti), Verga received 600 lire, which he passed on to Dina. The success of his films aroused public interest in Verga himself, but he was not inclined to oblige; typically, he wrote to Dina on 11th May, 1916:

"Please do try and save me the ridicule of being caricatured by this cinema photography! Also, please confirm that neither you nor I possess any photographs. I am so averse to personal exhibitions, that I have always refused to take curtain-calls. The first and last time this happened was at Turin, when I let myself be dragged onto the stage by Rossi and the Duse, who said to me: "It looks as if you do not wish to condescend to appear among the likes of us!'

"At the moment I am arguing with those who want my name on the bill of that *Cavalleria* film. I am only prepared to figure as the author of the story and of the play. That's enough. I am a storyteller, not a puppet showman!"

Salvatore Paola, his friend and trusted legal adviser, died in 1916, seventy-nine years old, while the court cases with Mascagni and Sonzogno were still in progress. In a letter to Dina of 28th June, 1916, Verga referred to a new incident in this dispute: "That other *'mascagnana sonzognata'** you mention I don't even bother with. My solicitors will see to that . . ."

On 19th July, 1916, he wrote that his court case was going well and that he hoped his opponents would have to "spit the bone out". He added that "the cinema, too, which has taken the place of the theatre, is only a phantasmagoria."

A letter of 23rd August, 1918, shows that in spite of his belief in victory, the outcome of the war greatly worried him. "You know I have now become a Socialist, in this war in which the lower classes have set the best example and given the best blood". He distrusted the Yugoslavs: hitherto they had been only chatterboxes, or little more. But once they were "made", it would be worse to have them on the other side of the Adriatic than the Austrians.

Further blows were in store: Arrigo Boito, the last of his Milan friends, died on 10th June, 1918, and his young niece Caterina Catalano died on 15th February, 1919, during the terrible epidemic of Spanish flu which followed the end of the war, leaving an infant son.**

*"*Cagnana*" means "bitchy". "*Menzogna*" means "lie". To join the two names of his adversaries together, to mean "a bitchy lie", is an extremely vicious pun.

**As a wedding present, he had given his niece the ex-capellaneria at Mineo, the piece of land mentioned on pp. 47 and 183. After her death it became the property of her son, at present Italy's Ambassador to Egypt, who still owns it.

Once more Dina was anxious to come and comfort him but he requested her not to do so. As far as he was concerned, he wrote to her on 7th June, 1919, he could only be "alone, alone, alone."

In August 1919, Verga wrote to Dina about the engagement of his only surviving nephew, Giovanni, to a young lady from Venice, a match of which he never fully approved.

At about the same time he wrote his last short story, *Una capanna e il tuo cuore* (*A Hut and Your Heart*), about a group of destitute actors; the story appeared in the *Illustrazione italiana,* after his death, with a sad dedication to De Roberto.

Towards the end of the war, some public interest in the almost completely forgotten Verga returned. To begin with only one or two articles of little importance appeared. They were followed by Luigi Russo's book,* *Giovanni Verga,* in October 1919.

This was the first full literary evaluation of Verga's work, and was based on a thorough study and critical assessment. It was, in fact, the first serious assessment of his work since Benedetto Croce's essay of 1903.

On 9th July, 1920, Luigi Pirandello presided at a meeting in honour of Verga's eightieth birthday at the Teatro del Valle in Rome. Benedetto Croce, Minister of Education at the time, was present. The weekly *Illustrazione italiana* devoted a whole issue to Verga. Even his financial position was now—for the first time in his life, and rather late in the day—no longer a worry to him; Bemporad, the Florence publishers, had paid 100,000 lire for the rights to publish his *opera omnia.*

Celebrations of his 80th birthday were arranged in Catania for 2nd September. At the Teatro Massimo, his play *Dal tuo al mio* was to be performed, and Pirandello was to be the official speaker at a meeting in his honour. Verga refused to attend the celebrations. The president of the committee in charge of the arrangements tried his hardest to persuade Verga to come, and, attributing Verga's reluctance to his well-known shyness, asked him to overcome this shyness "just for once."

"How do you know that it is shyness which makes me not want to come?" asked Verga coolly.

"What else could it be?"

"Contempt", said Verga, "because you all left it too late."

The celebrations took place without him. Pirandello, who had

*First published by Ricciardi, Naples, later by Laterza, Bari, 1966.

travelled the considerable distance from his home in Agrigento to Catania in order to deliver his address, was to spend the night there. Late at night and tired, he returned to his hotel. He felt disappointed, and Verga's absence had cast a shadow over the festivities. On entering his bedroom in the hotel, he saw to his surprise Verga, sitting quietly in a chair. He walked towards him. Verga rose slowly, and with outstretched hand came to meet him. He firmly gripped Pirandello's right hand and looked sadly, with tears in his eyes, into Pirandello's face. They both stood silently for a minute or so—and, without saying a word, Verga left.

The next morning a deputation from the Committee, together with the writer Niccodemi, who represented the Italian Society of Authors, came to Verga's house to offer their homage. Niccodemi had wished "to kiss the hand which had written *I Malavoglia*". Available accounts differ to some extent, but agree about Verga's marked uneasiness, and his obvious suffering. After the visitors had departed, Verga left his house and went to his club—which was quite deserted at that hour—and remained there, alone, in extreme need of solitude.

A short time before, on 17th July, 1920, Verga had written to Dina that his eightieth birthday "honours" were weighing even more heavily on him than his eighty years.

By now the "recognition" had really begun: on 3rd October, Giolitti, President of the Council (Prime Minister) sent a telegram to Verga to inform him that he had been appointed a Senator. Verga replied, as his biographers report, "with extreme brevity". The full story of this reply is contained in a letter to his brother Mario of 4th October, 1920.

"My dearest brother,
"This morning I had a telegram which I enclose, as I know that it will give you pleasure. In fact, as soon as friend De Roberto had seen it, he said, 'This is going to please brother Mario more than it will please you'. Here it is:
"'Rome October 3. 7.30 p.m. Verga Giovanni Catania.
'Pleased to inform you that acting on my proposal and following the vote in the Cabinet, H.M. the King has with today's decree nominated you a Senator of the Realm.
'Giolitti, Prime Minister.'
"This means much less to me than it will to you, but I did not want to appear a poseur by not accepting, or a villain by not thanking, and I have tried to evade both these pitfalls by replying as follows:
'To H.E. Giolitti, Rome.
Am grateful to His Majesty, to Your Excellency and the Council

of Ministers for the honour awarded to me, and thank you for informing me of it.

Verga.'

"My friends here thought this telegram far too dry, but that is exactly what I wanted. I wished to act neither like a snob, nor like a cad towards those rulers of ours, high and low, who carry us to ruin and dishonour. However, let us change to a more pleasant subject, and that is my hope to see you here again soon."

Attached to this letter was a separate sheet of paper, which read:

"But all alone with you, dear brother, I want, if that Senatorship of mine gives you any pleasure, to recall with tears of gratitude in my eyes our courageous father. With five children and insufficient means, and his vision dimmed by the conditions of the time, he allowed me to go ahead beyond the extent of his limited horizon. And I want to recall our mother, who did so much, always helped us in every way she could, and willingly made a mother's greatest sacrifice: to let me go away, so that I could try to pursue my ideals. Also our dear grandmother who let me have all her savings, starting with those thousand lire which she gave me in 1867 to enable me to live away from home! And then I want to thank *you* as well, for the help *you* have given me so readily. And that's that. Glory and paradise to the dead, and my gratitude to you. As far as I am concerned, I am finished and shall soon be at the end. I greet you with a heavy heart."

The title of Senator carries the address of "Your Excellency" and, jokingly, Dina used this mode of address in her letter of congratulation. In his reply, Verga said that he would not write to her any more if she did that again; that she had always been "a naughty little girl" and would remain a naughty little girl at 60, 70, and at 80 years as well. Again she asked for a meeting, but on 14th October, 1920, Verga replied:

"After ten years? What are you saying? What should we do? After all this time? However, ten years later, or earlier, believe me, I always am yours, only yours, your most afffffectionate* Verga."

Dina's reply to this letter has survived. It is a remarkable letter; a sad but perfectly controlled outcry of an utterly disappointed friend. This is how she wrote, on 18th October, 1920:

"What a cold shower your letter was. In the winter, it is quite enough to give one a bad chill.

*The multiplication of the f's is a jocular reference to Dina's earlier teasing about his Sicilian accent.

"During these last few days, which I have been spending mostly at the dentist's, the hairdresser's and the shoemaker's in order to get myself smartened up as much as possible, it did not even occur to me that such a thing could happen! And yet, in its crudeness it is really quite straightforward, and obviously so.

"You see, not only have I, as you always say, remained a little girl, but a very simple one as well.

"Those ten long years of trial should have opened my eyes to the fact that the old saying *passata la festa; gabbato lu santo* (when his feast day has passed, the saint soon goes by the board) applies very justly to you, as well.

"But if one is made differently, if one thinks from the middle upwards, thinks with the heart as well as with the head? I was just going to continue: 'All the worse for the likes of us,' but it isn't so! No! All the worse for people like you, who no longer enjoy a single ray of light. As for me, I shall always remain grateful to you for those sparks, those flashes of light, which—even if only for a short time—have lifted me out of the hurly-burly of life.

"And now, granted for the sake of argument that I still feel the disappointment, I am trying to comfort myself with the thought that the journey would not only have been long, but most probably full of delays as well! Blessed philosophy comes to my aid! Let's not think about it any more. I accept that it is possible to remain affectionate friends without the desire to see one another. And what now? I switch off my light, and I say

"Buona notte, Senatori."

The last words of this letter form an ingenious pun. *Buona notte, Senatore* means *Good night, Senator*. To change the final e of *Senatore* into an i not only makes it sound Sicilian, but effects a double meaning as well; it now resembles *Buona notte, Suonatori*, the traditional dismissal of the players, after a serenade under the beloved's window.

Verga continued to be silent and depressed; at times he became very emotional. When he received a letter informing him that in a book which was about to be published* his relationship with Giselda would be discussed, he collapsed as if seized by a stroke.

On 11th December, 1920, he went to Rome to be sworn in as a Senator. He met Dina, and upon his return wrote that the journey had taken five hours longer than it should have done, that the luggage was delayed for two days, and that no cabs were available at Catania

*In Alfio Tomaselli's *Epistolario di Mario Rapisardi* (see p. 126).

station. In 1921 his brother Mario died. "If only I could run away, but I hardly can—where could I escape to from myself? Forgive the bitterness I spread around me, and pity me." Later the correspondence with Dina reverted to a quietly affectionate tone. He sent her a demijohn of wine and asked her to return the empty carboy.

His last letter to Dina was written on 28th December, 1921. Verga had promised that he would come to Rome to see her, but just now he could "neither face a night in the sleeper nor one in a hotel". The Countess had read press reports of a new decoration he had been awarded and he explained that this was the "Cross of Savoy, just another cross on top of the cross of my years". He sent her a senator's free railway pass "to and from Rome", the last he had left after satisfying the demands of various friends, in spite of his protest that "such free tickets were meant only for the members of the family".

On the night of 24th January, 1922, Verga returned from his club, dismissed his servant and, as was his habit, locked the door of his room. He put his spectacles and the latest book which had been presented to him, *Natio borgo selvaggio* (*My Savage Home*), by the Sicilian writer F. Paolieri, on his dressing table. While undressing, he suffered an attack of cerebral haemorrhage, and collapsed slowly. Not a sound was heard, no injury was found on his body. All night he lay on the floor. At eight o'clock the next morning the maid raised the alarm. His friend De Roberto came and for the next three days hardly left his bedside, until, in De Roberto's words, "immortality began" at 1.22 on the morning of 27th January.

Later, De Roberto published a moving account of the death of his great friend.

*   *   *

Verga had pretended for many years that he was working on the next book in the cycle of the doomed, *The Duchess of Leyra*. He had frequently referred to the progress of the work. Early publication of the book was expected, and a translation into French had been discussed. De Roberto made a thorough search for the manuscript, but could only find the first chapter and a few pages of the second.

This came as a complete surprise. Those who knew of Verga's honesty and integrity found it difficult to reconcile his comments regarding the book's progress with De Roberto's discovery of so little. Some requested that another thorough search for the missing parts of the manuscript should be made; there were various other suggestions, ranging from the assumption that Verga had, in a mood of despair, destroyed his own work to insinuations of jealous dishonesty against De Roberto.

We now know that there was no need for surprise: Verga had attempted to conceal from others the inactivity which his mental state imposed on him. In other words it was an act of deliberate dissimulation. This fits the pattern of Verga's depression and there is no incongruity.

He was psychologically of cyclothymian temperament, but only early on in life had there been any evidence of periods of exultation and, after he left Florence, such phases did not recur. His tendency to melancholia became in middle age quite obvious. His lack of success—a success which at least four of his books amply deserved—intensified by the loss of his *Cavalleria* and the triumph of D'Annunzio, made his melancholy progress to a severe reactive depression. This imposed an overwhelming desire for solitude. It also made him feel, and even exhibit, a dislike of literature which amounted almost to hatred; this is how in self-punishment he punished the love which had withheld its prize from him.

He was by nature shy and rather reserved, but once he made friends he sincerely felt linked to them, and remained always loyal. He was a man of upright character, and adhered with firmness and resolution to his convictions. He was never prepared to "trim", and not a single instance is known in which he changed, or pretended to change, his views for the sake of a material advantage.

At a period when practically every penny counted, he declined to join the salaried selection committee of a literary prize, because he regarded the awarding of literary prizes as nonsensical.

He was accepted by society, but did not take a very active part in social activities. He liked and he loved women, and was liked and loved in return. He was sexually promiscuous in a rather organized way, and it seems probable that, in his youth, he avoided marriage in order freely to enjoy numerous affairs. Despite the fact that descriptions of the tragic results of adultery were a favourite theme in his stories, he obviously thought that affairs with married women suited his personality best. At one stage he must have had a concomitant sexual relationship with three married women.

His deepest feeling was his affection for Dina, but he was in the end quite prepared to restrict this relationship to an exchange of letters. This exchange remained, however, in spite of their not seeing one another for ten years, on a frank, intimate and affectionate level.

He felt sincere remorse for his behaviour towards Giselda, not because he had been responsible for the break-up of her marriage, but because he tired of her so soon afterwards. He did not hurt her feelings too severely, and a beautiful wreath of violets from her arrived immediately after his death: hers and De Roberto's were the only flowers that went with him to his grave.

The sad effect of his depression was that it put its seal on his mental outlook, and precluded sustained work on a major literary subject.

If the contemporary public and critics had accepted his work in a more enlightened manner, we might well have had many more of his books and his stories; those stories which he was able to tell with a perfection never attained by anyone else in his homeland, and by very few in the rest of the world.

Verga was one of the world's great storytellers. His misfortune lay in the failure of his contemporaries to recognize an artist who was unduly sensitive and unexpectedly vulnerable to rejection and disappointment. His tragedy was that his contemporaries wounded him too deeply. Posterity too has neglected him. One may well ask— in Verga's own words:

Is time going to be a gentleman?

A POSTSCRIPT IN PICTURES

The missing Verga

La Traviata is taken from Dumas' La dame aux camélias,

but the source of Cavalleria *is not revealed*

GIACOMO PUCCINI

TOSCA

Opera in three acts

Libretto by G. GIACOSA and L. ILLICA
based on the drama by V. SARDOU

The vocal scores of Ricordi editions always mention the source of an opera;

GIACOMO PUCCINI

LA BOHÈME

(Founded upon "LA VIE DE BOHÈME,, by Henry Murger)

An opera in four acts

by

GIUSEPPE GIACOSA and LUIGI ILLICA

GUGLIELMO RATCLIFF

TRAGEDIA IN QUATTRO ATTI

DI

ENRICO HEINE

TRADUZIONE DI

ANDREA MAFFEI

MUSICA DI

PIETRO MASCAGNI

Riduzione per CANTO E PIANOFORTE

DI

AMINTORE GALLI

Prezzo L. 40.
(aumento compreso)

CASA MUSICALE SONZOGNO

Sonzogno editions, too, mention the source if it is Heine . . .

CAVALLERIA RUSTICANA

MELODRAMMA IN UN ATTO
DI
G. TARGIONI - TOZZETTI e G. MENASCI

MUSICA DI
PIETRO MASCAGNI

RIDUZIONE PER CANTO E PIANOFORTE
DI
LEOPOLDO MUGNONE

CASA MUSICALE SONZOGNO - MILANO

. . . but not if it is Verga

To mark the 50th anniversary of Verga's death, a commemorative postage stamp was issued, and a special postal imprint used . . .

. . . but the space for the monument in Catania's Piazza Verga remains empty

BIBLIOGRAPHICAL NOTE

Only two items of significance regarding his work appeared during Verga's lifetime. Benedetto Croce's essay (34 pages) in 1903 and Luigi Russo's book in 1919. This work of almost 400 pages deals thoroughly with Verga's writings—but gives hardly any biographical information: Russo probably knew little about Verga as a man, and his reputation as a somewhat mysterious philanderer made the well-disposed steer clear of his private life.

The friends who had known Verga intimately enough to write about him, among them Boito, Giacosa, Gualdo and Capuana, all died before him, with the exception of Federico De Roberto.

De Roberto's articles, 18 in all, printed in different newspapers and periodicals which soon became unobtainable, form therefore the only available first-hand evidence. Carmelo Musumarra eventually published them in a collected edition. They provided, and will continue to provide, the basic ingredients for every Verga biography; the first was Natale Scalia's *Giovanni Verga* in 1922.

The two volumes of *Studi verghiani*, edited by Lina Perroni and first published in 1929, form an important source of information, whatever one may think about the method by which the material was procured (see p. 83).

Parallel with the increasing recognition went the publication of a good deal of literary criticism of Verga's work—with scanty biographical notes. Maria Borgese's *Anime scompagnate* (*Souls apart*) 1937, gave the first full account of the Giselda affair, Nino Capellani's book *Vita di Giovanni Verga* followed in 1940.

In 1950 appeared Ermanno Scuderi's book *Verga* (Camene, Catania) and in 1954 Fredi Chiappelli's edition of the letters to Rod, with an interesting introduction and a chronological register of biographical dates which result from this correspondence. This book much advanced our knowledge of Verga.*

*It is amusing to note that among the words in *I Malavoglia* for which Rod required information was "pizza". Verga explained: "it is a type of Neapolitan focaccia (cake or bun), but it seems best to leave the word in Italian!"

The enormous growth of literature on Verga, often only some-what superficial critical comment, can be judged from Gino Raya's bibliography *Un secolo di bibliografia verghiana*, an excellent and complete reference book which appeared in 1960 containing about 3,000 entries; its second edition (1972) has 6,000! Raya's *Ottocento inedito* with interesting letters from Verga and his friends also appeared in 1960, and his *La lingua del Verga* as well as his edition of *Verga's Letters to Dina* (*Lettere a Dina*) in 1962.

In 1963 appeared Giulio Cattaneo's *Giovanni Verga*, by far the best of the biographies so far published, and the first biographical work to benefit from the information Raya's *Letters to Dina* had provided. This book also contains an excellent *Nota bibliografica*, sub-divided into subjects and much to be recommended.

In 1970, Raya republished the *Lettere a Dina* in a complete edition under the title *Lettere d'Amore*.

The first work by Verga which was translated into English was *The Blackcap's Story* (*Capinera*) which appeared in 1888 in the English monthly magazine *Italia*, published in Rome and now defunct.

In 1891 appeared *I Malavoglia* under the title *The House by the Medlar Tree*, followed in 1893 by *Master Don Gesualdo*, both translated by Mary Craig, and published by Osgood in London.

Alma Strettel's *Cavalleria Rusticana and Other Tales of Sicilian Peasant Life*, were published by Unwin in London in 1893.

D. H. Lawrence translated *Cavalleria Rusticana and other stories* [from *Vita dei Campi*], Cape, London, 1928, *Little Novels of Sicily* [*Novelle rusticane*], T. Seltzer, New York, 1925, and *Mastro-don Gesualdo*, T. Seltzer, New York, 1923.

A selection of Verga's short stories was translated by Giovanni Cecchetti, and published by the University of California Press in 1958.

Verga's works are briefly surveyed in J. H. Whitfield's history of Italian literature (1960) and the Manchester University Press published in 1962 a student's edition of *Pane Nero and other short stories*, edited by D. Maxwell White with an introduction containing a few pages of biographical notes on Verga.

With the exception of the youthful efforts, all Verga's works are readily available in Italian.

*   *   *

For the convenience of the reader, an alphabetical list of works quoted in this volume follows.

Alexander, Alfred, *Luigi Capuana's Comparatico*, Ciranna, Rome, 1970.

Barbiera, Raffaello, *Il salotto della Contessa Maffei*, Treves, Milan, 1895.

Borgese, Maria, *La Contessa Lara*, Treves, Milan, 1936.

Borgese, Maria, Anime scompagnate, *Nuova Antologia*, Rome, Nov.-Dec., 1937.

Cappellani, Nino, *Vita di Giovanni Verga*, Le Monnier, Florence, 1940.

Capuana, Luigi, *Il marchese di Roccaverdina*, Garzanti, Milan, 1969.

Capuana, Luigi, *Homo*, Brigola, Milan, 1883 (containing *Comparatico* and *Lu cumpari*).

Capuana, Luigi, *C'era una volta*, Bemporad, Florence, 1967.

Carner, Mosco, *Puccini*, Duckworth, London, 1958.

Cattaneo, Giulio, *Giovanni Verga* (*La vita sociale della Nuova Italia*, vol. vi), UTET, Turin, 1963.

Cattermole, Evelyn, *Canti e Ghirlande*, Florence, 1867.

Cattermole, Evelyn, see also Lara, Contessa

Cellamare, Daniele, *Pietro Mascagni*, Flli. Palombi, Rome, 1965.

Chiappelli, Fredi (ed.), Giovanni Verga, *Lettere al suo traduttore*, Le Monnier, Florence, 1954.

Croce, Benedetto, *Giovanni Verga*, La letteratura della Nuova Italia, III, Laterza, Bari, 1964.

Croce, Benedetto, *La Contessa Lara*, La letteratura della Nuova Italia, IV, Laterza, Bari, 1948.

D'Ambra, Lucio, see Perroni (*Studi verghiani*).

De Felice, Francesco, *Verga e la tradizione verista in Sicilia*, Giannotta, Catania, 1966.

De Roberto, Federico, *Casa Verga* (ed. C. Musumarra), Le Monnier, Florence, 1964.

Disraeli, Benjamin, *Sybil, or The Two Nations*, Warne, London, 1845.

Gandolfo, Antonino, *La Cavalleria rusticana in tribunale*, Studio editoriale, Catania, 1936.

Gatti, Carlo, *Il teatro alla Scala nella storia e nell'arte*, Ricordi, Milan, 1964.

Giacosa, Giuseppe. His plays are available in a complete edition, and some as paperbacks.

Lara, Contessa (Cattermole, Evelyn), *Versi*, Sommaruga, Rome, 1883.

Ojetti, Ugo, *Cose viste*, Mondadori, Milan, 1934.

Paternò, Giuseppe, *Giovanni Verga*, Tip. Etna, Catania, 1964.

Perroni, Lina (ed.), D'Ambra, Lucio, Incontro di Verga con Zola, *Studi verghiani*, Edizioni del Sud, Palermo, 1929.

Perroni, Lina, Preparazione dei "Malavoglia", *Studi verghiani*, Edizioni del Sud, Palermo, 1929.

Perroni, L. & V., Storia dei Malavoglia, carteggio con l'editore e con L. Capuana, *Nuova Antologia*, Rome, Mar.-Apr., 1940.

Rapisardi, Mario, *Antologia*, (ed. Ermanno Scuderi), Giannotta, Catania, 1968.

Raya, Gino, I fagiani di Emilio Zola, *Nuova Antologia*, Rome, May 1968.

Raya, Gino, *La lingua del Verga*, Le Monnier, Florence, 1962.

Raya, Gino (ed.), *Lettere a Dina*, Ciranna, Rome, 1962.

Raya, Gino (ed.), Giovanni Verga, *Lettere d'Amore*, Tindalo, Rome, 1970.

Raya, Gino, *Ottocento inedito*, Ciranna, Rome, 1960.

Raya, Gino, *Un secolo di bibliografia verghiana*, Cedam, Padua, 1960.

Russo, Luigi, *Giovanni Verga*, Laterza, Bari, 1966.

Scalia, Natale, *Giovanni Verga*, STET, Ferrara, 1922.

Scarfoglio, Edoardo, *Il libro di Don Chisciotte*, Quattrini, Florence, 1911.

Ternois, René, *Zola et ses amis italiens*, Publications de l'Université de Dijon, XXXVIII, Société les Belles Lettres, Paris, 1967.

Tomaselli, Alfio, *Epistolario di Mario Rapisardi*, Battiato, Catania, 1922.

Vigo, Lionardo, *Raccolta amplissima di canti populari Siciliani*, Galàtola, Catania, 1870-74.

Whitfield, John Humphreys, *A Short History of Italian Literature*, Cassell, London, 1962.

INDEX OF NAMES